Books on Egypt and Chaldaea

Vol. XXI. OF THE SERIES

THE

EGYPTIAN HEAVEN AND HELL

Vol. II.

THE SHORT FORM OF THE BOOK ÅM-ṬUAT

AND

THE BOOK OF GATES

E. A. Wallis Budge

ISBN: 978-1-63182-828-7

Printed: March 2023

Published and Distributed By:
Lushena Books
607 Country Club Drive, Unit E
Bensenville, IL 60106
www.lushenabks.com

ISBN: 978-1-63182-828-7

NOTE

This volume is the second of a series of three volumes which treat of the Egyptian Heaven and Hell. It contains the complete hieroglyphic text of the Summary, or short form of the Book Ȧm-Ṭuat, and the complete hieroglyphic text of the Book of Gates, with translations and reproductions of all the illustrations. A series of Chapters dealing with the origin and contents of Books of the Other World, with prefatory remarks, and a full index to the whole work, will be found in the third volume.

CONTENTS

ERRATA

P. 10, l. 3, for "Then-ṭent-baiu" read "Tent-baiu"; p. 20, l. 10, for "Nebt-mu-ṭuatiu" read "Metchet-mu-nebt-Ṭuatiu"; p. 18, l. 2, for [hieroglyphs] read [hieroglyphs]; p. 23, l. 3, for [hieroglyph] read [hieroglyph]; p. 34, l. 1, for [hieroglyphs] read [hieroglyphs]; p. 57, l. 3, for "the magical powers" read "her magical powers to those"; p. 113, l. 26, for [hieroglyphs] read [hieroglyphs]; p. 115, l. 11, for [hieroglyphs] read [hieroglyphs] p. 119, l. 3, for "Tchetbi" read "Nebt-tchefau"; p. 147, l. 7. for [hieroglyph] read [hieroglyph].

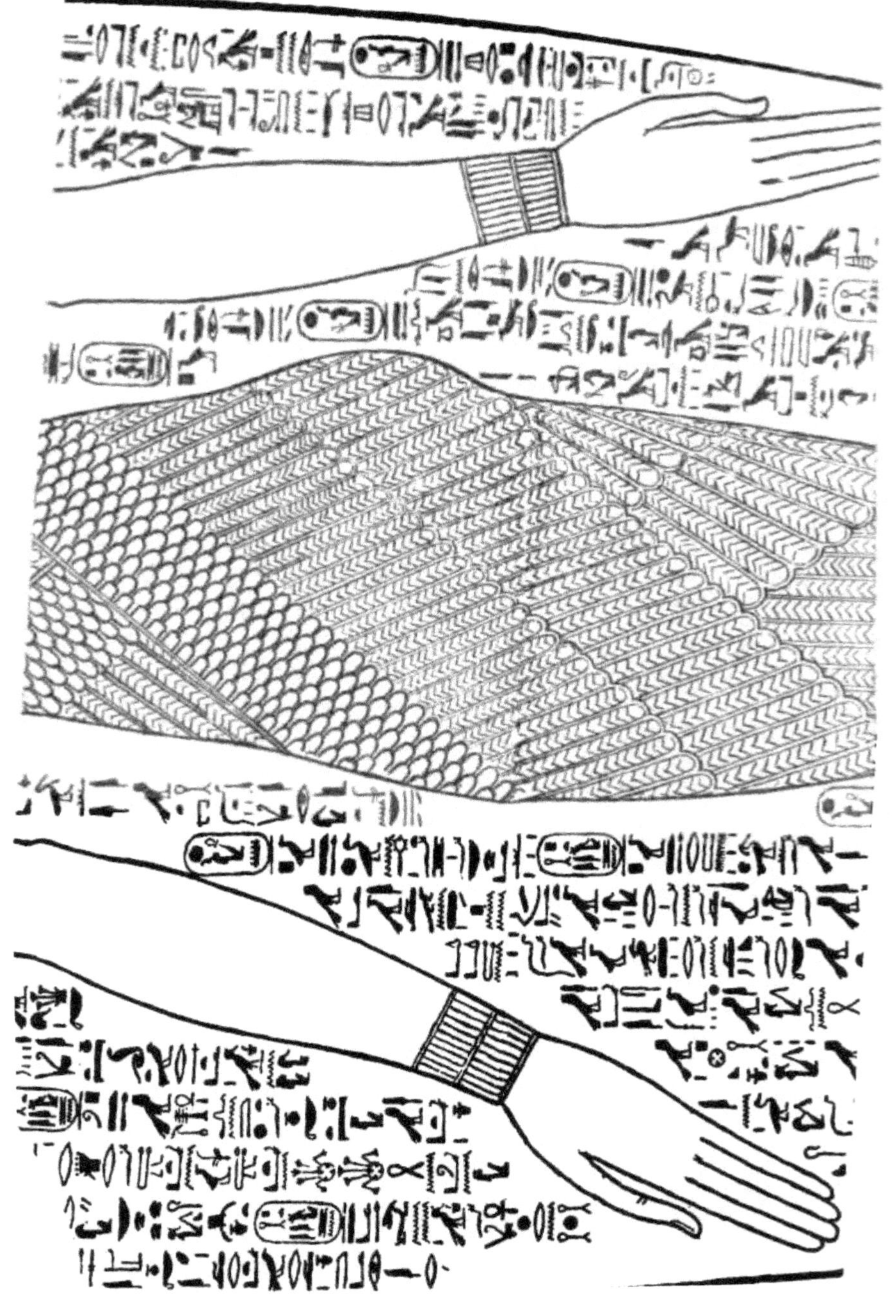

THE SHORT FORM

OF THE

BOOK OF ȦM-ṬUAT

THE SUMMARY OF THE BOOK OF WHAT IS IN THE UNDERWORLD.

THE BEGINNING OF THE HORN OF ȦMENTET, [WHICH IS] THE UTTERMOST POINT OF THE DEEPEST DARKNESS.

THE FIRST HOUR.

THIS god entereth into the earth through the Hall of the horizon of Ȧmentet. There are one hundred and twenty ȦTRU to journey over in this Hall before a man arriveth at the gods of the Ṭuat.

The name of the first Field of the Ṭuat is NET-RĀ. He (i.e., Rā) allotteth fields to the gods who are in [his] following, and he beginneth to send forth words to and to work out the plans of the divine beings of the Ṭuat in respect of this Field.

Whosoever shall have these made (i.e., copied)

according to the similitude which is in Ȧment of the Ṭuat, [and] whosoever shall have knowledge of these similitudes, [which are] the copies of this great god himself, they shall act as magical protectors for him upon earth regularly and unfailingly, and they shall act as magical protectors for him in the Great Ṭuat.

USHEMET-ḤĀTU-KHEFTI-RĀ is the name of the [first] hour of the night which guideth this great god through this Hall.

THE FIRST HOUR.

I.—FROM THE TOMB OF SETI I. (lines 1—22).

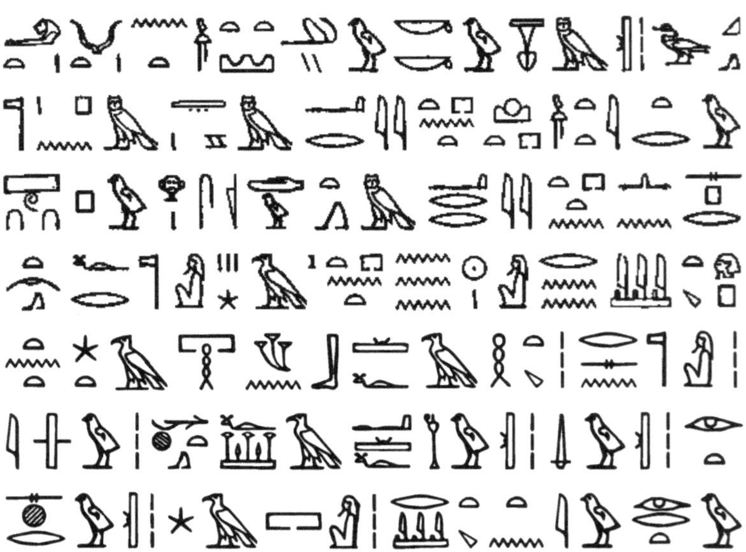

[1] In this word, [hieroglyph] is usually written for [hieroglyph] *ti*.

THE FIRST HOUR.

II.—From the Leyden Papyrus, T. 71.

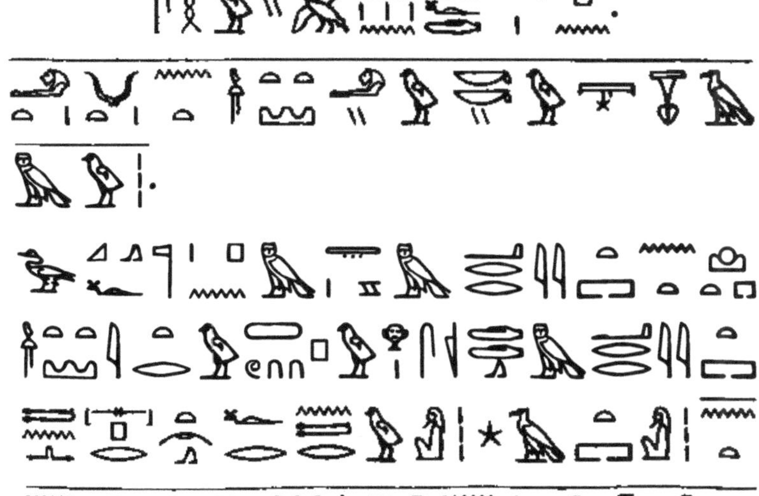

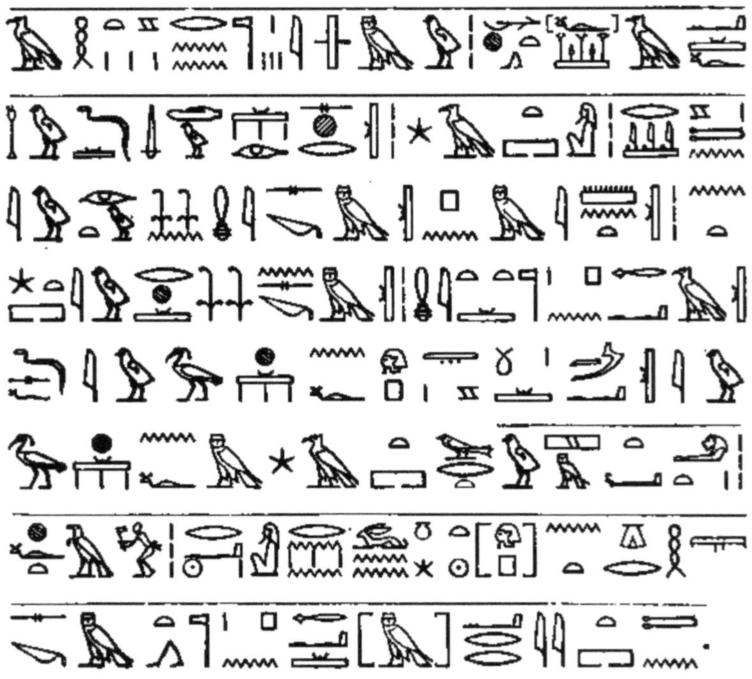

THE SECOND HOUR.

This great god afterwards taketh up his position in UR-NEST, which is three hundred and nine ÀTRU in length, and one hundred and twenty ÀTRU in width.

The name of the gods who are in this Field is BAIU-ṬUATI. Whosoever knoweth their names shall have his existence with them, and unto him shall this great god allot fields in the place wherein they are in the FIELD OF URNES. He shall stand up with the Gods who Stand Up (ĀḤĀU), he shall travel on in the following of this great god, he shall enter into the earth, he shall force a way through the Ṭuat, he shall cleave a passage through the tresses of the gods with flowing hair (ḤENKSU), he shall travel on by the EATER OF THE ASS (ĀM-ĀA) after the emptying of the lands, he shall eat bread-cakes in the Boat of the Earth, and there shall be given unto him the fore-part of TATUBȦ.

Whosoever shall have made in writing (or, in drawing) similitudes of the BAIU-ṬUATI (i.e., the Souls of the Ṭuat) in the forms in which they are in Ȧment of the Ṭuat—now the beginning of such representations should be from Ȧmentet,—and whosoever shall make offerings unto them upon earth in their names, [these things I say] shall act as magical protectors to that person upon earth, regularly and unfailingly.

And whosoever shall know the words which the gods of the Ṭuat speak to this god, and the words which are saiḍ by him to them when he is approaching the gods of the Ṭuat, [these words I say] shall act as magical protectors to him that knoweth them upon earth, regularly and unfailingly.

SHESAT-MĀKET-NEB-S is the name of the hour of the night which guideth this great god through this Field.

THE SECOND HOUR.

I.—FROM THE TOMB OF SETI I. (lines 23—61).

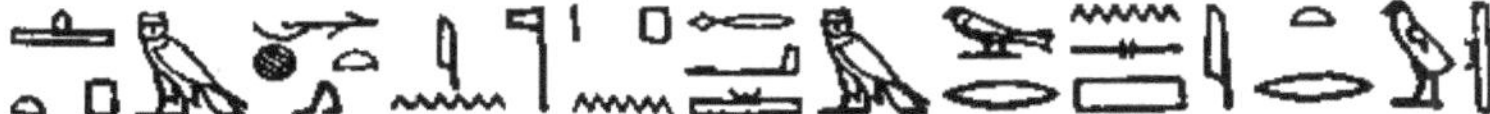

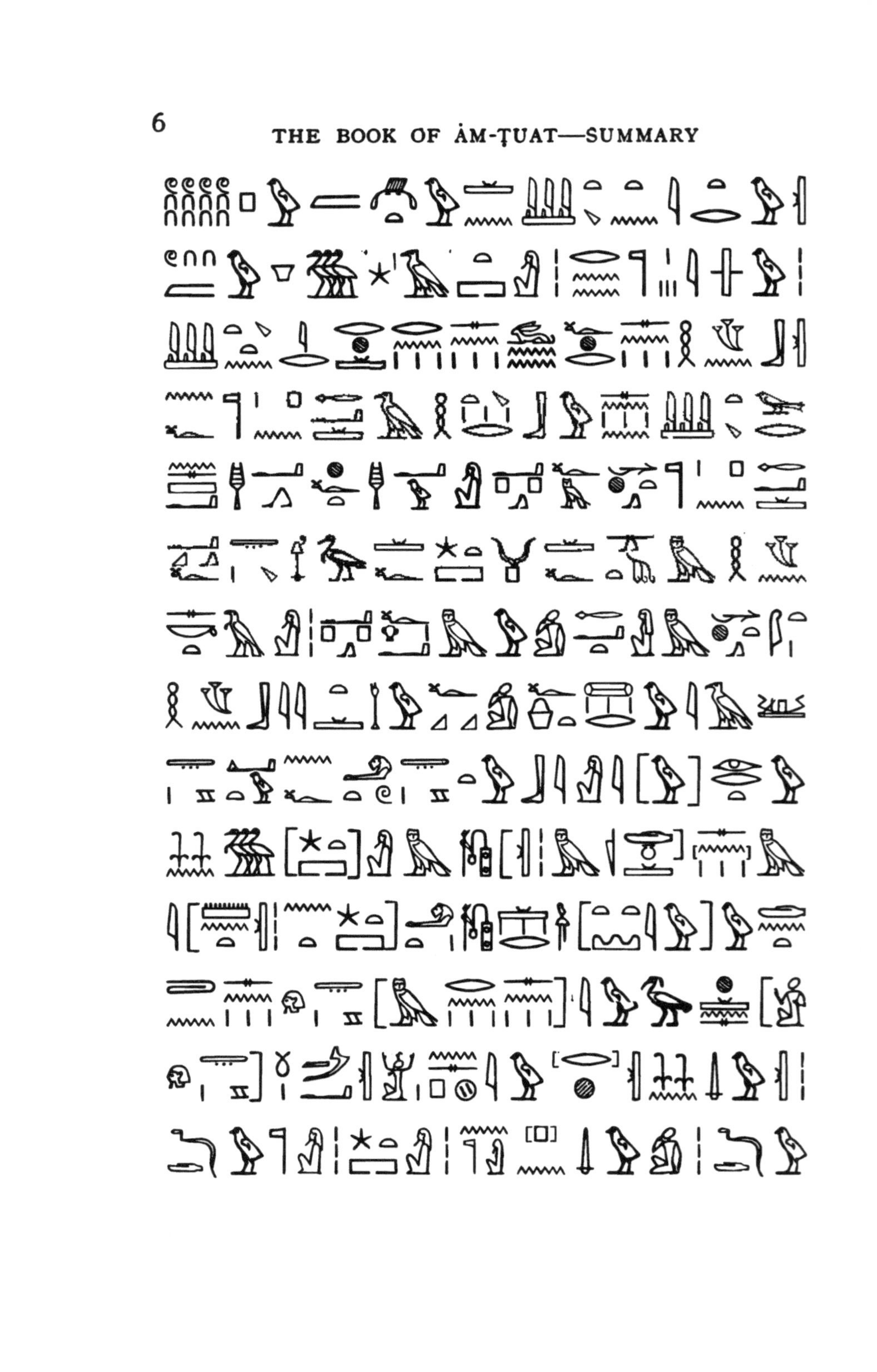

THE SECOND HOUR.

II.—From the Leyden Papyrus, T. 71.

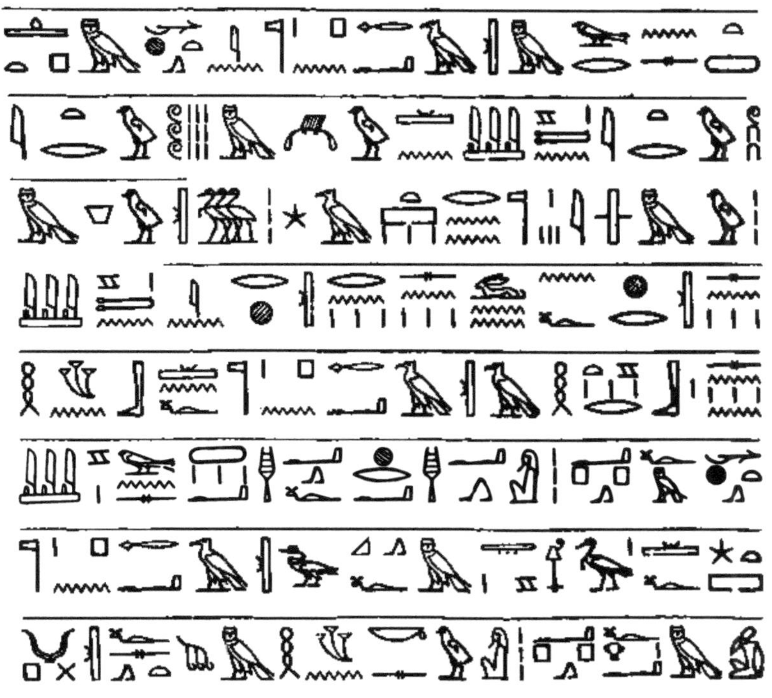

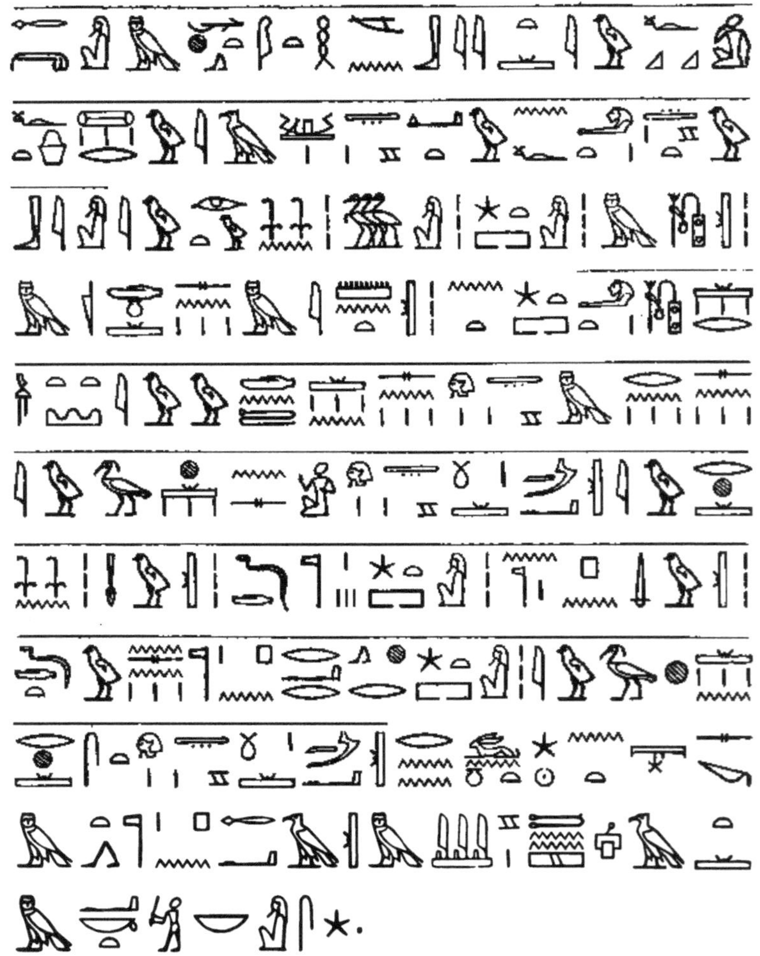

THE THIRD HOUR.

This great god afterwards taketh up his position in the Fields of the PERU-gods (i.e., the Fighters), and this great god paddleth his way over the STREAM OF OSIRIS (NET-ÅSÅR) in sailing up this Field, which is three hundred and nine ÅTRU long, and one hundred and twenty ÅTRU wide. This great god uttereth words to those who are in the following of Osiris to this City, and he allotteth unto them estates which are situated in this Field.

BAIU-SHETAIU (i.e., Hidden Souls) is the name of the gods who are in this Field, and whosoever knoweth their names upon earth shall be able to approach to the place where Osiris is, and there shall be given unto him water for his Field.

NET-NEB-UA-KHEPER-ÅUĀTU is the name of this Field. Whosoever shall know these hidden similitudes of the Hidden Souls in the correct forms wherein they are depicted in Åment of the Ṭuat—now the beginning of such representations should be from Åmentet—[these figures I say] shall act as magical protectors to that man upon earth, [and] in Neter-khert, regularly and unfailingly.

Whosoever knoweth these, when he is making his journey past them shall escape from their roarings, and he shall not fall down into their furnaces (or, pits).

Whosoever knoweth this, when he is keeping ward over [his] seat (or, place), his bread-cake shall be with Rā; and whosoever knoweth this, being soul [and] spirit, shall have the mastery over his legs, and shall never enter into the place of destruction, but he shall come forth with his attributes (or, forms), and shall snuff the air for his hour.

THENṬENT-BAIU is the name of the hour of the night which guideth this great god through this Field.

THE THIRD HOUR.

I.—FROM THE TOMB OF SETI I. (lines 62—105).

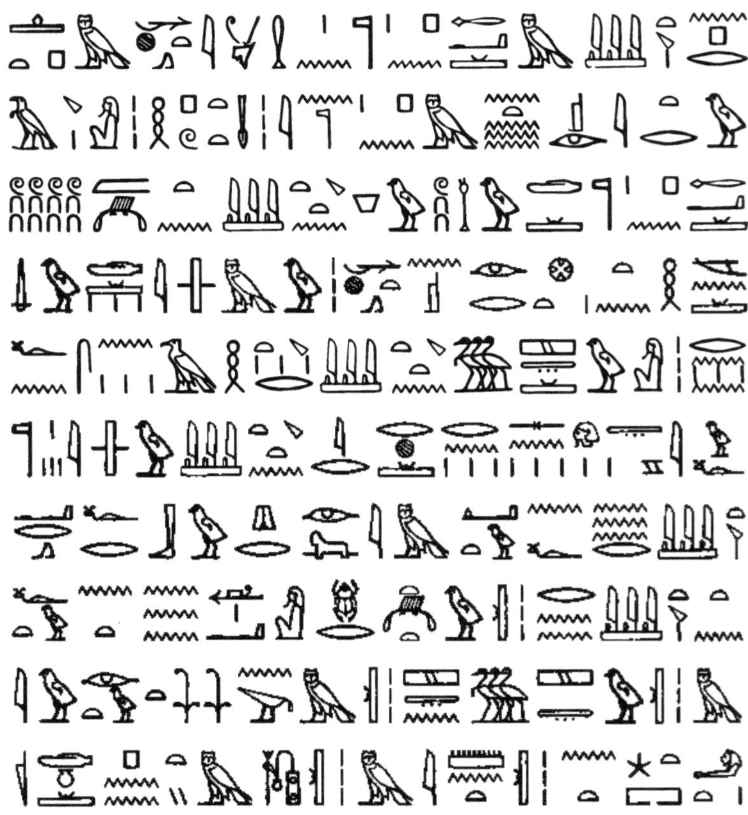

THE THIRD HOUR.

II.—From the Leyden Papyrus, T. 71.

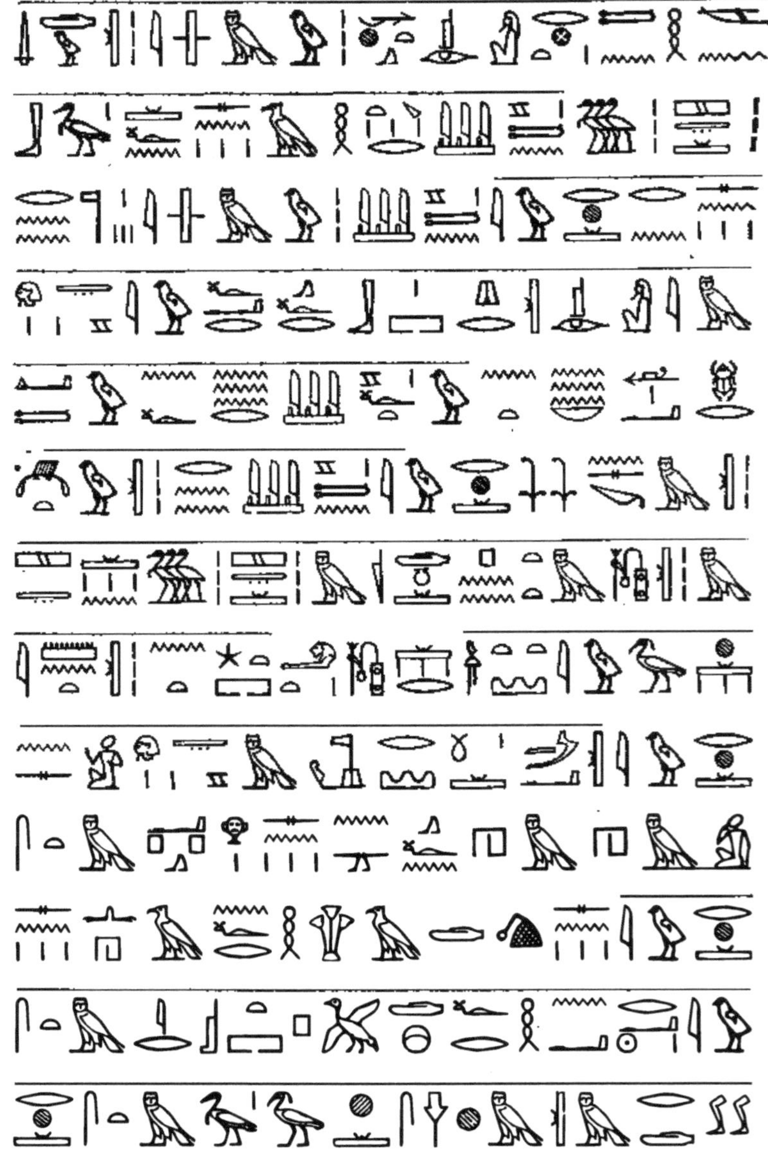

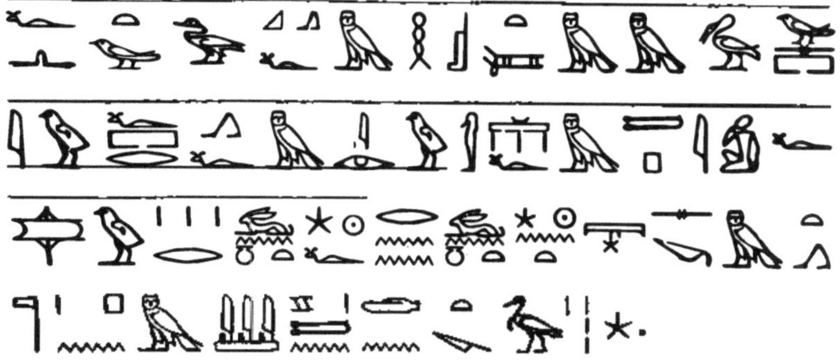

THE FOURTH HOUR.

The majesty of this great god, having been towed along, afterwards taketh up his position in the secret Circle of ÅMENTET, and he performeth the affairs of the gods of the Ṭuat who are therein by means of his voice, but he seeth them not.

ÅNKH-KHEPERU is the name of the gate of this Circle.

ÅMENT-SETHAU is the name of this Circle.

Whosoever knoweth this representation of the hidden roads of RE-STATET, and the holy paths of the ÅMMEḤET, and the secret doors which are in the Land of SEKER, the god who is upon his sand, shall be in the condition of him that eateth the bread-cakes which are [made] for the mouth of the LIVING gods in the Temple of Tem.

Whosoever knoweth this shall be in the condition of him that is *maāt* on the ways, and he shall journey over the roads of RE-SETHAU, and he shall see the representations of the ȦMMEḤET.

URT-EM-SEKHEMU-SET is the name of the hour of the night which guideth this great god.

THE FOURTH HOUR.

I.—FROM THE TOMB OF SETI I. (lines 106—138).

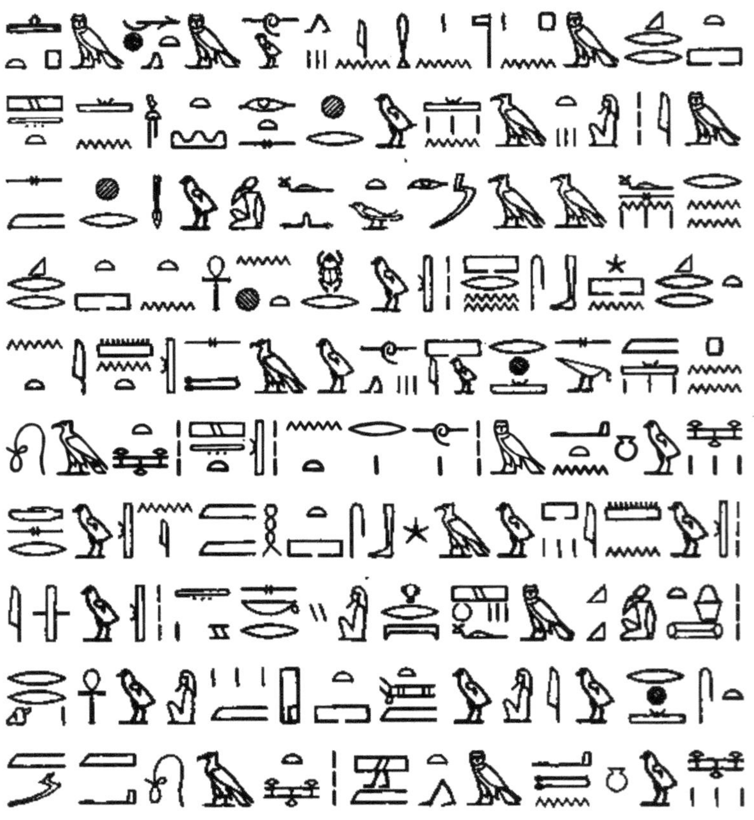

THE FOURTH HOUR.

II.—From the Leyden Papyrus, T. 71.

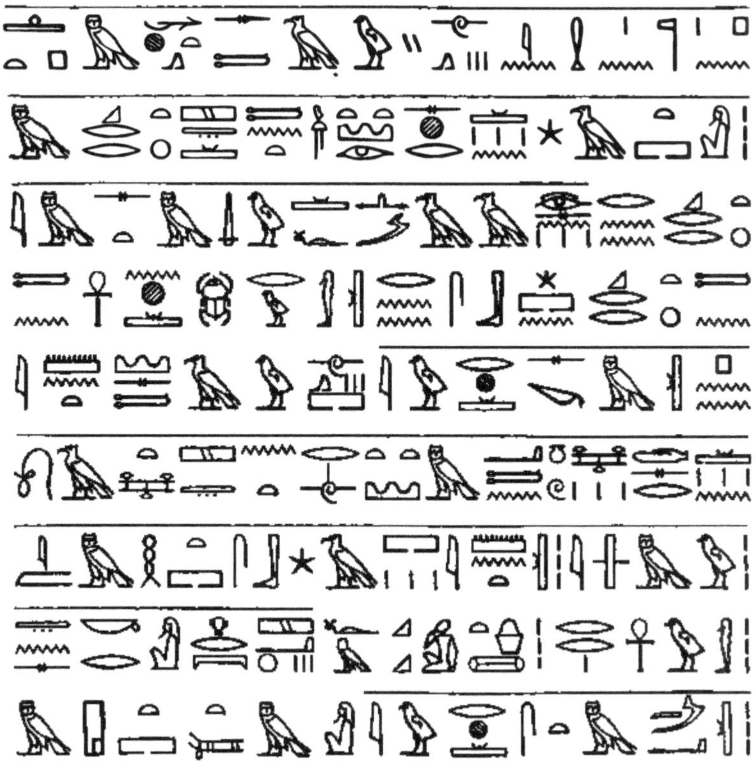

THE FIFTH HOUR.

This great god is towed along over the ways of Maāt of the Ṭuat through the upper half of this secret Circle of the god Seker, who is upon his sand, and he neither looketh upon nor gazeth at the secret figure of the earth which containeth the flesh of this god. The gods who are in [the train of] this god hear the words of Rā, who crieth unto them from where this god is.

Āḥā-neteru is the name of the door [of this City].

Åment is the name of the Circle of this god, [and in it are] the secret path of Åmentet, and the doors of the hidden palace, and the holy place of the Land of Seker [with his] flesh, and [his] members, [and his] body, in the divine form which they had at first.

Baiu-Åmu-Ṭuat is the name of the gods who are in [this] Circle. Their forms (*åru*) who are in their hour, and their secret shapes (*kheperu*) neither know, nor look upon, nor see this image (or, similitude) of SEKER (or, the hawk) himself.

Whosoever shall make these representations according to the image which is in writing in the hidden places of the Ṭuat, at the south of the Hidden Palace, and whosoever shall know them shall be at peace, and his soul shall unite itself to the offerings of SEKER, and the goddess KHEMIT shall not hack his body in pieces, and he shall go on his way towards her in peace. Whosoever shall make offerings to these gods upon earth—[these offerings, I say, shall act as magical protectors to that man upon earth, and in NETER-KHERT, regularly and unfailingly].

SEM-ḤER-ÅB-UÅA-S is the name of the hour of the night which guideth this great god through this Field.

THE FIFTH HOUR.

I.—FROM THE TOMB OF SETI I. (lines 139—173).

THE FIFTH HOUR.

II.—From the Leyden Papyrus, T. 71.

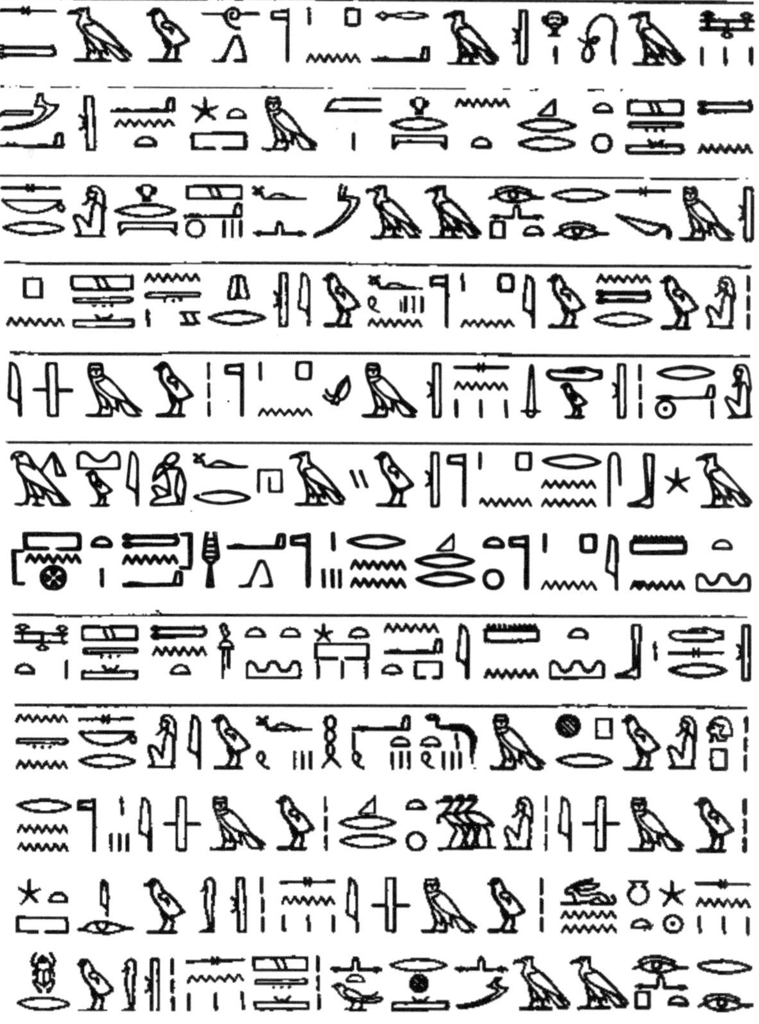

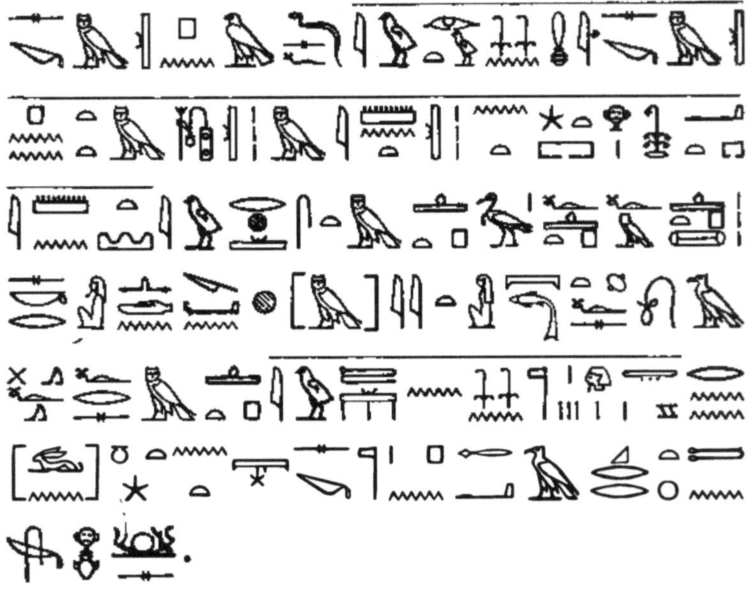

THE SIXTH HOUR.

The majesty of this great god taketh up his position in the stream of NEBT-MU-ṬUATIU (i.e., the Lord of the waters of the gods of the Ṭuat), and he sendeth forth words to the gods who are therein, and he commandeth that they have the mastery over their divine offerings in this City. He maketh his way through this Field, being provided with his Boat, and he setteth apart by his words the estates which are [to produce] their offerings in this City, and he giveth to them water for their lakes, and he travelleth through the Ṭuat every day.

SEPṬ-METU is the name of the door of this City.

The secrĕt roads of Ámentet, and the manner wherein this great god is being rowed along over the water therein in his boat to perform the plans (or, affairs) of the gods of the Ṭuat, the gathering together [of them] by their names, the manifestations of their shapes (or, forms), and [their] secret hours, such are the things of which the secret representation of the Ṭuat is not known to men and women.

Whosoever shall make [a copy of] this image in writing, according to the representation of the same which is in the hidden things of the Ṭuat, at the south of the Hidden Palace, and whosoever shall know them shall be in the condition of one who awardeth offerings in abundance in the Ṭuat, and he shall be united to the offerings of the gods who are in the following of Osiris, and his parents (or, kinsfolk) shall make the offerings which are obligatory on the earth.

The majesty of this great god sendeth forth words, and he giveth divine offerings to [the gods of] the Ṭuat, and he standeth up by them; and they see him, and they have dominion over their Fields and over the gifts made to them, and they effect their transformations by reason of the words which this great god hath spoken unto them.

METCHET-NEBT-ṬUATIU is the name of this Field, which is the road of the Boat of Rā.

MESPERIT-ÁR-MAĀT is the name of the hour of the night which guideth this great god through this country.

THE SIXTH HOUR.

I.—From the Tomb of Seti I. (lines 174—210).

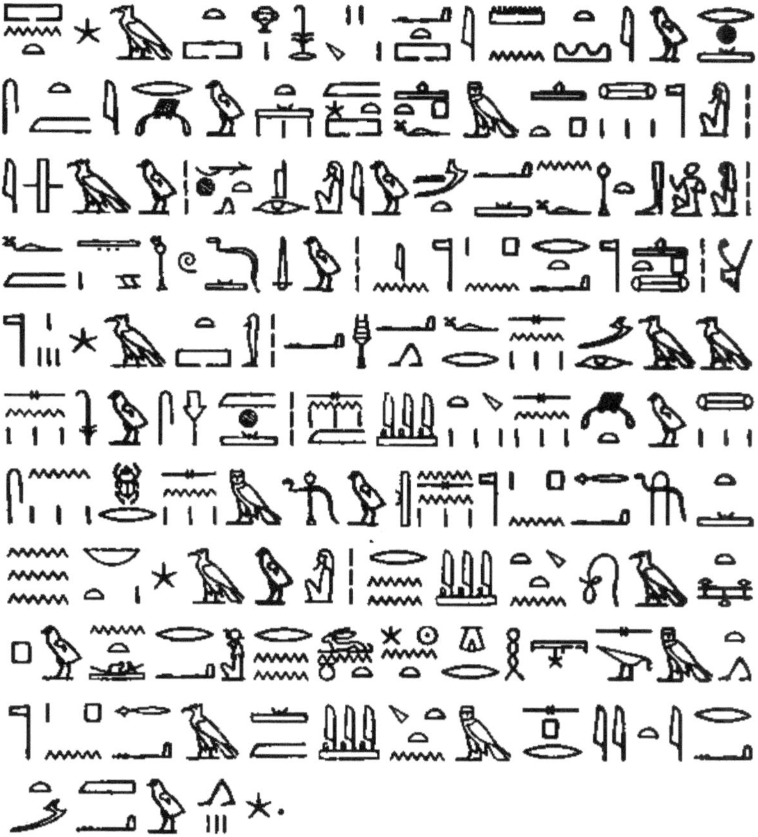

THE SIXTH HOUR.

II.—From the Leyden Papyrus, T. 71.

THE SEVENTH HOUR.

The majesty of this great god taketh up his position in the secret place of Osiris, and the majesty of this great god sendeth forth words into this to the gods who dwell therein. This god maketh to himself other forms for this hidden place in order to drive out of his path the serpent fiend ĀPEP by means of the words of power of ISIS, and the words of power of SEMSU (?).

RUTI-ȦSȦR is the name of the gate of this City through which this god passeth.

TEPḤET-SHETA is the name of this City.

This great god maketh his way over the road of Åment in the holy boat, and he passeth in it over this road which is without water, without being towed along. He maketh his way by means of the words of power of ISIS, and by means of the words of power of SEMSU (?), and the utterances of this great god himself [act as] magical protectors, and perform the slaughters of Åpep in the Ṭuat, in this Circle, in his windings in the sky.

Whosoever shall make [a copy of] these [pictures] according to the similitudes which are in writing at the northern side of the Hidden Palace in the Ṭuat, they shall act as magical protectors for him that maketh them in heaven and in earth. And whosoever knoweth them shall be a soul of souls with Rā. And whosoever shall make (i.e., recite) the words of power of ISIS and the words of power of SEMSU, shall make to be driven back the Åpep of Rā in Åmentet. Whosoever shall do [this] in the Hidden Palace of the Ṭuat, and whosoever shall do [this] upon earth, [the result is] the same. Whosoever knoweth this shall be in the Boat of Rā, both in heaven and upon earth; but he that hath no knowledge of this representation shall not know how to drive back NEḤA-ḤRÅ (i.e., Stinking-Face).

Now the ridge of earth of NEḤA-ḤRÅ in the Ṭuat is four hundred and fifty cubits in length, and he filleth it with the undulations of his body. The regions which belong to him are made (i.e., kept) for him, and the great god doth not make his way over him when he maketh him to turn aside out of the way for him, from the secret place of Osiris, when this god maketh his way through this city in the form of the serpent **Meḥen**.

Whosoever shall know this upon earth, the serpent Neḥa-ḥrȧ shall not drink his water, and the soul of him that knoweth it shall not be evilly entreated by the gods who are in this Circle; and whosoever knoweth it the crocodile Āb-shau shall not devour his soul.

Khesef-hai-ḥeseq-Neḥa-ḥrȧ is the name of the hour of the night which guideth this great god through this Circle.

THE SEVENTH HOUR.

I.—From the Tomb of Seti I. (lines 210—213).

THE SEVENTH HOUR.

II.—From the Leyden Papyrus, T. 71.

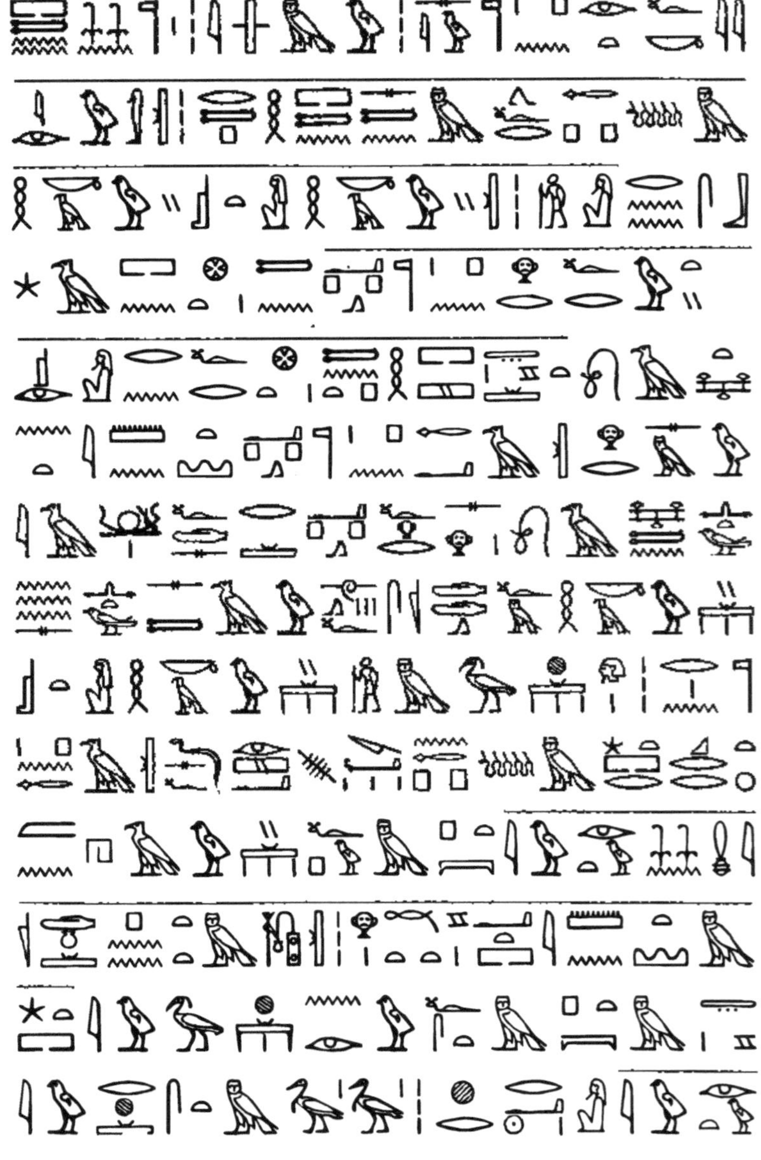

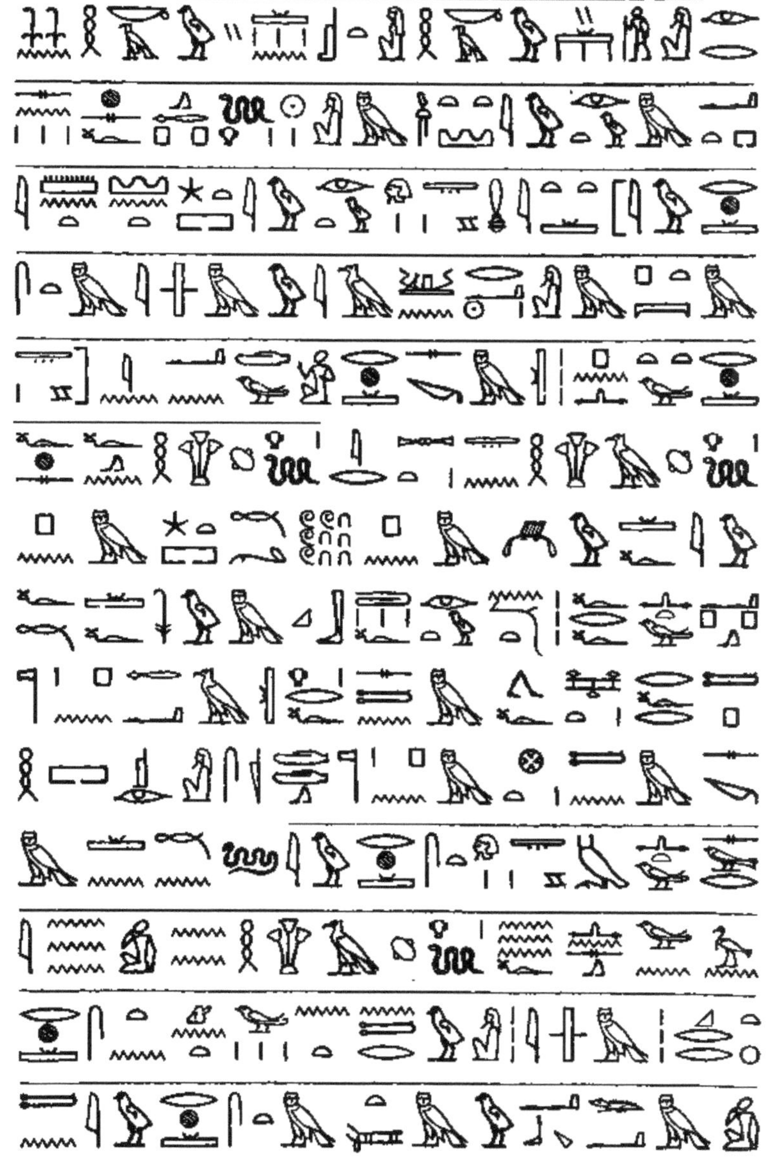

THE EIGHTH HOUR.

When the majesty of this great god hath taken up his position in the secret Circles of those who are in their sand, he sendeth forth words to them from out of his Boat, and the gods tow along him that is in the holy embrace (?) of the serpent MEḤEN.

ÅḤĀ-ÅN-URṬ-F is the name of the gate of this City.

ṬEBAT-NETERU-SET is the name of this City.

As for the secret Circle of ÅMENTET, this great god maketh his way over it in his Boat, by means of the towing of the gods who are in the Ṭuat.

Whosoever shall make [a copy of] these things according to the similitude which is in writing on the north [wall] of the Hidden Palace in the Ṭuat, and whosoever shall know them by their names, shall be in the condition of one who is fully provided with swathings on the earth, and he shall never be repulsed at the secret gates, and he shall have abundant offerings in the great funeral hall regularly and unfailingly for millions of years.

NEBT-USHA is the name of the hour of the night which guideth this great god.

THE EIGHTH HOUR.

From the Leyden Papyrus, T. 71.

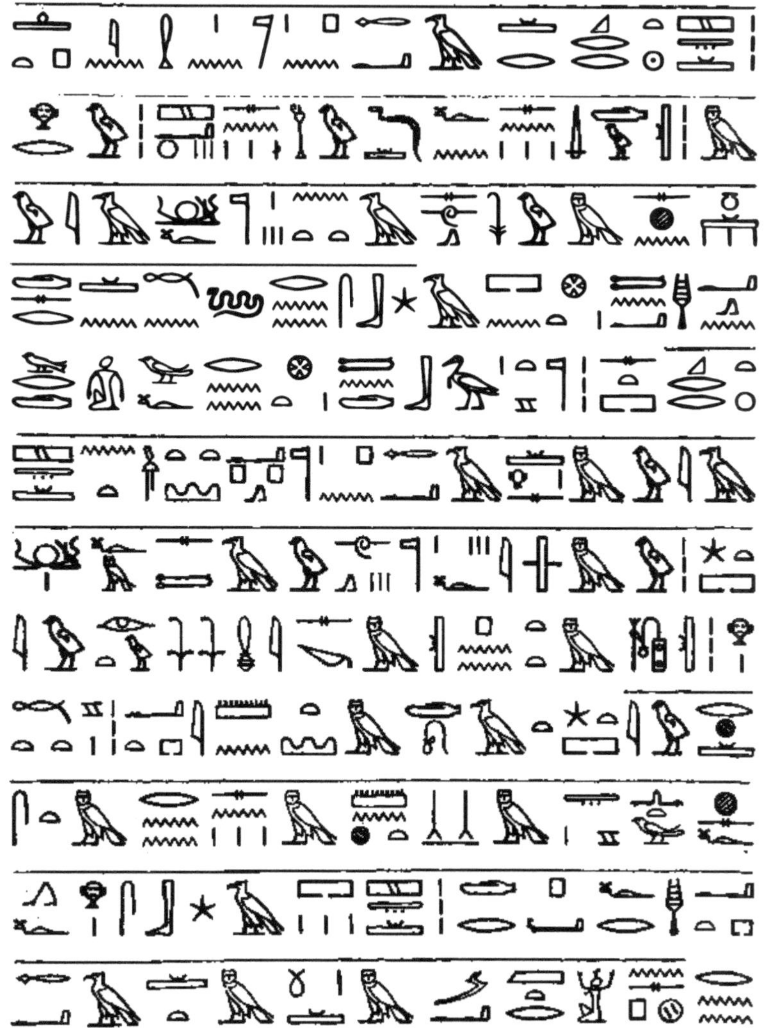

THE NINTH HOUR.

When the majesty of this great god hath taken up his position in this Circle, he sendeth forth words from his Boat to the gods who dwell therein, and the sailors join the Boat of this great god in this City.

SAA-ḲEB is the name of the gate of this City through which this great god passeth to take up his position on the stream which is in this City.

BES-ȦRU is the name of this City, which is the secret Circle of ȦMENTET, wherein take up their positions in the Ṭuat this great god and his sailors.

Whosoever maketh [a copy of] these things in their names according to the similitudes which are in writing on the east [wall] of the Hidden Palace of the Ṭuat, and whosoever knoweth their names upon earth, and knoweth their habitations in Ȧmentet, shall rest in his habitation in the Ṭuat, and he shall stand up among the lords of the provisions of the gods, and his voice shall be *maāt* before the *tchatcha* beings on the day of the reckoning of Pharaoh (literally, the thrice great house). And these things shall act as magical protectors to him that knoweth them upon earth.

MĀK-NEB-S is the name of the hour of the night which guideth this great god in this Circle.

THE NINTH HOUR.

FROM THE LEYDEN PAPYRUS, T. 71.

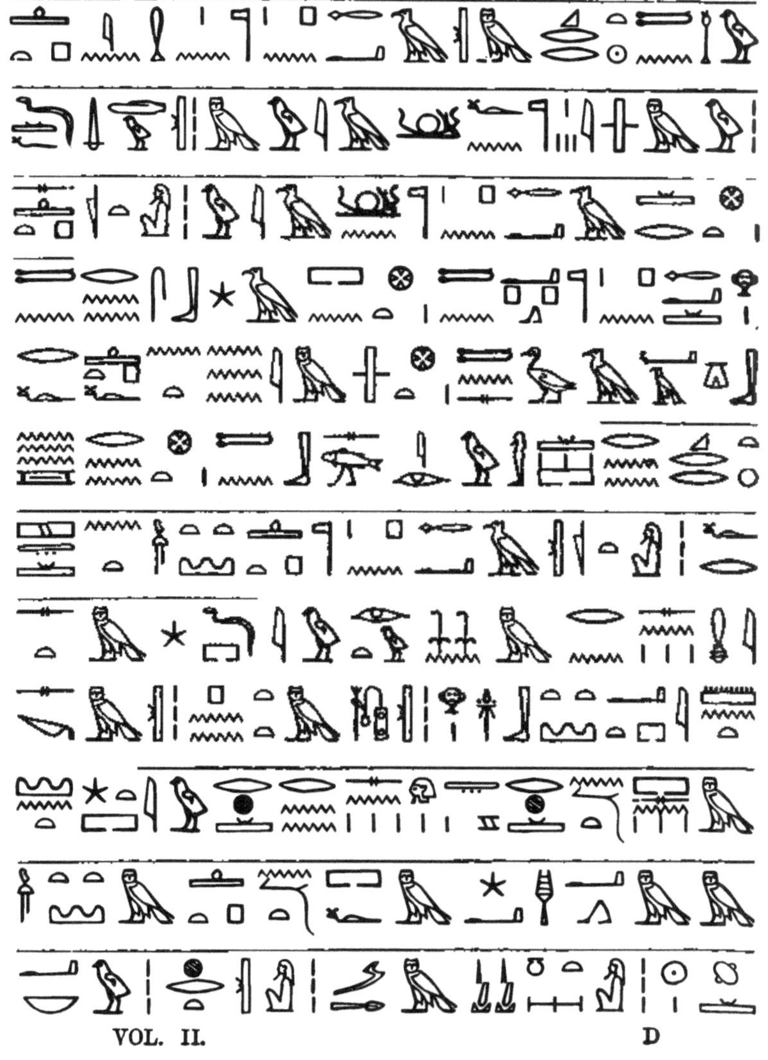

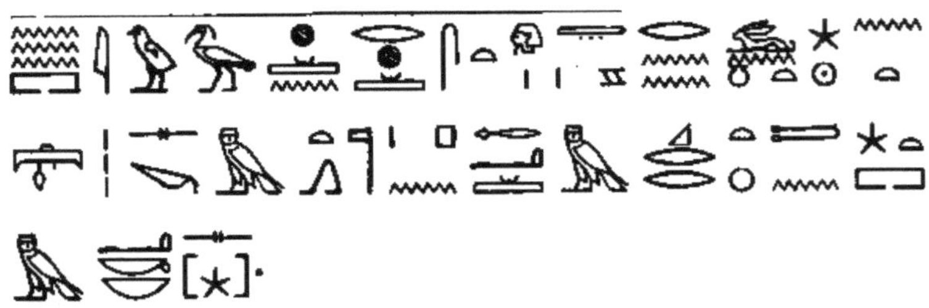

THE TENTH HOUR.

The majesty of this great god taketh up his position in this Circle, and he sendeth forth words to the gods who are in it.

AA-KHEPERU-MES-ÅRU is the name of the gate of this City through which this great god passeth.

METCH-QA-UṬEBU is the name of this City. [This is] the secret Circle of Åmentet whereto KHEPERÅ joineth himself before Rā, and the gods, and the spirits, and the dead cry out from it over the secret representations (or, images) of ÅḲERT.

Whosoever shall make [a copy of] these [representations] according to the figures which are depicted on the east [wall] of Åment, and whosoever knoweth them by their names shall journey round about in the Ṭuat, and shall travel through it, and he shall not be driven back, and he shall flourish with Rā.

ṬENṬENIT-ḤESQ-KHAKÅBU is the name of the hour of the night which guideth this great god through the secret ways of this City.

THE TENTH HOUR.

From the Leyden Papyrus, T. 71.

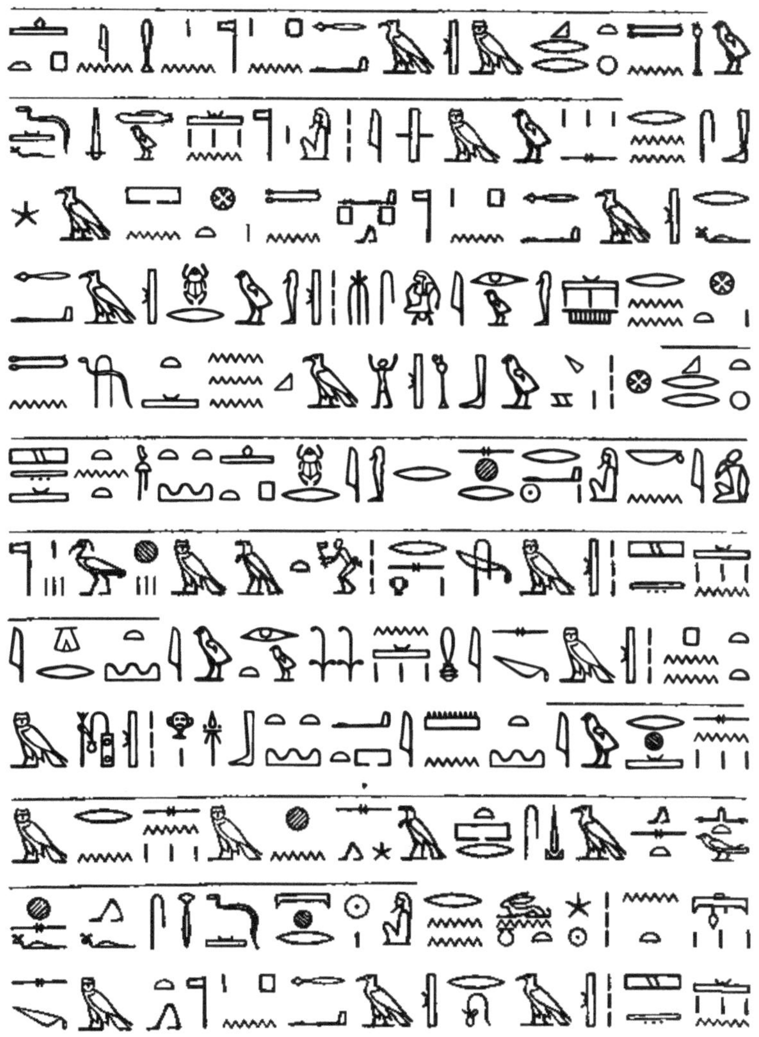

THE ELEVENTH HOUR.

The majesty of this great god taketh up his position in this Circle, and he sendeth forth words unto the gods who are therein.

SEKHEN-ṬUATIU is the name of the gate of this City through which this great god passeth.

RE-EN-QERERT-ÅPT-KHAT is the name of this City. [This is] the secret Circle of the Ṭuat into which this great god passeth on his way, and [he] cometh forth at the eastern mountain of the sky, the eater of eternity. The form thereof is in the presence of the serpent PETRA, which dwelleth in this City, and they (i.e., the gods) place themselves in the train of [Rā] when the birth of KHEPER upon earth is about to take place.

Whosoever shall make [a copy] of these [representations] according to the figures which are depicted on the east [wall] of the palace of Åment in the hidden [places] of the Ṭuat, and whosoever knoweth them shall be in the position of him that divideth his offering, and of him who is a spirit who is suitably equipped [to travel] both in heaven and upon earth, regularly and unceasingly.

SEBIT-NEB-UÅA-KHESEF-SEBIU-EM-PERT-F is the name of the hour of the night which guideth this great god in this Circle.

THE ELEVENTH HOUR.

From the Leyden Papyrus, T. 71.

THE TWELFTH HOUR.

The majesty of this great god taketh up his position in this Circle at the limits of the thick darkness, and this great god is born under the form of KHEPERÀ in this Circle. The gods NU and ÀMMUI, and ḤEḤ and ḤEḤ[UT] are in this Circle at the birth of this great god, when he maketh his appearance from the Ṭuat, and taketh up his place in the Māṭeṭ Boat, and riseth from between the thighs of the goddess Nut.

THENEN-NETERU is the name of the gate of this City. KHEPER-KEKUI-KHĀ-MESTI is the name of this City. [This is] the secret Circle of the Ṭuat, wherein this great god is born, when he maketh his appearance in NU, and taketh up his place in the body of NUT.

Whosoever shall make [a copy] of these [representations] according to the figures which are depicted on the east [wall] of the palace of Àment of the Ṭuat, they shall be magical protectors to him that knoweth them upon earth, both in heaven and on earth.

At this point the light beginneth [to come], and it is the end of the thick darkness which Rā travelleth through in Àmentet, and of the secret matters which this great god performed therein. He who hath no knowledge of the whole (?) or part (?) of the secret representations of the Ṭuat, shall be condemned to destruction.

Whosoever shall make [a copy] of these [representations] according to this copy of what is in the Ȧment of the Ṭuat, [which] cannot be looked at or seen, and whosoever shall know these secret images shall be in the condition of the spirit who is equipped [for journeying], and shall come forth [from] and shall descend into the Ṭuat, and shall hold converse with the men and women who live [there] regularly and unfailingly, millions of times.

THE TWELFTH HOUR.

FROM THE LEYDEN PAPYRUS, T. 71.

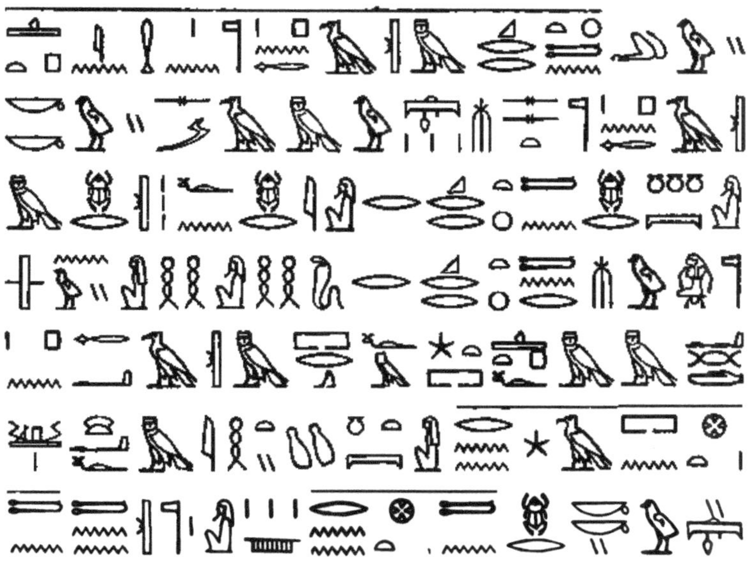

THE BOOK OF GATES

THE BOOK OF GATES

CHAPTER I.

THE ALABASTER SARCOPHAGUS OF SETI I.

THE text of the "Book of Gates," printed in the following pages, is taken from the alabaster sarcophagus of king Seti I., B.C. 1370, which is preserved in the Museum of Sir John Soane, at 13, Lincoln's Inn Fields. This sarcophagus is, undoubtedly, one of the chief authorities for the text of that remarkable book; but before any attempt is made to describe the arrangement of the scenes and the inscriptions which accompany them, it will be well to recall the principal facts connected with its discovery by Giovanni Battista Belzoni, who has fortunately placed them on record in his *Narrative of the Operations and recent discoveries within the pyramids, temples, tombs and Excavations in Egypt and Nubia*, London, 1820, p. 233 ff. In October, 1815, Belzoni began to excavate in the Bibân-al-Mulûk, i.e., the Valley of the Tombs of the Kings, on the western bank of the Nile at Thebes, and in the bed of a watercourse he found a spot where the ground bore traces of having been "moved." On the 19th of the month his workmen made a way through the sand and fragments of stone which had been piled up there, and entered the first corridor or passage of a magnificent tomb, which he soon discovered to have been made for one of the great kings of Egypt. A second corridor led him to a square chamber which, being thirty feet deep, formed a serious obstacle in the way of any unauthorized intruder, and served to catch any rain-water which might make its way down the corridors from the entrance. Beyond this chamber are two halls, and from the first of these Belzoni passed through other corridors and rooms until he entered the vaulted chamber in which stood the sarcophagus.[1] The sarcophagus chamber is situated at a distance of 320 feet from the entrance to the first corridor, and is 180 feet below the level of the ground. Belzoni succeeded in bringing the sarcophagus from its chamber into the light of day without injury, and in due course it arrived in England; the negotiations which he opened with the Trustees of the British Museum, to whom its purchase was first proposed, fell through, and he subsequently sold it to Sir John Soane, it is said for the sum of £2000. An examination of the sarcophagus shows that both it and its cover were hollowed out of monolithic blocks of alabaster,

[1] As Belzoni's narrative is of interest, his account of his discovery of Seti's tomb is given in the Appendix to this Chapter.

and it is probable, as Mr. Sharpe says,[1] that these were quarried in the mountains near Alabastronpolis, i.e., the district which was known to the Egyptians by the name of Ḥet-nub, , and is situated near the ruins known in modern times by the name of Tell al-'Amarna. In the Ḥet-nub quarries large numbers of inscriptions, written chiefly in the hieratic character, have been found, and from the interesting selection from these published by Messrs. Blackden and Fraser, we learn that several kings of the Ancient and Middle Empires carried on works in them, no doubt for the purpose of obtaining alabaster for funeral purposes. The sarcophagus is 9 ft. 4 in. long, 3 ft. 8 in. wide, in the widest part, and 2 ft. 8 in. high at the shoulders, and 2 ft. 3 in. at the feet; the cover is 1 ft. 3 in. high. The thickness of the alabaster varies from 2½ to 4 inches. The skill of the mason who succeeded in hollowing the blocks without breaking, or even cracking them, is marvellous, and the remains of holes nearly one inch in diameter suggest that the drill was as useful to him as the chisel and mallet in hollowing out the blocks. When the sarcophagus and its cover were finally shaped and polished, they were handed over to an artisan who was skilled in cutting hieroglyphics and figures of the gods, &c., in stone, and both the insides and outsides were covered by him

[1] *The Alabaster Sarcophagus of Oimenepthah I., King of Egypt.* London, 1864, p. 14.

with inscriptions and vignettes and mythological scenes which illustrated them. Both inscriptions and scenes were then filled in with a kind of paint made from some preparation of copper, and the vivid bluish green colour of this paint must have formed a striking contrast to the brilliant whiteness of the alabaster when fresh from the quarry. At the present time large numbers of characters and figures are denuded of their colour, and those in which it still remains are much discoloured by London fog and soot.

The first to attempt to describe the contents of the texts and scenes on the sarcophagus of Seti I. was the late Samuel Sharpe, who, with the late Joseph Bonomi, published "The Alabaster Sarcophagus of Oimenepthah I., King of Egypt," London, 1864, 4to; the former was responsible for the letterpress, and the latter for the plates of scenes and texts. For some reason which it is not easy to understand, Mr. Sharpe decided that the hieroglyphic characters which formed the prenomen of the king for whom the sarcophagus was made were to be read "Oimenepthah," a result which he obtained by assigning the phonetic value of O to the hieroglyphic sign for Osiris . The prenomen is sometimes written , or , and , and is to be read either SETI-MER-EN-PTAḤ, or SETI-MEN-EN-PTAḤ. Mr. Sharpe did not, apparently, realize that both the signs and were to be read "Set," and he gave to the first the phonetic value of A and to the second the value of O; he next identified "Aimenepthah" or "Oimenepthah" with the Amenophath of Manetho, and the Chomaepthah of Eratosthenes, saying, "hence arises the support to our reading his name (i.e., the king's) Oimenepthah." Passing over Mr. Sharpe's further remarks, which assert that the sarcophagus was made in the year B.C. 1175 (!), we must consider briefly the arrangement of the texts and scenes upon the insides and outsides of the sarcophagus and its covers. On the upper outside edge of the sarcophagus runs a single line of hieroglyphics which contains speeches supposed to be made to the deceased by the four children of Horus; this line is in two sections, each of which begins at the right hand side of the head, and ends at the left hand side of the foot. Below this line of hieroglyphics are five large scenes, each of which is divided into three registers, and these are enclosed between two dotted bands which are intended to represent the borders of the "Valley of the Other World." On the inside of the sarcophagus are also five scenes, but there is no line of hieroglyphics running along the upper edge. On the bottom of the sarcophagus is a finely cut figure of the goddess Nut, and round and about her are texts selected from the Theban Recension of the *Book of the Dead;* on the inside of the cover is a figure of the goddess Nut, with arms outstretched. On the outside of the cover, in addition to the texts which record the names and titles of the deceased, are inscribed two large scenes, each of which is divided into three registers, like those inside and outside the sarcophagus.

The line of text on the upper outside edge reads:—

I.

I. Speech of Mesthȧ: "I am Mesthȧ, I am [thy] son, "O Osiris, king, lord of the two lands, Men-Maāt-Rā, "whose word is *maāt*, son of the Sun, Seti Mer-en-Ptaḥ, "whose word is *maāt*, and I have come so that I "may be among those who protect thee. I make to "flourish thy house, which shall be doubly established, "by the command of Ptaḥ; by the command of Rā "himself."

Speech of Ȧnpu: "I am Ȧnpu, who dwelleth in (or, "with) the funeral chest." He saith, "Mother Isis "descendeth . . . . bandages for me, Osiris, king "Men-Maāt-Rā, whose word is *maāt*, son of the Sun, "Seti Mer-en-Ptaḥ, whose word is *maāt*, from him "that worketh against me."

Speech of Ṭuamātef: "I am Ṭuamātef, I am thy "son Horus, I love thee, and I have come to avenge "thee, Osiris, upon him that would work his wicked-

"ness upon thee, and I will set him under thy feet "for ever, Osiris, king, lord of the two lands, Men-"Maāt-Rā, son of the Sun, [proceeding] from his "body, loving him, lord of crowns (or, risings) Seti "Mer-en-Ptaḥ, whose word is *maāt*, before the Great "God."

To be said: "Rā liveth, the Tortoise dieth! Strong "are the members of . . . . . Osiris, king Men-Maāt-"Rā, whose word is *maāt*, for Qebḥsennuf guardeth "them. Rā liveth, the Tortoise dieth! In a sound "state is he who is in the sarcophagus, in a sound state "is he who is in the sarcophagus, that is to say, the "son of the Sun, Seti Mer-en-Ptaḥ, whose word is "*maāt*."

Speech of NUT: Nut, the great one of Seb, saith: "O Osiris, king, lord of the two lands, Men-Maāt-Rā, "whose word is *maāt*, who loveth me, I give unto "thee purity on the earth, and splendour (or, glory) "in the heavens, and I give unto thee thy head for "ever."

II. Speech of NUT, who is over the ḤENNU BOAT: "This is my son, Osiris, king, Men-Maāt-Rā, whose "word is *maāt*. His father Shu loveth him, and his "mother Nut loveth him, Osiris, son of Rā, Seti Mer-"en-Ptaḥ, whose word is *maāt*."

Speech of ḤĀPI: "I am Ḥāpi. I have come that I "might be among those who protect thee, I bind "together for thee thy head, [and thy members, smiting "down for thee thine enemies beneath thee, and I give "thee][1] thy head, O Osiris, king, Men-Maāt-Rā, whose "word is *maāt*, son of Rā, Seti Mer-en-Ptaḥ, whose "word is *maāt*."

Speech of ÂNPU, the Governor of the divine house: "I am Ânpu, the Governor of the divine house. O "Osiris, king, lord of the two lands, Men-Maāt-Rā, "whose word is *maāt*, son of the Sun, [proceeding] "from his body, the lord of crowns, Seti Mer-en-Ptaḥ, "whose word is *maāt*, the *Shennu* beings go round "about thee, and thy members remain uninjured, O "Osiris, king, Men-Maāt-Rā, whose word is *maāt* for "ever."

Speech of QEBḤSENNUF: "I am thy son, I have "come that I might be among those who protect "thee. I gather together for thee thy bones, and "I piece together for thee thy limbs. I bring unto "thee thy heart, and I set it upon its seat in thy "body. I make to flourish (or, germinate) for thee thy "house after thee, [O thou who] liv[est] for ever."

To be said: "Rā liveth, the Tortoise dieth! Let "enter the bones of Osiris, king Men-Maāt-Rā, whose "word is *maāt*, the son of the Sun, Seti Mer-en-Ptaḥ, "whose word is *maāt*, let them enter into their founda-"tions. Pure is the dead body which is in the earth,

[1] Supplying the words [hieroglyphs] from the well-known speech on the Canopic jars.

"and pure are the bones of Osiris, king Men-Maāt-Rā, "whose word is *maāt,* like Rā [for ever!]."

On the bottom of the sarcophagus is a large, full-length figure of the goddess NUT, who is depicted in the form of a woman with her arms ready to embrace the body of the king. Her face and the lower parts of the body below the waist are in profile, but she has a front chest, front shoulders, and a front eye. Her feet are represented as if each was a right foot, and each only shows the great toe. One breast is only shown. The hair of the goddess is long and falls over her back and shoulders; it is held in position over her forehead by a bandlet. She wears a deep collar or necklace, and a closely-fitting feather-work tunic which extends from her breast to her ankles; the latter is supported by two shoulder straps, each of which is fastened with a buckle on the shoulder. She has anklets on her legs, and bracelets on her wrists, and armlets on her arms. The inscriptions which are cut above the head, and at both sides, and under the feet of the goddess contain addresses to the king by the great gods of the sky, and extracts from the *Book of the Dead;* they read:—

THE SARCOPHAGUS OF SETI I.

INSCRIPTION ON THE BOTTOM OF THE SARCOPHAGUS OF SETI I.

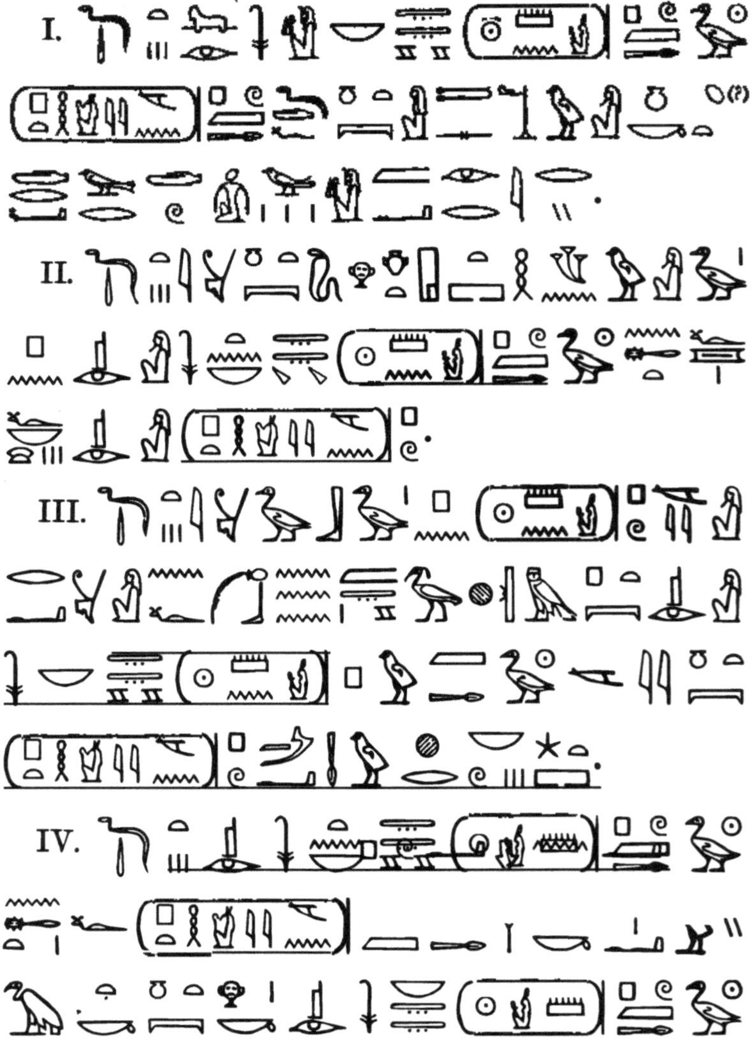

INSCRIPTION ON THE BOTTOM OF THE SARCOPHAGUS OF SETI I.

The words of Osiris the king, the lord of the two lands, MEN-MAĀT-RĀ, whose word is *maāt*, the son of Rā (i.e., the Sun), SETI MER-EN-PTAḤ, whose word is *maāt*, who saith, "O thou goddess NUT, support thou "me, for I am thy son. Destroy thou my defects of "immobility, together with those who produce them."

II. The goddess NUT, who dwelleth in ḤET-ḤENNU, saith, "This [is my] son Osiris, the king, the lord "of the two lands, MEN-MAĀT-RĀ, whose word is "*maāt*, the son of Rā, [proceeding] from his body, "who loveth him, the lord of crowns, Osiris, SETI "MER-EN-PTAḤ."

III. The god SEB saith, "This [is my] son MEN-"MAĀT-RĀ, who loveth me. I have given unto him "purity upon earth, and glory in heaven, him the "Osiris, king, the lord of the two lands, MEN-MAĀT-RĀ, "whose word is *maāt*, the son of Rā, the lover of Nut, "that is to say, SETI MER-EN-PTAḤ, whose word is "*maāt*, before the lords of the Ṭuat."

IV. Words which are to be said:—"O Osiris, king, "lord of the two lands, MEN-MAĀT-RĀ, whose word is "*maāt*, the son of Rā, [proceeding] from his body, that "is to say, SETI MER-EN-PTAḤ, whose word is *maāt*. "Thy mother NUT putteth forth [her] two hands and "arms over thee, Osiris, king, lord of the two lands, "MEN-MAĀT-RĀ, whose word is *maāt*, son of Rā,

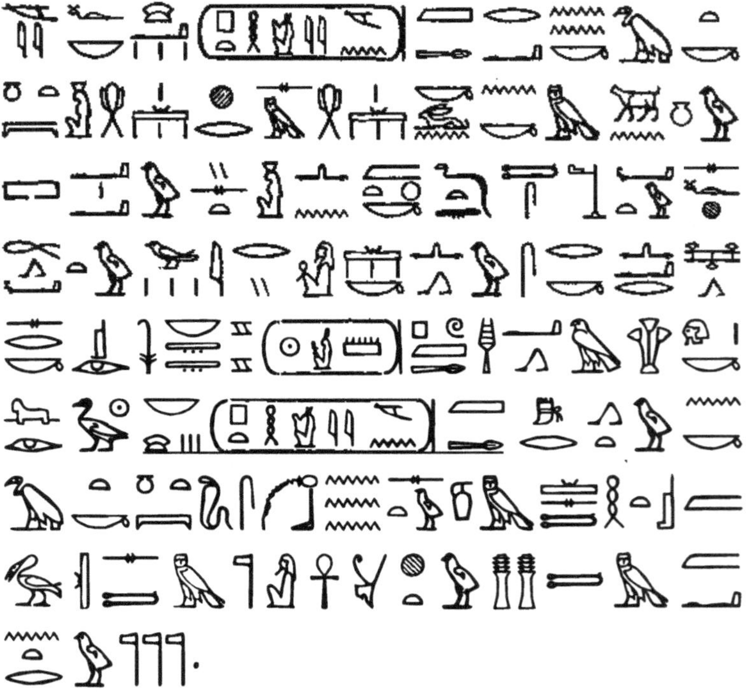

V.

"whom he loveth, lord of diadems, SETI MER-EN-"PTAḤ, whose word is *maāt.* Thy mother NUT "hath added the magical powers which are thine, "and thou art in her arms, and thou shalt never "die. Lifted up and driven away are the calamities "which were to thee, and they shall never [more] "come to thee, and shall never draw nigh unto "thee, Osiris, king, the lord of the two lands, MEN-"MAĀT-RĀ, whose word is *maāt.* Horus hath taken "up his stand behind thee, Osiris, son of Rā, lord "of diadems, SETI MER-EN-PTAḤ, whose word is "*maāt,* for thy mother NUT hath come unto thee; "she hath purified (or, washed) thee, she hath united "herself to thee, she hath supplied thee as a "god, and thou art alive and stablished among the "gods."

V. The great goddess NUT saith, "I have endowed "him with a soul, I have endowed him with a spirit, "and I have given him power in the body of his "mother TEFNUT, I who was never brought forth. I "have come, and I have united myself to OSIRIS, "the king, the lord of the two lands, MEN-MAĀT-RĀ, "whose word is *maāt,* the son of Rā, the lord of "diadems, SETI MER-EN-PTAḤ, whose word is *maāt,* "with life, stability, and power. He shall not "die. I am NUT of the mighty heart, and I took "up my being in the body of my mother TEFNUT "in my name of Nut; over my mother none hath

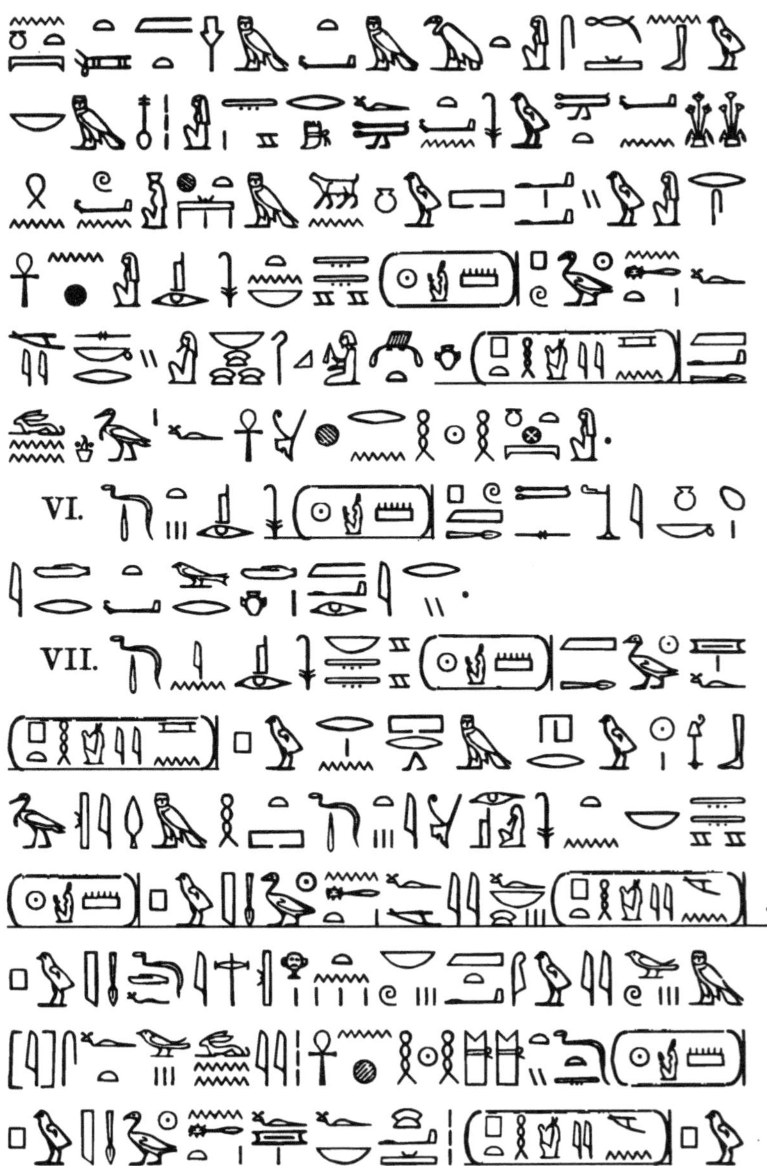
VI.
VII.

"gained the mastery. I have filled every place with my "beneficence, and I have led captive the whole earth; "I have led captive the South and the North, and I "have gathered together the things which are into my "arms to vivify Osiris, the king, the lord of the two "lands, MEN-MAĀT-RĀ, the son of the Sun, [proceeding] "from his body, the lover of SEKER, the lord of diadems, "the governor whose heart is glad, SETI MER-EN-PTAḤ, "whose word is *maāt*. His soul shall live for ever!"

VI. ["Nut,"] saith Osiris, the king MEN-MAĀT-RĀ, whose word is *maāt*, "Raise thou me up! I am [thy] "son, set thou free him whose heart is at rest from "that which maketh [it to be still]."

VII. Osiris, the king, the lord of the two lands, MEN-MAĀT-RĀ, whose word is *maāt*, the son of the Sun, loving him, SETI MER-EN-PTAḤ, saith the

CHAPTER OF COMING FORTH BY DAY AND OF MAKING A WAY THROUGH ĀMMEḤET.[1]

Saith Osiris, the king, the lord of the two lands, MEN-MAĀT-RĀ, whose word is *maāt*, the son of the Sun, [proceeding] from his body, loving him, the lord of crowns, SETI MER-EN-PTAḤ, whose word is *maāt*, "Homage to "you, O ye lords of *maāt*, who are free from iniquity, "who exist and live for ever and to the double *ḥenti* "period of everlastingness, MEN-MAĀT-RĀ, whose word "is *maāt*, the son of the Sun, [proceeding] from his body, "loving him, the lord of diadems, SETI MER-EN-PTAḤ,

[1] This is Chapter LXXII. of the *Book of the Dead.*

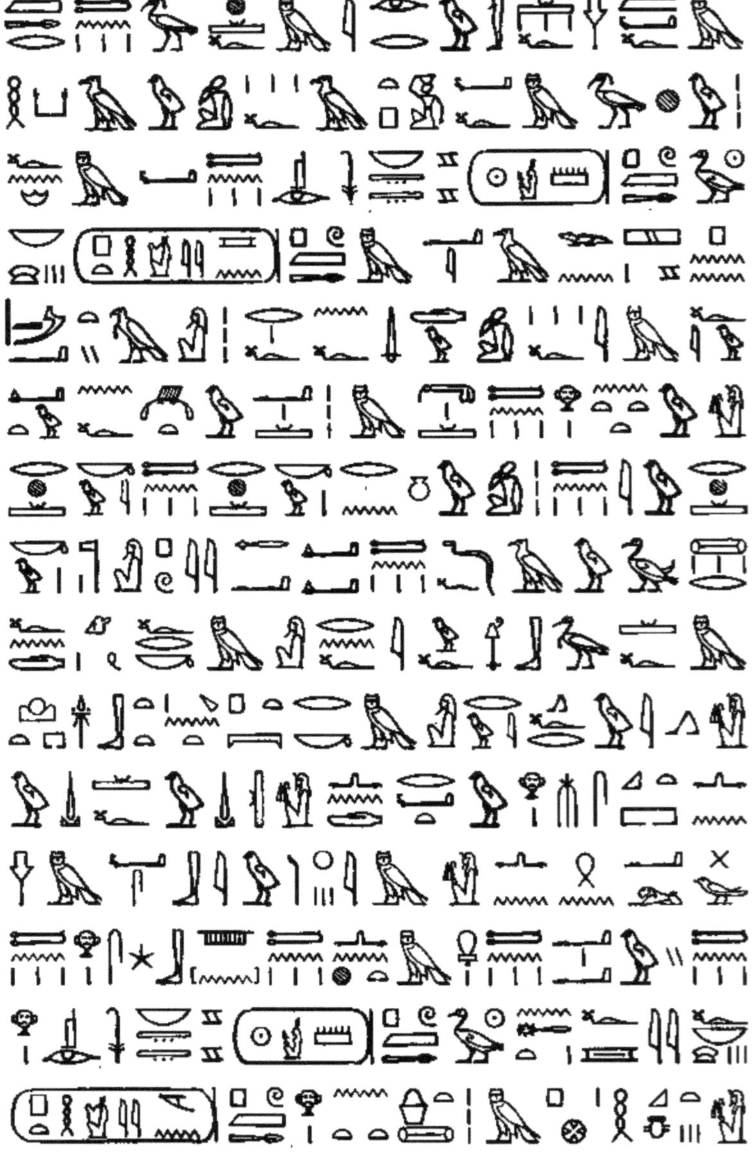

"whose word is *maāt*, before you hath become a "*khu* (i.e., a spirit) in his attributes, he hath gained "the mastery through his words of power, and he "is laden with his splendours. O deliver ye the "Osiris, the king, the lord of the two lands, MEN-"MAĀT-RĀ, whose word is *maāt*, the son of the sun, "the lord of diadems, SETI MER-EN-PTAḤ, whose "word is *maāt*, from the Crocodile of this Pool of "Maāti. He hath his mouth, let him speak there-"with. Let there be granted unto him broad-handed-"ness in your presence, because I know you, and I "know your names. I know this great god unto "whose nostrils ye present offerings of *tchefau*. "REKEM is his name. He maketh a way through "the eastern horizon of heaven. REKEM departeth "and I also depart; he is strong and I am strong. "O let me not be destroyed in the MESQET Chamber. "Let not the Sebȧu fiends gain the mastery over "me. Drive not ye me away from your Gates, "and shut not fast your arms against the Osiris, "the king, the lord of the two lands, MEN-MAĀT-"RĀ, whose word is *maāt*, the son of the Sun, [pro-"ceeding] from his body, loving him, the lord of "diadems, SETI MER-EN-PTAḤ, whose word is *maāt*, "because [my] bread is in the city of PE,[1] and my "ale is in the city of ṬEP, and my arms are united

[1] Pe and Ṭep formed a double city in the Delta.

VIII.

"in the divine house which my father hath given unto "me. He hath stablished for me a house in the high "place of the lands, and there are wheat and barley "therein, the quantity of which is unknown. The son "of my body acteth for me there as *kher-ḥeb.*[1] Grant "ye unto me sepulchral offerings, that is to say, "incense, and *merḥet* unguent, and all beautiful and "pure things of every kind whereon the God liveth. "Osiris, the king, MEN-MAĀT-RĀ, whose word is *maāt*, "the son of the Sun, [proceeding] from his body, loving "him, the lord of diadems, the ruler of joy of heart, "SETI MER-EN-PTAḤ, whose word is *maāt*, existeth for "ever in all the transformations which it pleaseth "[him to make]. He floateth down the river, he saileth "up into SEKHET-ÅARU,[2] he reacheth SEKHET-ḤETEP.[3] "I am the double Lion-god."[4]

VIII. Saith Osiris, the king, the lord of the two lands, MEN-MAĀT-RĀ, whose word is *maāt*, son of the Sun, loving him, SETI MER-EN-PTAḤ, whose word is *maāt* :—"O ward off that destroyer from my father "Osiris, the king, the lord of the two lands, MEN-MAĀT-"RĀ, whose word is *maāt*, and let his divine protection "be under my legs, and let them live. Strengthen "thou Osiris, son of the Sun, lord of diadems, SETI MER-"EN-PTAḤ, whose word is *maāt*, with thy hand. Grasp "thou him with thy hand, let him enter thy hand, let

1 The *kher-ḥeb* was the priestly official who read the funeral service.

2 I.e., the Field of Reeds.

3 I.e., the Field of Peace.

4 I.e., Shu and Tefnut.

IX.

"him enter thy hand, O Osiris, king, lord of the two "lands, MEN-MAĀT-RĀ, whose word is *maāt,* thou shalt "not perish. NUT cometh unto thee, and she fashioneth "thee as the Great Fashioner, and thou shalt never "decay; she fashioneth thee, she turneth thy weak-"ness into strength, she gathereth together thy "members, she bringeth thy heart into thy body, and "she hath placed thee at the head of the living doubles "(*kau*), O Osiris, king, lord of the two lands, MEN-"MAĀT-RĀ, whose word is *maāt,* before the beautiful "god, the lord of TA-TCHESERT."

IX. Saith Osiris, the king, the lord of the two lands, MEN-MAĀT-RĀ, whose word is *maāt,* the son of the Sun, [proceeding] from his body, loving him, the lord of diadems, SETI MER-EN-PTAḤ, whose word is *maāt,*

[THE CHAPTER OF CAUSING THE SOUL TO BE UNITED TO ITS BODY IN THE UNDERWORLD][1]

"Hail, ye gods who bring (ÅNNIU)! [Hail] ye gods "who run (PEḤIU)! [Hail] thou who dwellest in "his embrace, thou great god, grant thou that may "come unto me my soul from wheresoever it may be. "If it would delay, then let my soul be brought unto "me from wheresoever it may be, for thou shalt find "the Eye of Horus standing by thee like those "watchful gods. If it lie down, let it lie down in "ÅNNU (Heliopolis), the land where [souls are joined "to their bodies] in thousands. Let my soul be brought

[1] This is Chapter LXXXIX. of the *Book of the Dead.*

X.
XI.

"unto me from wheresoever it may be. Make thou "strong, O guardian of sky and earth, this my soul. "If it would tarry, do thou cause the soul to see its "body, and thou shalt find the Eye of Horus standing "by thee even as do those [gods who watch]."

"Hail, ye gods who tow along the boat of the lord of "millions of years, who bring [it] into the upper regions "of the Ṭuat, who make it to pass over Nut, and who "make the soul to enter into its *sāḥu* (i.e., spiritual body), "let your hands be full of weapons, and grasp them "and make them sharp, and hold chains in readiness to "destroy the serpent enemy. Let the Boat rejoice, and "let the great god pass on in peace, and behold, grant "ye that the soul of Osiris, king MEN-MAĀT-RĀ, whose "word is *maāt*, may emerge from the thighs [of Nut] in "the eastern horizon of heaven, for ever and for ever."

X. Osiris, the king, the lord of the two lands, MEN-MAĀT-RĀ SETEP-[EN]-RĀ, whose word is *maāt*, the son of Rā, loving PTAḤ-SEKRI, the lord of diadems, SETI MER-EN-PTAḤ, whose word is *maāt*, saith:—"O ye "*shennu* beings, go ye round behind me, and let not "these my members be without strength."

XI. Osiris, the king, the lord of the two lands, MEN-MAĀT-RĀ AA-RĀ, whose word is *maāt*, the son of the sun, [proceeding] from his body, loving him, lord of diadems, SETI MER-EN-PTAḤ, saith:—"O Nut, lift thou "me up. I am thy son. Do away from me that which "maketh me to be without motion." [Nut saith]:— "O Osiris, the king, the lord of the two lands, MEN-

"MAĀT-RĀ AA-RĀ, whose word is *maāt*, the son of "the sun, [proceeding] from his body, loving him, "the lord of diadems, SETI MER-EN-PTAḤ, whose "word is *maāt*, I have given thee thy head to be "on thy body, and all the members of him that is "SETI MER-EN-PTAḤ, whose word is *maāt*, shall never "lack strength."

On the outside of the cover, beneath the two scenes and texts which occupied the upper part of it, was a horizontal line of hieroglyphics which contained two short speeches, the one by the goddess Nut, and the other by Thoth. The speech of Nut is a duplicate of the opening lines of that found on the bottom of the sarcophagus (see above § v., p. 55); the speech of Thoth is much mutilated, and can have contained little except the promise to be with the king, and a repetition of the royal name and titles. On the inside of the cover were texts, many portions of which are identical, as we see from the fragments which remain, with the Chapters from the *Book of the Dead* which are found on the bottom of the sarcophagus, and which have been transcribed above. At each side of the figure of the winged goddess which was cuṭ on the breast was a figure of the god Thoth, who is seen holding a staff surmounted by the symbol of "night," [hieroglyph]. When the cover was complete there were probably four such figures upon it, and the texts which accompanied them were, no doubt, identical with those found in Chapter CLXI. of the *Book of the Dead.*

The scenes and inscriptions which cover the inside and outside of the sarcophagus are described and transcribed in the following chapters.

APPENDIX TO CHAPTER I.

BELZONI'S ACCOUNT OF HIS DISCOVERY OF THE TOMB OF SETI I.

"ON the 16th (of October) I recommenced my excava-"tions in the Valley of Beban el Malook, and pointed "out the fortunate spot, which has paid me for all the "trouble I took in my researches. I may call this a "fortunate day, one of the best perhaps of my life; "I do not mean to say, that fortune has made me rich, "for I do not consider all rich men fortunate; but she "has given me that satisfaction, that extreme pleasure, "which wealth cannot purchase; the pleasure of "discovering what has been long sought in vain, and "of presenting the world with a new and perfect "monument of Egyptian antiquity, which can be "recorded as superior to any other in point of "grandeur, style, and preservation, appearing as if just "finished on the day we entered it; and what I found "in it will show its great superiority to all others. "Not fifteen yards from the last tomb I described, I "caused the earth to be opened at the foot of a steep "hill, and under a torrent, which, when it rains, pours "a great quantity of water over the very spot I have "caused to be dug. No one could imagine, that the "ancient Egyptians would make the entrance into "such an immense and superb excavation just under a "torrent of water; but I had strong reasons to suppose, "that there was a tomb in that place, from indications "I had observed in my pursuit. The Fellahs who "were accustomed to dig were all of opinion, that "there was nothing in that spot, as the situation of "this tomb differed from that of any other. I con-"tinued the work, however, and the next day, the "17th, in the evening we perceived the part of the "rock that was cut, and formed the entrance. On the "18th, early in the morning, the task was resumed, "and about noon the workmen reached the entrance, "which was eighteen feet below the surface of the "ground. The appearance indicated, that the tomb "was of the first rate; but still I did not expect to "find such a one as it really proved to be. The Fellahs "advanced till they saw that it was probably a large "tomb, when they protested they could go no further, "the tomb was so much choked up with large stones, "which they could not get out of the passage. I "descended, examined the place, pointed out to them "where they might dig, and in an hour there was "room enough for me to enter through a passage that "the earth had left under the ceiling of the first "corridor, which is 36 ft. 2 in. long, and 8 ft. 8 in. wide, "and, when cleared of the ruins, 6 ft. 9 in. high. "I perceived immediately by the painting on the "ceiling, and by the hieroglyphics in *basso relievo,* "which were to be seen where the earth did not reach, "that this was the entrance into a large and magnifi- "cent tomb. At the end of this corridor I came to a "staircase 23 ft. long, and of the same breadth as the "corridor. The door at the bottom is 12 ft. high. "From the foot of the staircase I entered another "corridor, 37 ft. 3 in. long, and of the same width and "height as the other, each side sculptured with "hieroglyphics in *basso relievo,* and painted. The "ceiling also is finely painted, and in pretty good "preservation. The more I saw, the more I was eager "to see, such being the nature of man; but I was "checked in my anxiety at this time, for at the end of "this passage I reached a large pit, which intercepted "my progress. This pit is 30 ft. deep, and 14 ft. by "12 ft. 3 in. wide. The upper part of the pit is "adorned with figures, from the wall of the passage "up to the ceiling. The passages from the entrance "all the way to this pit have an inclination downward "of an angle of eighteen degrees. On the opposite side "of the pit facing the entrance I perceived a small "aperture 2 ft. wide and 2 ft. 6 in. high, and at the "bottom of the wall a quantity of rubbish. A rope "fastened to a piece of wood, that was laid across the "passage against the projections which formed a kind "of door, appears to have been used by the ancients "for descending into the pit; and from the small "aperture on the opposite side hung another, which "reached the bottom, no doubt for the purpose of "ascending. We could clearly perceive, that the water "which entered the passages from the torrents of rain "ran into this pit, and the wood and rope fastened to "it crumbled to dust on touching them. At the "bottom of the pit were several pieces of wood, placed "against the side of it, so as to assist the person who "was to ascend by the rope into the aperture. I saw "the impossibility of proceeding at the moment. Mr. "Beechey, who that day came from Luxor, entered the "tomb, but was also disappointed.

"The next day, the 19th, by means of a long beam "we succeeded in sending a man up into the aperture, "and having contrived to make a bridge of two beams, "we crossed the pit. The little aperture we found to "be an opening forced through a wall, that had "entirely closed the entrance, which was as large as "the corridor. The Egyptians had closely shut it up, "plastered the wall over, and painted it like the rest "of the sides of the pit, so that but for the aperture, "it would have been impossible to suppose, that there "was any further proceeding; and anyone would "conclude, that the tomb ended with the pit. The "rope in the inside of the wall did not fall to dust, but "remained pretty strong, the water not having reached "it at all; and the wood to which it was attached was "in good preservation. It was owing to this method "of keeping the damp out of the inner parts of the "tomb, that they are so well preserved. I observed "some cavities at the bottom of the well, but found "nothing in them, nor any communication from the "bottom to any other place; therefore we could not "doubt their being made to receive the waters from "the rain, which happens occasionally in this moun- "tain. The valley is so much raised by the rubbish, "which the water carries down from the upper parts, "that the entrance into these tombs is become much "lower than the torrents; in consequence, the water "finds its way into the tombs, some of which are "entirely choked up with earth.

"When we had passed through the little aperture "we found ourselves in a beautiful hall, 27 ft. 6 in. by "25 ft. 10 in., in which were four pillars 3 ft. square. "I shall not give any description of the painting, till I "have described the whole of the chambers. At the "end of this room, which I call the entrance-hall, and "opposite the aperture, is a large door, from which "three steps lead down into a chamber with two "pillars. This is 28 ft. 2 in. by 25 ft. 6 in. The pillars "are 3 ft. 10 in. square. I gave it the name of the "drawing-room; for it is covered with figures, which, "though only outlined, are so fine and perfect, that "you would think they had been drawn only the day "before. Returning into the entrance-hall, we saw "on the left of the aperture a large staircase, which "descended into a corridor. It is 13 ft. 4 in. long, "7 ft. 6 in. wide, and has 18 steps. At the bottom we "entered a beautiful corridor, 36 ft. 6 in. by 6 ft. 11 in.

"We perceived that the paintings became more perfect "as we advanced farther into the interior. They "retained their gloss, or a kind of varnish over the "colours, which had a beautiful effect. The figures are "painted on a white ground. At the end of this "corridor we descended ten steps, which I call the "small stairs, into another, 17 ft. 2 in. by 10 ft. 5 in. "From this we entered a small chamber, 20 ft. 4 in. by "13 ft. 8 in., to which I gave the name of the Room of "Beauties; for it is adorned with the most beautiful "figures in *basso relievo*, like all the rest, and painted. "When standing in the centre of this chamber, the "traveller is surrounded by an assembly of Egyptian "gods and goddesses. Proceeding farther, we entered "a large hall, 27 ft. 9 in. by 26 ft. 10 in. In this hall "are two rows of square pillars, three on each side of "the entrance, forming a line with the corridors. At "each side of this hall is a small chamber; that on the "right is 10 ft. 5 in. by 8 ft. 8 in., that on the left "10 ft. 5 in. by 8 ft. 9½ in. This hall I termed the "Hall of Pillars; the little room on the right, Isis' "Room, as in it a large cow is painted, of which I "shall give a description hereafter; that on the left, "the Room of Mysteries, from the mysterious figures "it exhibits. At the end of this hall we entered a "large saloon, with an arched roof or ceiling, which is "separated from the Hall of Pillars only by a step "so that the two may be reckoned one. The saloon "is 31 ft. 10 in. by 27 ft. On the right is a small "chamber without anything in it, roughly cut, as if "unfinished, and without painting; on the left we "entered a chamber with two square pillars, 25 ft. 8 in. "by 22 ft. 10 in. This I called the Sideboard Room, "as it has a projection of 3 ft. in form of a sideboard "all round, which was perhaps intended to contain the "articles necessary for the funeral ceremony. The "pillars are 3 ft. 4 in. square, and the whole beautifully "painted as the rest. At the same end of the room, "and facing the Hall of Pillars, we entered by a large "door into another chamber with four pillars, one of "which is fallen down. This chamber is 43 ft. 4 in. by "17 ft. 6 in.; the pillars 3 ft. 7 in. square. It is covered "with white plaster, where the rock did not cut "smoothly, but there is no painting on it. I named it "the Bull's, or Apis' Room, as we found the carcass "of a bull in it, embalmed with asphaltum; and also, "scattered in various places, an immense quantity of "small wooden figures of mummies 6 or 8 in. long, "and covered with asphaltum to preserve them. "There were some other figures of fine earth baked, "coloured blue, and strongly varnished. On each side "of the two little rooms were wooden statues standing "erect, 4 ft. high, with a circular hollow inside, as if to "contain a roll of papyrus, which I have no doubt "they did. We found likewise fragments of other "statues of wood and of composition.

"But the description of what we found in the centre "of the saloon, and which I have reserved till this place, "merits the most particular attention, not having its "equal in the world, and being such as we had no idea "could exist. It is a sarcophagus of the finest oriental "alabaster, 9 ft. 5 in. long, and 3 ft. 7 in. wide. Its "thickness is only 2 in., and it is transparent, when a "light is placed in the inside of it. It is minutely "sculptured within and without with several hundred "figures, which do not exceed 2 in. in height, and "represent, as I suppose, the whole of the funeral "procession and ceremonies relating to the deceased, "united with several emblems, &c. I cannot give an "adequate idea of this beautiful and invaluable piece "of antiquity, and can only say, that nothing has been "brought into Europe from Egypt that can be com-"pared with it. The cover was not there; it had been "taken out, and broken into several pieces, which we "found in digging before the first entrance. The "sarcophagus was over a staircase in the centre of the "saloon, which communicated with a subterraneous "passage, leading downwards, 300 ft. in length. At the "end of this passage we found a great quantity of bats' "dung, which choked it up, so that we could go no "farther without digging. It was nearly filled up too "by the falling in of the upper part. One hundred feet "from the entrance is a staircase in good preservation; "but the rock below changes its substance, from a beau-"tiful solid calcareous stone, becoming a kind of black "rotten slate, which crumbles into dust only by touching. "This subterraneous passage proceeds in a south-west "direction through the mountain. I measured the "distance from the entrance, and also the rocks above, "and found that the passage reaches nearly halfway "through the mountain to the upper part of the valley. "I have reasons to suppose, that this passage was used "to come into the tomb by another entrance; but this "could not be after the death of the person who was "buried there, for at the bottom of the stairs just "under the sarcophagus a wall was built, which "entirely closed the communication between the tomb "and the subterraneous passage. Some large blocks of "stone were placed under the sarcophagus horizontally, "level with the pavement of the saloon, that no one "might perceive any stairs or subterranean passage "was there. The doorway of the sideboard room had "been walled up, and forced open, as we found the "stones with which it was shut, and the mortar in the "jambs. The staircase of the entrance-hall had been "walled up also at the bottom, and the space filled "with rubbish, and the floor covered with large blocks "of stone, so as to deceive any one who should force "the fallen wall near the pit, and make him suppose, "that the tomb ended with the entrance-hall and the "drawing-room. I am inclined to believe, that who-"ever forced all these passages must have had some "spies with them, who were well acquainted with the "tomb throughout. The tomb faces the north-east, "and the direction of the whole runs straight south-"west."

CHAPTER II.

THE ANTE-CHAMBER OF THE ṬUAT.

IN the FIRST DIVISION of the "Book of Gates of the Ṭuat," according to the sarcophagus of Seti I., we see the horizon of the west, or the mountain of the west, , divided into two parts, , and the boat of the sun is supposed to sail between them, and to enter by this passage into the Ṭuat. On the right hand is fixed a jackal-headed standard, and on each side of it kneels a bearded god; one god is called ṬAT, , and is a personification of the region which is beyond the day, and the other SET, , and represents the funeral mountain. On the left hand is a ram-headed standard, and on each side of it also kneels a bearded god; as before, one is called Ṭat and the other Set. The ram's head has the horizontal, wavy horns, which belong to the particular species of ram that was the symbol of the god Khnemu; this animal disappeared from Egypt before the XIIth Dynasty, but the tradition of him remained. In the middle of the scene sails the boat of the sun. The god is symbolized by a beetle within a disk, which is enveloped in the folds of a

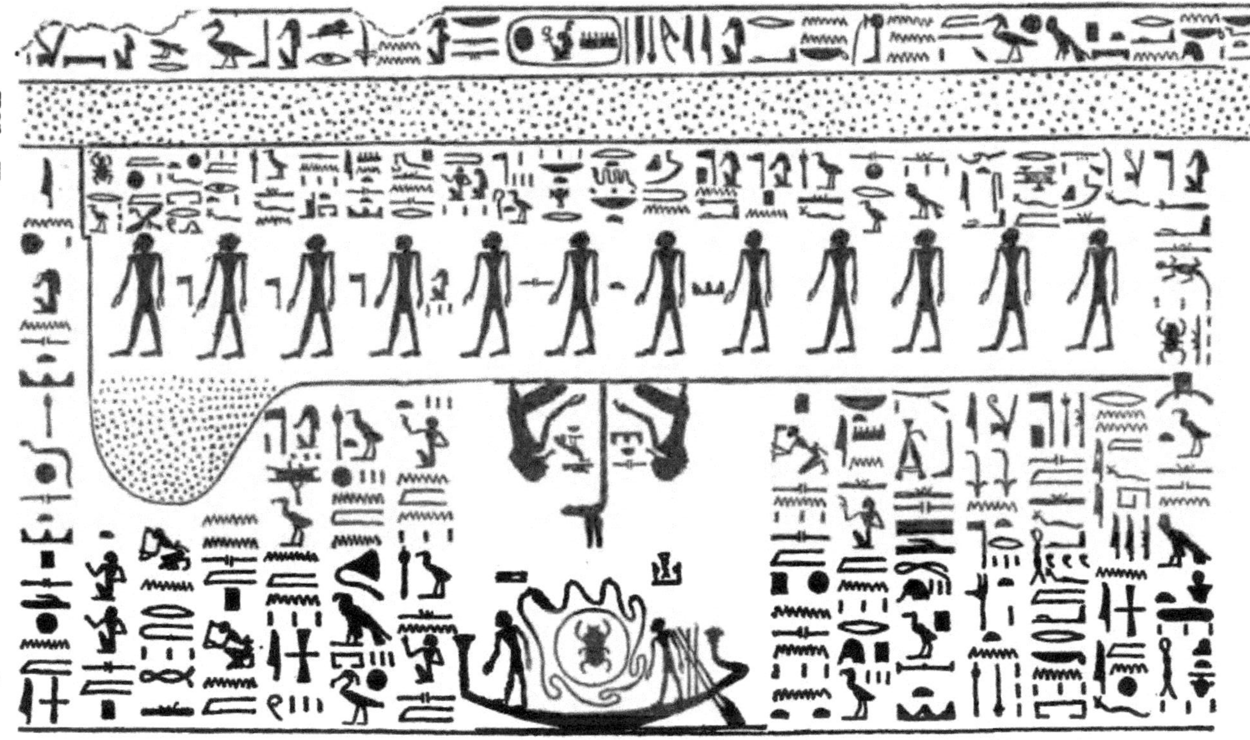

Part of the horizon over which the Boat of the Sun passes to enter the Ṭuat at eventide.
In it are Twelve Gods of the Funeral Mountain.

serpent having its tail in its mouth. In the bows stands the god of divine intelligence, whose name is SA, , and in the stern, near the two paddles, stands ḤEKA, , i.e., the personification of the word of power, or of magical utterance. The god who usually accompanies SA is ḤU. The text which refers to the Sun-god reads:—

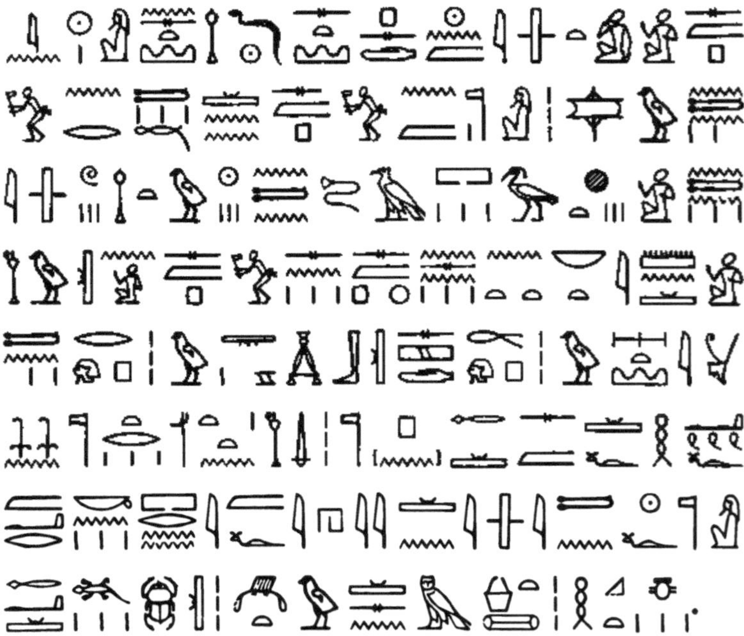

"Rā saith unto the Mountain:—Send forth light, O "Mountain! Let radiance arise from that which hath "devoured me, and which hath slain men and is filled "with the slaughter of the gods. Breath to you, O "ye who dwell in the light in your habitations, my

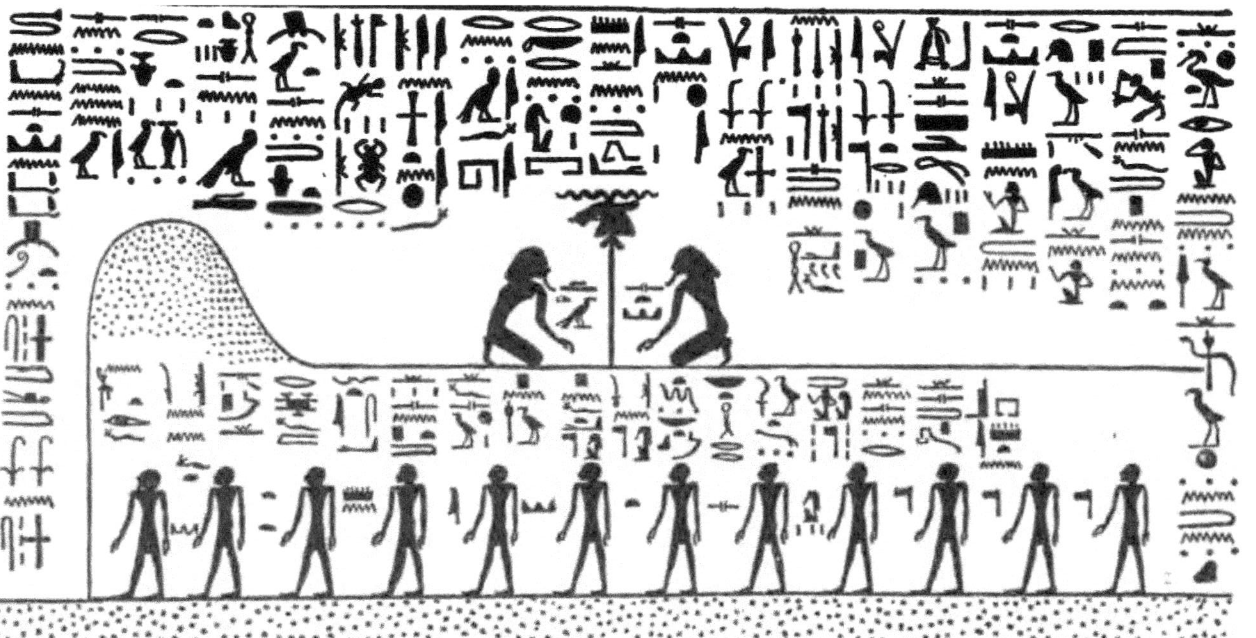

Part of the horizon over which the Boat of the Sun passes to enter the Ṭuat at eventide.
In it are twelve Gods of Set-Ȧmentet.

"splendours shall be to you. I have decreèd their "slaughter, and they have slaughtered everything "which existeth. I have hidden you from those who "are upon the earth, restoring the crown (or, tiara) to "those who are on the Mountain. The gods say:— "'Let this jackal-headed sceptre ( ) emit the words "of this great god who joineth together his members. "Come then unto us, O thou from whom we have come "forth! Cries of joy are to thee, O thou who art in "thy disk, thou great god whose forms (or transforma- "tions) are manifold.' Their provisions [consist] of "bread-cakes and beer."

The paragraph below the above text is practically a duplicate of it, but it contains no mention of either the jackal-headed or the ram-headed sceptre, and it is unnecessary to give it here.

On the right of the boat stand twelve gods, who are called "gods of the mountain," , and the text referring to them reads:—

"[These gods] have come into being from **Rā**, and "from his substance, and have emerged from his eye. "He hath decreed for them [as] a place (or, abode) the "Hidden Mountain (*Åment Set*), which consumeth men, "and gods, and all cattle, and all reptiles which are "created by this great god. This great god hath decreed "the plans (or, designs) thereof having made [them] to "spring up in the earth which he created."

On the left of the boat stand twelve gods, who are called "gods of Set-Åmentet," [hieroglyphs], and the text referring to them reads:—

"The hidden place. [These are] those who have "consumed the men, and the gods, and all the cattle, "and all the reptiles which this great god hath created. "This great god hath decreed plans for them after "he made them to spring up in the land which he "created, that is to say, in the Åmentet which he "made."

CHAPTER III.

THE GATE OF SAA-SET.

THE SECOND DIVISION OF THE ṬUAT.

THE boat of Rā, having passed between the two halves of the horizon of the West, now approaches a gateway, the door of which is closed before him; the door of the second division of the Ṭuat is different from the doors of the other divisions, for it consists of a single leaf which turns upon a pivot working in holes in the top and bottom of the framework of the door. This door is guarded by a serpent called SAA-SET, , which stands upon its tail. The text referring to this serpent reads:—

[1] Var.

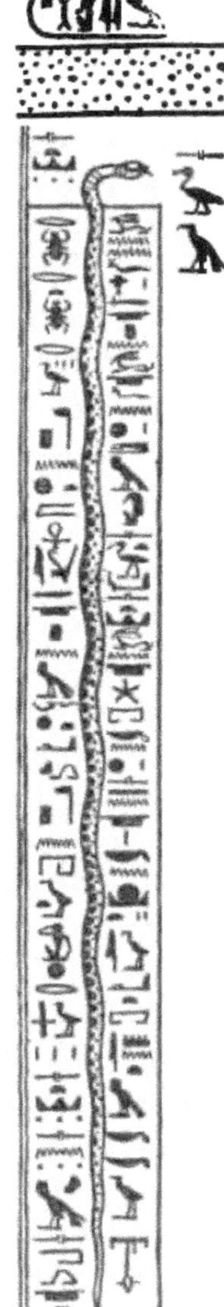

"He who is over (i.e., has the "mastery over) this door openeth to "Rā. SA saith unto SAT-SET, 'Open "thy door to Rā, throw wide open thy "door to KHUTI. The hidden abode is "in darkness, so that the transforma-"tions of this god may take place.' "This portal is closed after this god "hath entered in through it, and there "is lamentation on the part of those "who are in their mountain when "they hear this door shut."

In the centre of the scene we see the boat of Rā being towed along by four gods standing, each of whom grasps the tow-line with both hands. The god is now in the form of a ram-headed man, who holds the sceptre [hieroglyph] in his right hand, and has the solar disk above his horns. He stands within a shrine which is enveloped in the voluminous folds of the serpent Meḥen, [hieroglyph]; a serpent also stands on his tail before him. In front of the shrine stands SA, and behind it ḤEKAU. The gods who tow the boat are called ṬUAIU, [hieroglyphs].

The sun's boat is met in this section by a company of thirteen gods, who are under the direction of a god who holds a staff in his hand. The names of the first seven gods are:—NEPEMEḤ, [1] NENḤĀ, [2] BA, , ḤERU, , BEḤĀ-ÅB, , KHNEMU, , and SETCHET, ; the third has the head of a ram, and the fourth that of a hawk. The last six gods

The Boat of the Sun towed by Gods of the Ṭuat.

are described as "gods who are in the entrances," ; the god who bears the staff has no name. The text which refers to the Sun-god reads:—

[1] Var., NEPEN, .   [2] Var., NENĀ, .

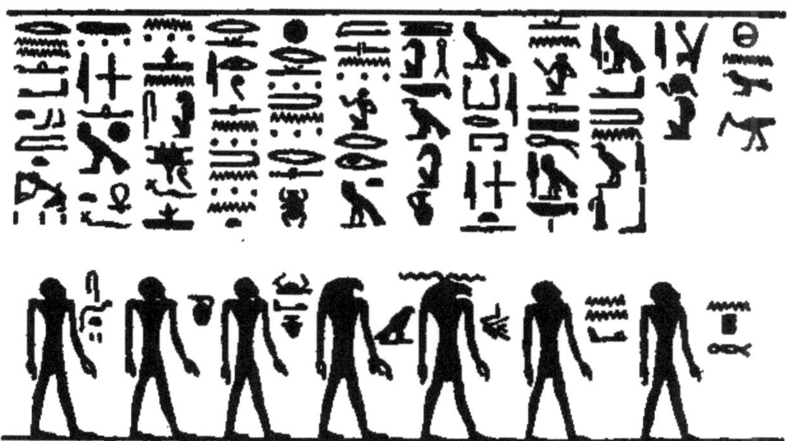

Seven of the Gods of the Entrances who tow the Boat of the Sun through Saa-Set.

Six of the Gods of the Entrances who tow the Boat of the Sun through Saa-Set, and a god who bears a staff.

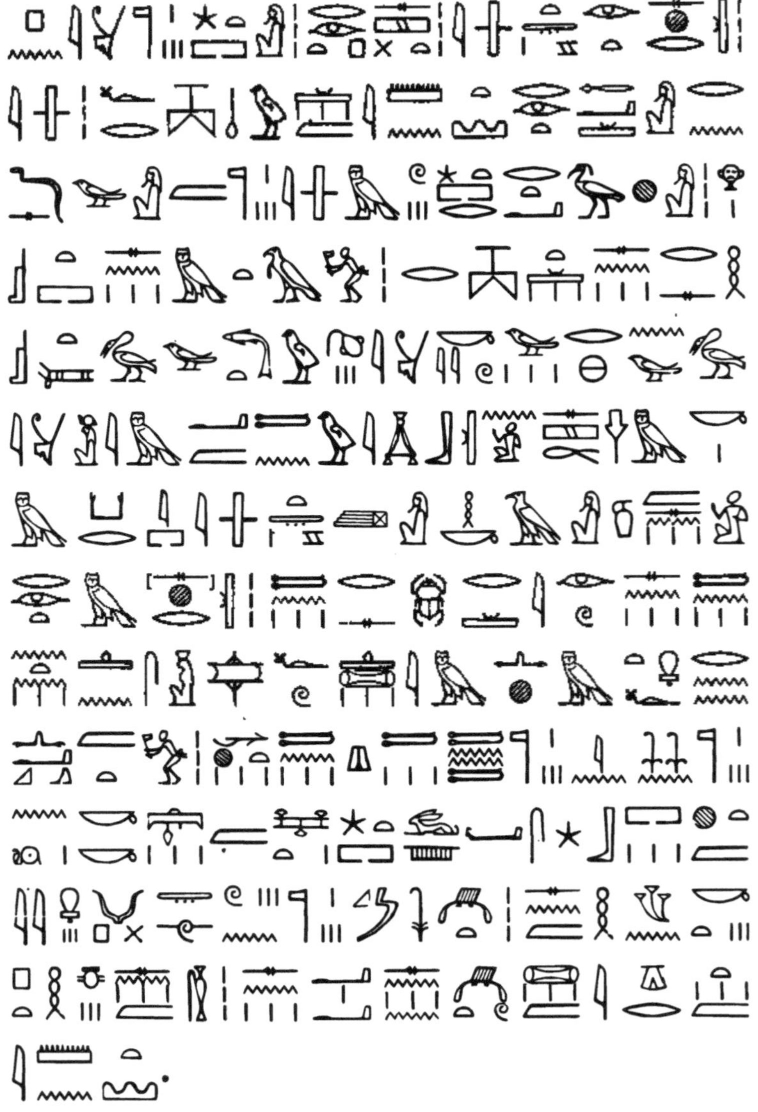

"This great god journeyeth along the roads of the

"Ṭuat. This god is drawn by the gods of the Ṭuat "in order to make divisions (or, distinctions) in the "earth, and to work out [his] designs therein, to weigh "words and deeds in Ȧment, to magnify the great god "above the little god among the gods who are in the "Ṭuat, to place the KHU (i.e., the blessed dead) upon "their thrones, and the damned [in the place] to which "they have been condemned in the judgment, and to "destroy their bodies by an evil death. Rā saith:—'O "grant ye to me that I may restore the tiara, and that "I may have possession of [my] shrine which is in the "earth. Let SA and ḤEKA unite themselves to me for "the working out of plans for you, and for making to "come into being their attributes (or, forms) ye [have] "what is yours. ISIS hath made to be at peace the "wind, and offerings are there. None shutteth [the "door] against you, and the damned do not enter in "after you. That which belongeth to you is to you, O "gods.' These gods say unto Rā, 'There is darkness "on the road of the Ṭuat, therefore let the doors "which are closed be unfolded, let the earth open, "so that the gods may draw along him that hath "created them.' Their food [i.e., the food of these "gods] is of the funeral offerings, and their drink "is from their cool waters, and their hands are "on meat offerings among the Ȧḳert regions of "Ȧment."

On the right of the boat are twenty-four gods, the first twelve of whom are described as "those who are at peace, the worshippers of Rā," [hieroglyphs], and the second twelve as "the righteous who are in the Ṭuat," [hieroglyphs], These beings are thus described by the accompanying text:—

[hieroglyphs]

Nine of the gods who adore Rā and are at peace.

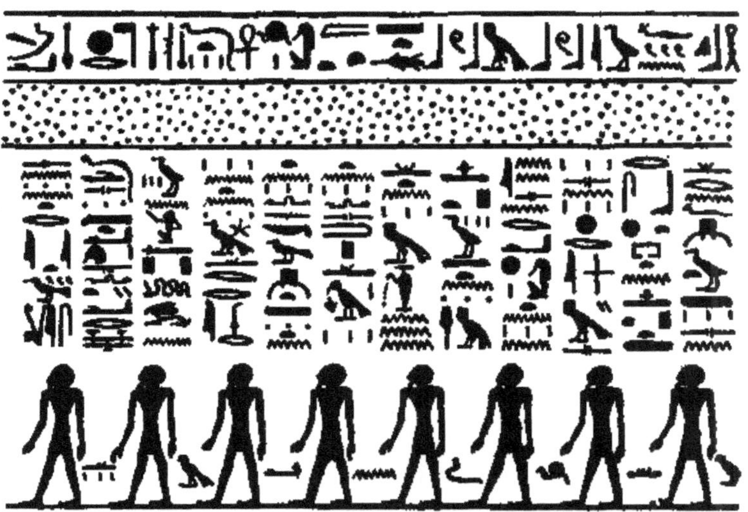

Five of the righteous gods of the Ṭuat.

Three of the gods who adore Rā and are at peace.

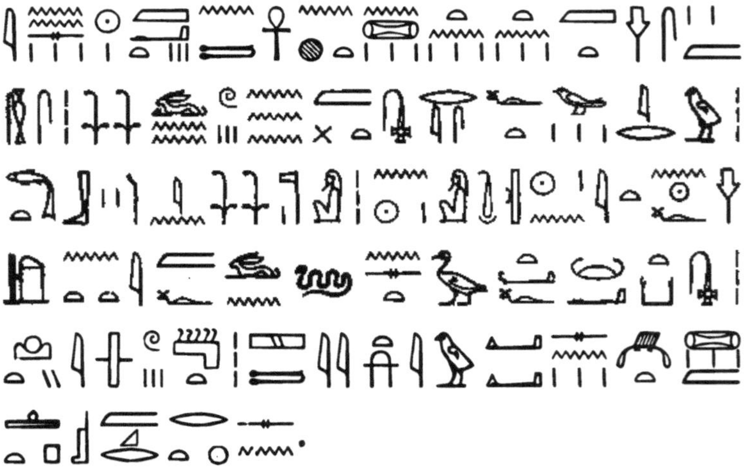

"These [are they who] have worshipped (or, praised) "Rā upon earth, who uttered words of power against "Āpep, who made their offerings unto him, and who "burnt (*literally,* made) incense to their gods on their "own behalf, after their offerings. They have gained "possession of their cool waters, and they receive their "meat, and they eat of their offerings in the gateway "of him whose name is hidden. Their meat is by the "gateway, and their offerings are with him who is "therein. And Rā saith unto them:—'Your offerings "are yours, ye have power over your cool waters, your "souls shall never be hacked to pieces, your meat "shall never fail, [O ye who have] praised [me], and "have vanquished Āpep for me.'"

The above passage refers to the "worshippers of Rā who are at peace."

"[These are] they [who] spake truth upon earth,

"and who were not addicted to evil thought about the "gods. They make their invocations in this gateway, "they live upon maāt (i.e., truth), and their cool "waters are in their cisterns. Rā saith unto them:— "'Truth is yours, live ye on your food. Ye yourselves "are truth;' and they have power over these their cool "waters, which are waters of fire to those who have

Seven of the righteous gods of the Ṭuat.

"guilt and sin. And these gods say to Rā:—'Let "there be stability to the Disk of Rā. Let him that is "in the shrine have the mastery over it, and let the "serpent [Meḥen] guard him well. May the flames of "Khuti which are in the corners of the hidden shrine "grow stronger.' And there shall be given to them "meat in the place of peace in their circle."

The above passage refers to the "righteous who are in the Ṭuat."

On the left side of the boat of Rā are: 1. The god TEM, [hieroglyphs], who is depicted in the form of an aged man, leaning heavily on a stick which he grasps in his right hand. 2. Four male beings who are lying prostrate on their backs. 3. Twenty male beings, with their backs bowed, and their arms tied together at their elbows behind their backs. The four beings are described as "the inert," [hieroglyphs], and the twenty as "the apos-"tates of the Hall of Rā, "who have blasphemed "Rā upon earth, who have "invoked evils upon him "that is in the Egg, who "have thrust aside the "right, and have spoken "words against KHUTI," [hieroglyphs].

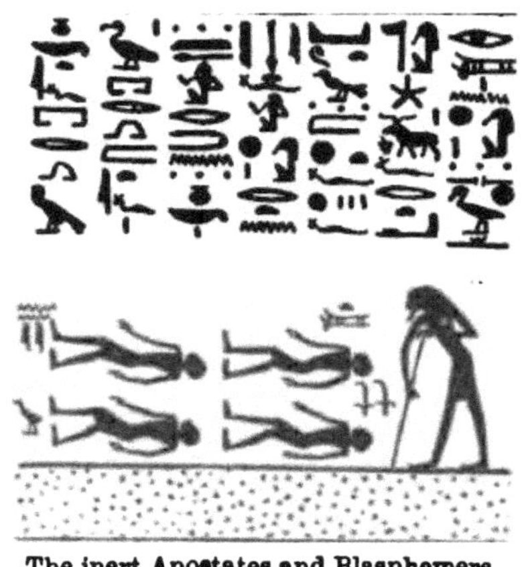
The inert Apostates and Blasphemers of Rā.

The text referring to the inert and the apostates reads:—

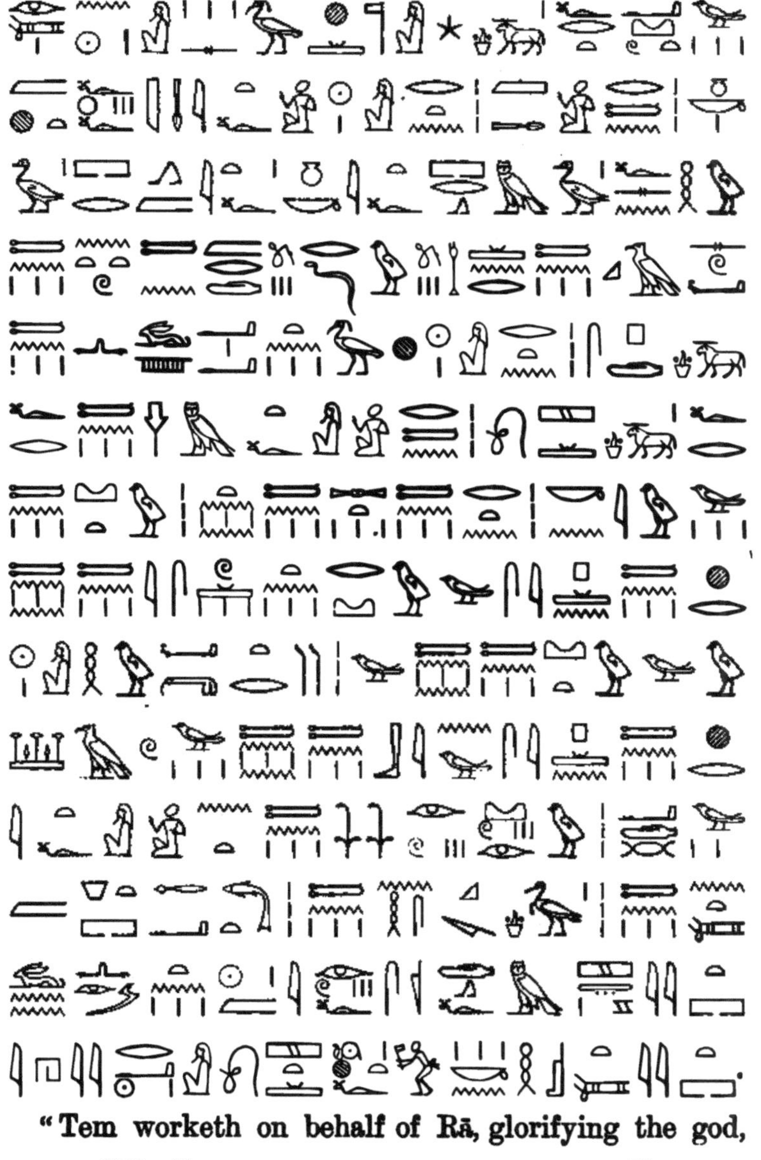

"Tem worketh on behalf of Rā, glorifying the god,

"and singing praises to his soul, and distributing evil "things to his enemies. [He saith]:—'The word of "my father Rā is right (*maāt*) against you, and my "word is right against you. I am the son who pro-"ceedeth from his father, and I am the father who "proceedeth from his son. Ye are fettered, and ye "are tied with strong cord, and it is I who have sent "forth the decree concerning you that ye should be

The Apostates and Blasphemers of Rā, who are doomed to destruction, with their arms bound.

"bound in fetters; your arms shall never more be "opened. Rā pronounceth the formula against you, "his soul is prepared to attack you; my father hath "gained the mastery over you, and his soul uttereth "words against you. Your evil deeds [have turned] "against you, your plottings [have come] upon you, "your abominable acts [have recoiled] upon you, your "destinies are for evil, and your doom hath been "decreed before Rā; your unjust and perverted judg-"ments are upon yourselves, and the wickedness of "your words of cursing are upon you. Evil is the doom "which hath been decreed for you before my father. "It is you who have committed sins, and who have "wrought iniquity in the Great Hall; your corruptible

The Apostates and Blasphemers of Rā, who are doomed to destruction, with their arms bound.

"bodies shall be cut in pieces, and your souls shall "have no existence, and ye shall never again see Rā "with his attributes [as] he journeyeth in the hidden "land. Hail, Rā! Adored be Rā! Thine enemies are "in the place of destruction.'"

CHAPTER IV.

THE GATE OF AQEBI.

THE THIRD DIVISION OF THE ṬUAT.

THE boat of the sun having passed through the Second Division of the Ṭuat arrives at the gateway which leads to the THIRD DIVISION. This gateway is unlike the first, which has already been described, for its opening is protected by an outwork, similar to that which protects the door of a fortified building. The outwork is guarded by nine gods, in the form of mummies, who are described as the "second company of the gods," [hieroglyphs], and in this wall, which completely divides the Second Division from the Third, is an opening, which leads to a corridor that runs between two walls, the tops of which are protected by rows of pointed stakes, [hieroglyphs]. At the entrance to the corridor stands a god, in mummied form, called ĀM-ĀUA, [hieroglyphs], and at the exit is a similar god called SEKHABESNEFUNEN, [hieroglyphs]; each is said to "extend his arms and hands to Rā," [hieroglyphs]. At each side of the angle, near

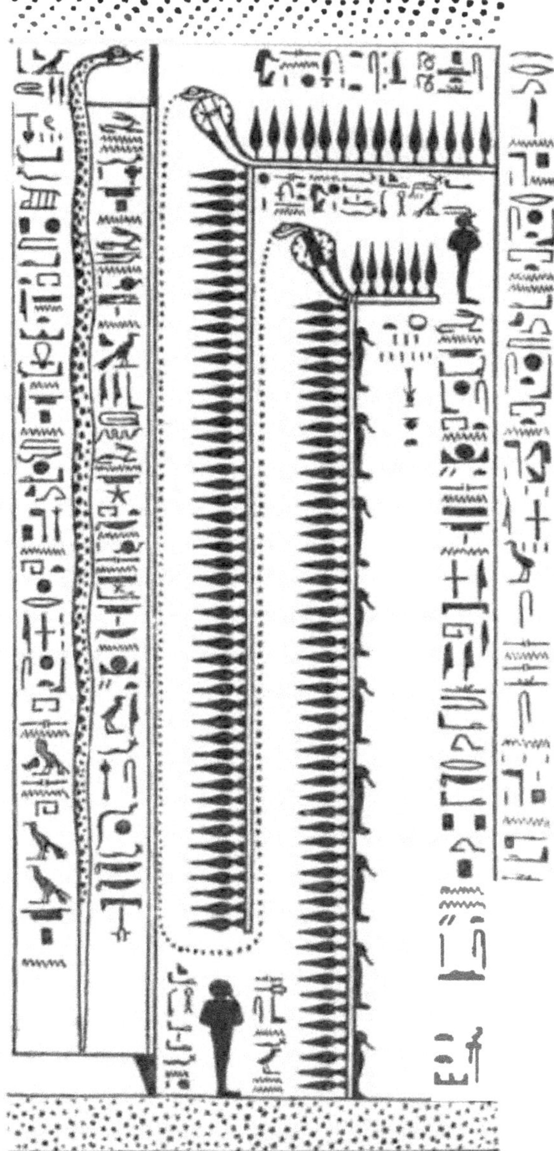

The Gate of the Serpent Aqebi.

the entrance to the corridor, is a serpent, who ejects flames from his mouth; the flame from the one sweeps along the corridor, at the end of which it is met by the flame from the other serpent which sweeps along the inside of the inner wall. The flames of these serpents are said to be for Rā, [hieroglyphs]. The gateway leading to the Third Division is called SEPṬET-UAUAU, [hieroglyphs], and the door thereof, which opens inwards, is guarded by the serpent standing on his tail, who is called AQEBI, [hieroglyphs], and faces outwards. The texts referring to the entrance of Rā through this gateway read:—

"[When] this god cometh to this gateway, to enter "in through this gateway, the gods who are therein "acclaim this great god, [saying], 'Let this gateway be "unfolded to KHUTI, and let the doors be opened to "him that is in heaven. Come then, O thou traveller, "who dost journey in Ȧmentet.' He who is over this "door openeth [it] to Rā. SA saith unto AQĒBI, 'Open "thy gate to Rā, unfold thy door to KHUTI. He shall "illumine the darkness, and he shall force a way for "the light in the habitation which is hidden.' This "door is closed after the great god hath entered "through it, and there is lamentation to those who are "in their gateway when they hear this door close "[upon them]."

Along the middle of the THIRD DIVISION we see the boat of the sun being drawn along by four gods, as before; the god Rā stands in a shrine, similar to that already described, and his companions are SA and ḤEKAU. The rope by which the boat is towed along is fastened to the two ends of a very remarkable object, in the form of a long beam, each end of which terminates in a bull's head. The accompanying text describes it as "his boat," , and from the fact that the four gods who tow the boat are seen again at the other end of the beam-like object, with the towing-rope in their hands, it is clear that the boat of Rā, and the god himself, were believed to pass *through* it, from one end to the other. The object is supported on the shoulders of eight gods, in mummied form, "who are called "Bearers of the gods," ; at each end, immediately behind the bull's head, stands a bull, and at intervals seven gods, who are called "the

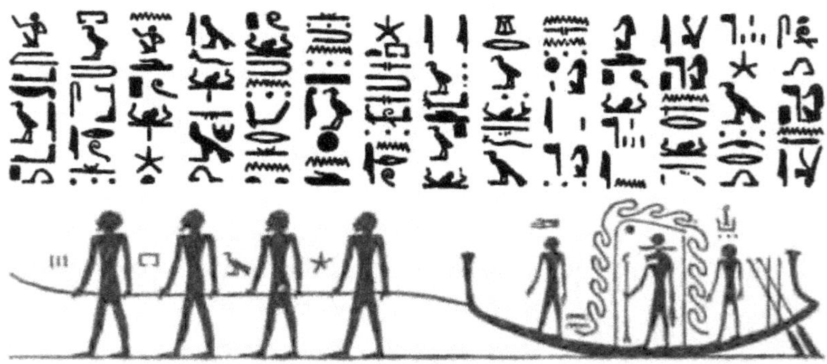

The Gods of the Third Division of the Ṭuat towing the Boat of Rā.

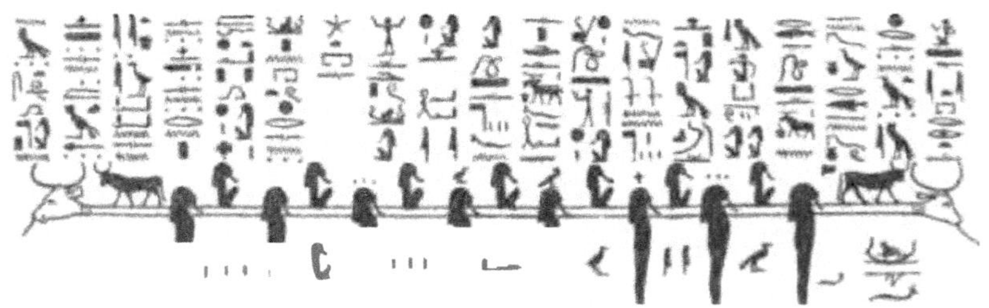

The Eight Bearers of the Boat of the Earth and its Seven Gods.

gods who are within," , are seated upon it. At the end of this Division stand four mummied forms, with their elbows projecting, and their hands crossed on their breasts. The text which refers to the passage of the boat of the sun reads:—

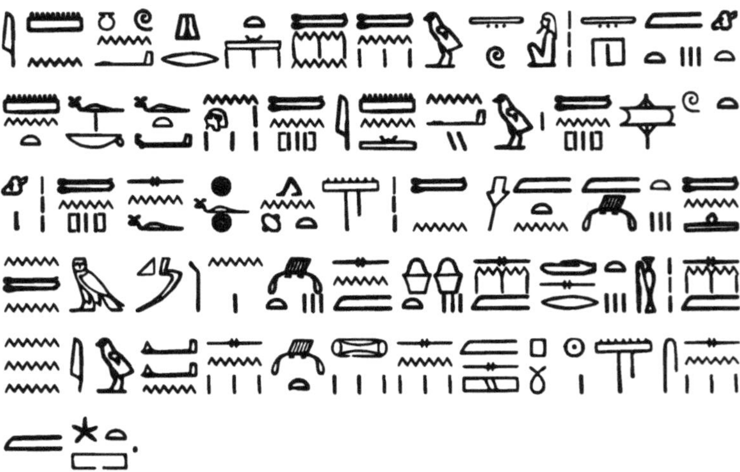

"This great god is towed along by the gods of the "Ṭuat, and this great god advanceth to the Boat of the "Earth, which is the bark of the gods. Rā saith unto "them:—'Hail, ye gods who bear up his Boat of "the Earth, and who lift up the Bark of the Ṭuat, "may there be support to your forms and light "unto your Bark. Holy is he who is in the Boat "of the Earth. I make to go back the Bark of "the Ṭuat which beareth my forms (or, attributes), "and verily I travel into the hidden habitation to "perform the plans which are carried out therein.' "ENNURKHATA, ENNURKHATA [saith], 'Praised be the "Soul which the Double Bull hath swallowed, and "let the god be at peace with that which he hath "created.'"

The effect of the above words is to allow the Sun-god and his boat to pass through the double bull-headed Boat of the Earth without any let or hindrance, and when he has done this,—

"These gods (i.e., the four gods at the other end of "the Boat of the Earth) say to Rā:—'Praised be Rā, "whose Soul hath been absorbed by the Earth-god! "Praised be the gods of Rā who hath rested [therein].' "This Boat of its Ṭuat rejoiceth, and there are cries "from them after Rā hath passed them as he journeyeth "on his way. Their offerings are the plants of the year,

The Ṭuat-gods address the Utau.

"and their offerings are given to them when they hear "the words of those who draw along this great god. "The gods of the Ṭuat (?) who [draw] the holy Boat "in the earth say unto the Utau, whose arms are "hidden:—'O ye Utau of the earth, whose duty it is to "stand (?) near his habitation, whose heads are uncovered, "and whose arms are hidden, may there be air to your "nostrils, O Utau, and may your funeral swathings "be burst open, and may you have the mastery over

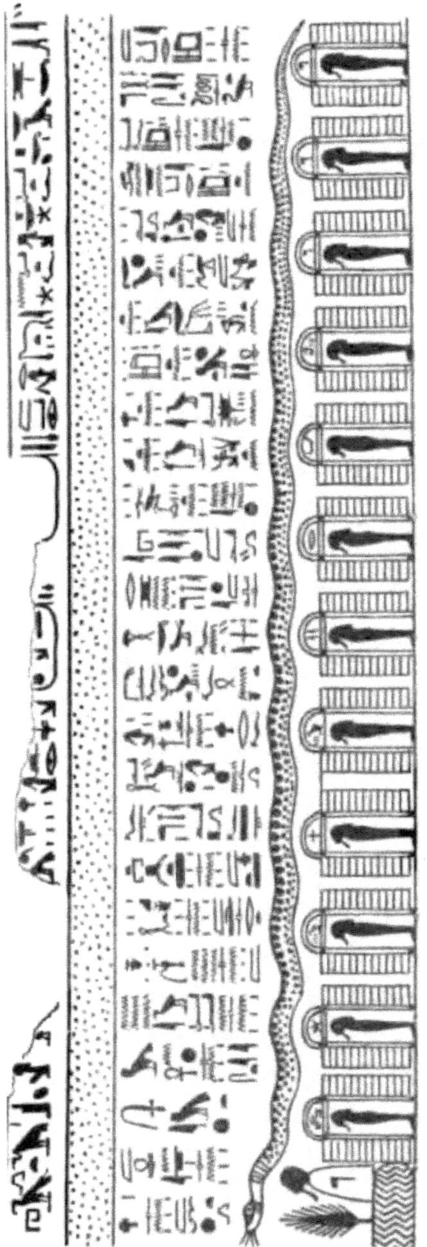

The Twelve holy Gods who are in the Ṭuat.

"your meats, and may "you have peace (or, "rest) in that which I "have created. Their "food is of bread "cakes, and their "bread is made of "the red grain, the "draughts which they "drink are of [cool] "water, and their meat "is given unto them "because of the white- "ness (or, brilliance) "of their apparel in "the Ṭuat."

On the right hand side of this Division of the Ṭuat the boat of the Sun passes twelve shrines, each of which has its doors thrown wide open, and so permits us to see a god in mummied form standing inside it these gods are described as "the holy gods who are in the

Ṭuat," [hieroglyphs]. Along the front of the twelve shrines stretches an enormous serpent, the duty of which is to protect those who stand in them. Beyond the shrines is a long basin or lake of boiling water, with rounded ends, in which stand up to their waists twelve mummied gods, with black heads, who either have white bodies, or are arrayed in white apparel; in front of each god grows a large ear of wheat. These gods are described as "the gods in the boiling lake," [hieroglyphs]. The texts which relate to both groups of beings are as follows:—

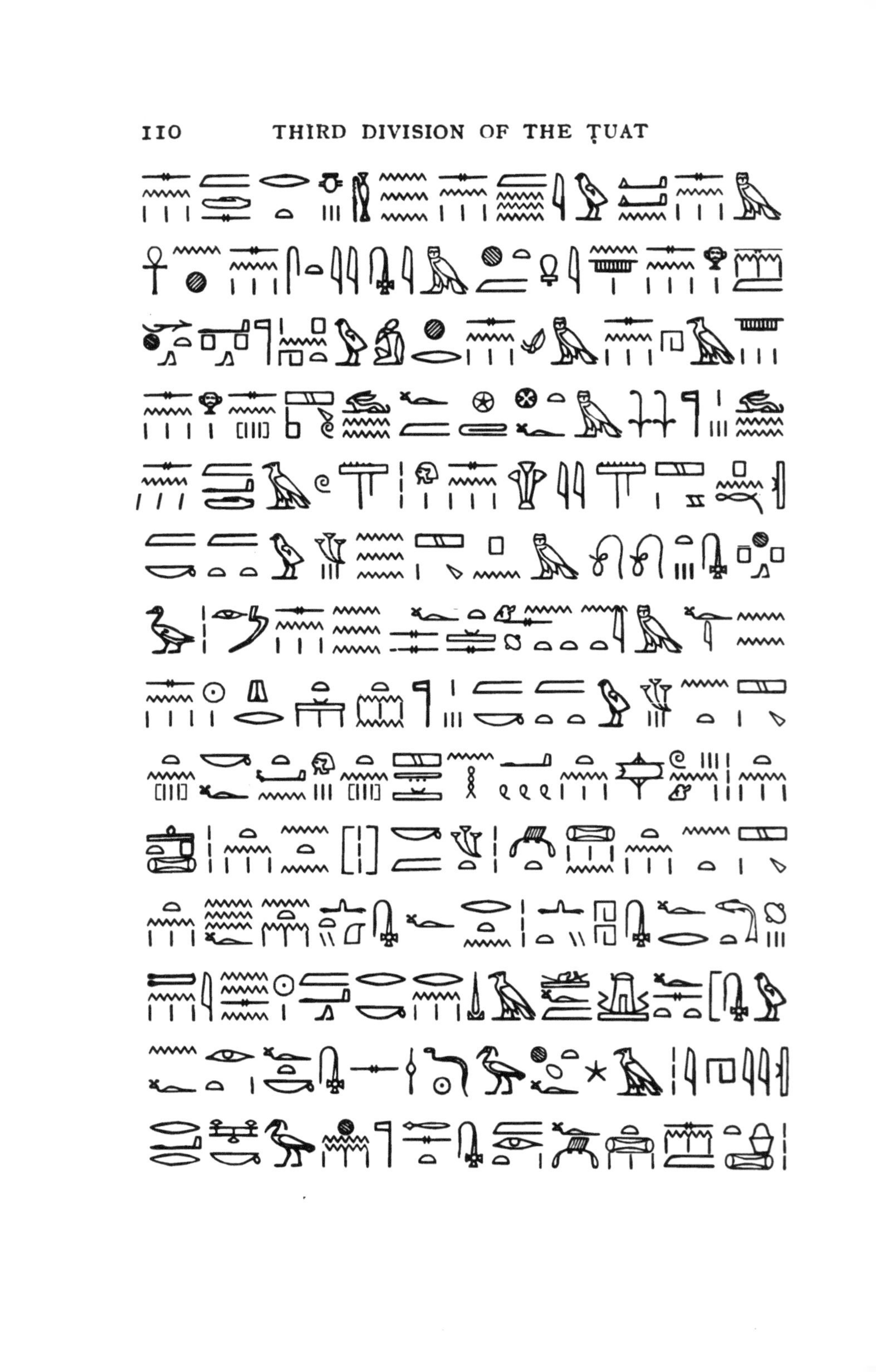

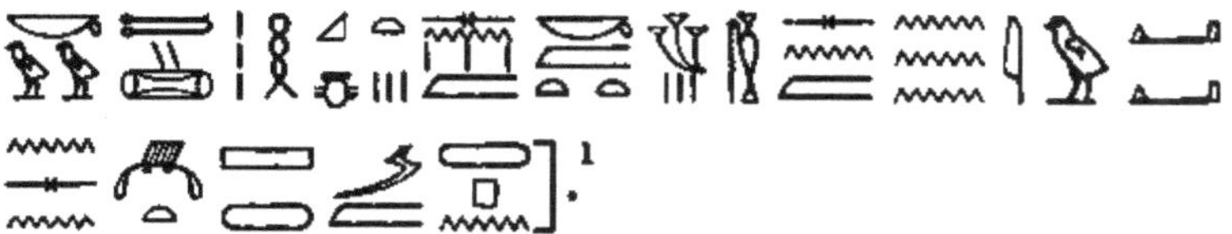

"[Those who are in] their shrines are the members "of the god whose shrines the serpent SETI guardeth. "Rā saith unto them:—'Open ye [the doors of] your "shrines, so that my radiance may penetrate the "darkness in which ye are! I found you weeping and "lamenting, with your shrines tightly closed, but air "shall be given to your nostrils, and I have decreed "that ye shall have abundance to overflowing [in all "things].' And these gods say unto Rā:—'Hail, Rā, "come thou into our lake, O thou great god who never "failest.' The *Shennu* gods who are before and behind "him pay homage to him, and they rejoice in Rā when "he traverseth [their] region, and when the great god "journeyeth through the secret place. Their food "consisteth of loaves of bread, their drink is made "from the red [barley], and their cool waters come "from [their cisterns of] water, and the serpent of fire, "SETI, giveth unto them the things whereon they live "there. The door which shutteth them in closeth "after this god hath passed through their midst, and "they utter cries of grief when they hear their doors "shut upon them."

[1] The text in brackets is supplied from Lefébure, *Les Hypogées Royaux de Thèbes* (Tombeau de Seti Ier, ive partie, pl. xiv.), Paris, 1886.

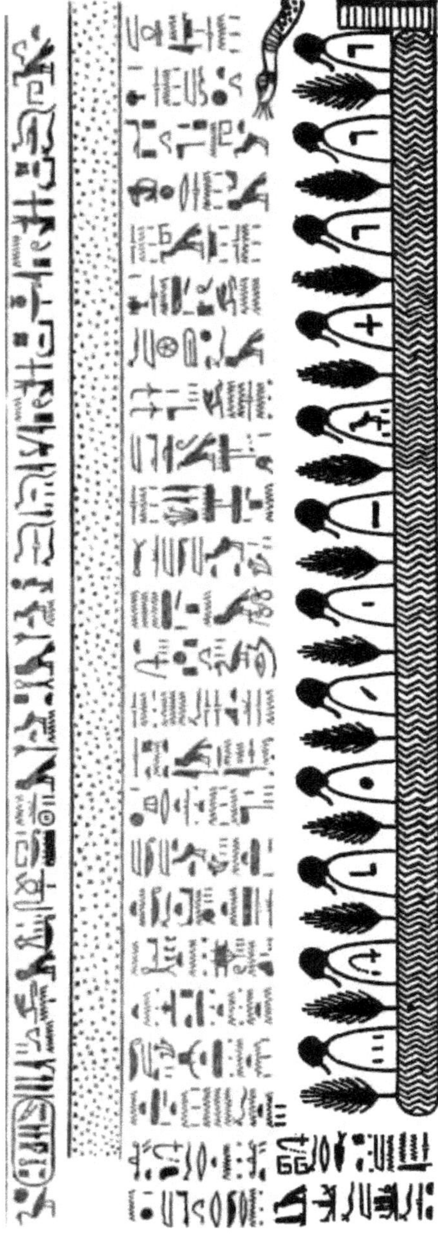

The Gods of the Boiling Lake.

The following refers to the lake of water in this Division:—

"[Here is] the "lake of water "which is in the "Ṭuat, and it is "surrounded by "the gods who are "arrayed in [their] "apparel, and who "have [their] heads "uncovered. This "lake is filled with "green herbs. The "water of this lake "is boiling hot, and "the birds betake "themselves to "flight when they "see the waters "thereof, and when "they smell the "fœtid smell which "is in it. Unto "these gods saith "Rā:—'O ye gods "whose duty it is "[to guard] the green herbs of your lake, whose heads "are uncovered, and whose limbs are covered with "garments, may there be air to your nostrils, and may "offerings be made to you of the green herbs, and may "your meat be from your lake. The water thereof "shall be yours, but to you it shall not be boiling, and "the heat thereof shall not be upon your bodies.' "These [gods] say unto Rā:—'Come thou unto us, O "thou who sailest in thy boat, whose eye is of blazing "fire which consumeth, and hath a pupil which sendeth "forth light! The beings of the Ṭuat shout with joy "when thou approachest; send forth thy light upon us, "O thou great god who hast fire in thine eye.' Their "food consisteth of loaves of bread and green herbs, and "their drink (or, beer) is of the *kemtet* plants, and their "cool water is from [their cisterns of] water. And food "shall be given unto them in abundance from this lake."

On the left of the path along which the boat of Rā passes in this Division of the Ṭuat are two groups of beings. In the first of these we see the god TEM, [hieroglyphs], in the form of an aged man, with bent shoulders, leaning upon a staff; coiled up before him in voluminous folds, with its head flat upon the ground, is the monster serpent ĀPEP, [hieroglyphs]. Behind Āpep stand nine men, with their arms hanging by their sides; these are called the "TCHATCHA who repulse ĀPEPI," [hieroglyphs]. In the second group is TEM,

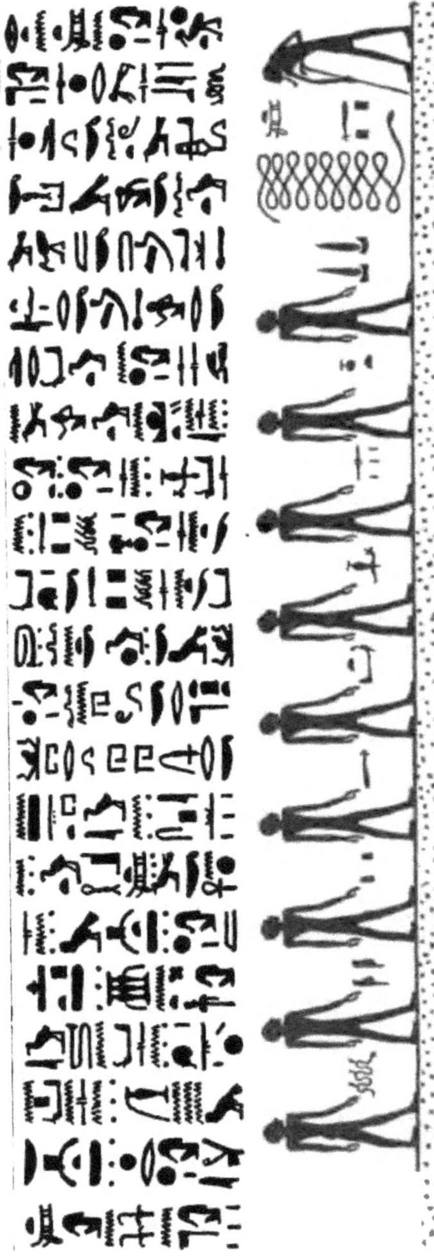

The Tchatcha who repulse Āpep.

in a similar attitude, and before him stand nine gods, each holding the symbol of life in the right hand, and the sceptre [hieroglyph] in the left; the nine gods are called "Nebu khert," i.e., "Lords of destinies," [hieroglyphs].

The texts which refer to these groups read:—

[hieroglyphs]

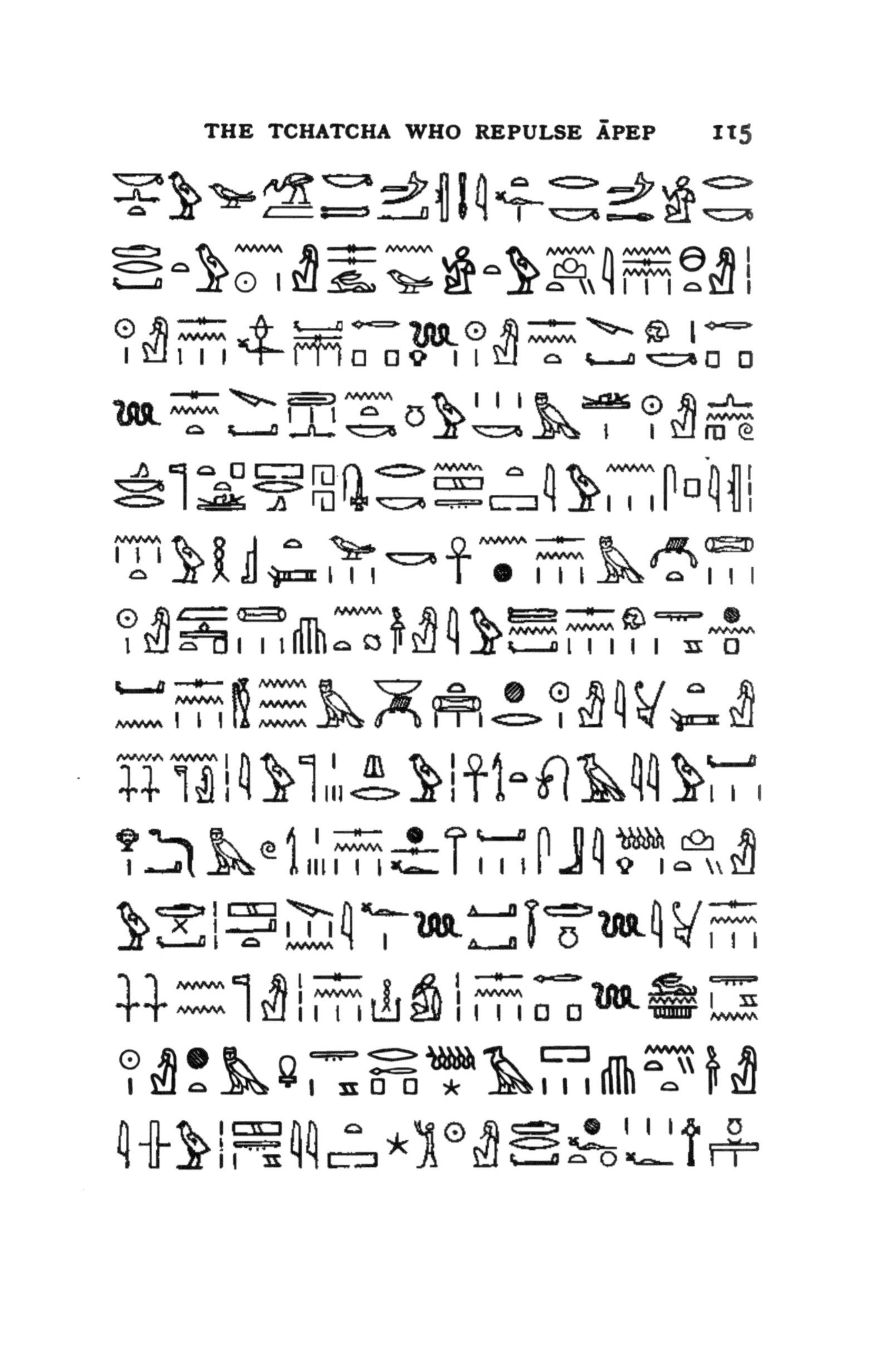

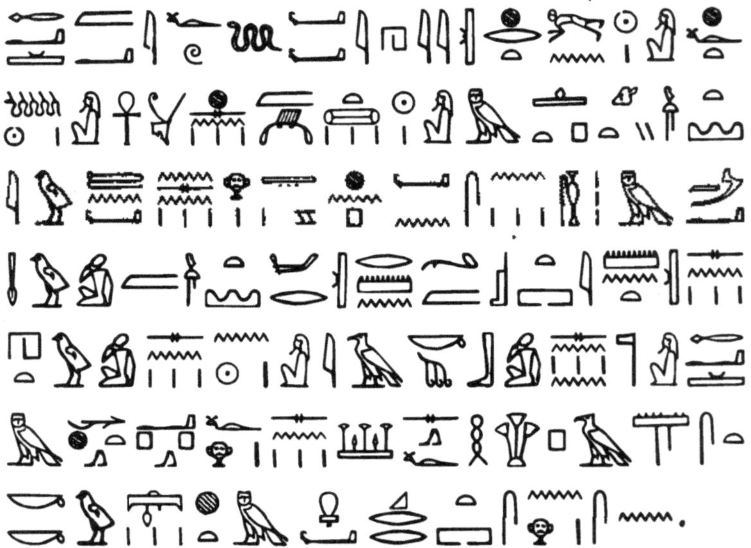

The first group shows us what "TEM hath done for "RĀ, and how he hath protected the god by words of "magical power, and hath overthrown the serpent "SEBȦ. [TEMU saith:—] 'Thou art prostrate, and thou "shalt never more rise up; thou art enchanted by [my "enchantments], and thou shalt never more be found. "The word of my father is *maāt* against thee, and my "word is *maāt* against thee; I have destroyed thee for "RĀ, and I have made an end of thee for KHUTI.'

"The company of the gods of Rā who repulse ĀPEP "say:—'Thy head is slit, O Āpep, thy folds are gashed, "thou shalt never more envelop the boat of Rā, and "thou shalt never again make a way into the divine "bark. A flame of fire goeth out against thee from "the hidden place, and we have condemned thee to thy "dire doom.' They (i.e., 'the nine gods of the "company of Rā) live "upon the food of Rā, "and upon the cakes "of KHENT-ÅMENTI, for "offerings are made on "their behalf upon "earth, and libations of "cool water are made "unto them by the lord "of food (or, as lords of "food) before Rā."

To the second group of nine gods "TEM saith:—'Inasmuch as "ye are the gods who "possess life and sceptre "(i.e., authority), and "who have mastery over "your sceptres, drive ye "back the serpent SEBÅ "from KHUTI, gash ye "with knives the foul "and evil serpent ÅF.' "These are the gods who "work enchantments on "ĀPEP, who open the "earth to RĀ, and who

The Lords of Destinies (?).

"shut it against APEP in the gates of KHENTI-ÅMENTI. "They are those who are in the hidden place, and they "praise Rā, and they destroy his enemies, and they "protect the great one against the serpent ÅFU, and "they utter cries of joy at the overthrow by Rā of the "enemy of Rā. They live upon the meat of Rā, and "on the cakes offered to KHENTI-AMENTI. Offerings "are made on their behalf upon earth, and they receive "libations through [their] word being *maāt* in Åment, "and holy are they of arm in their hidden place. "They utter cries to Rā, and they make lamentation "for the great god after he hath passed by them, for "when he hath departed they are enveloped in dark- "ness, and their circle is closed upon them."

CHAPTER V.

THE GATE OF TCHEṬBI.

THE FOURTH DIVISION OF THE ṬUAT.

THE boat of the sun having passed through the Third Division of the Ṭuat arrives at the gateway which leads to the Fourth Division. This gateway is like that which admitted the god into the Third Division, and its outwork is guarded by nine gods, in the form of mummies, who are described as the "third company of the gods of the great god who are within," . At the entrance to the corridor which runs between the two walls is a god in mummied form called ENUERKHATA, , and at the exit is a similar god called SEṬA-TA, ; each god has a uraeus over his brow, and each is said to "extend his arms and hands to Rā," . The corridor is swept by flames of fire which proceed from the mouths of two serpents, stationed each at an angle, and their "fire is for Rā." The gateway of the Fourth Division is called NEBT-S-TCHEFAU, , and the text says, "This great god cometh to this "gateway, and entereth in through it, and the gods "who are therein acclaim him," The company of gods say to Rā, "Open thou the earth, force thou a way through "the Ṭuat and the region which is above, and dispel "our darkness; hail, Rā, come thou to us," The monster serpent which stands on his tail and guards the gateway is called TCHEṬBI, , and the two lines of text which refer to his admission of Rā read, "He who is "over this door openeth to Rā. SA saith to TCHEṬBI:— "'Open [thy] gate to Rā, unfold thy doors to KHUTI, "that he may send light into the thick darkness, and "may make his radiance illumine the hidden habitation.' "This door is shut after this great god hath passed "through it, and there is lamentation to those who are "in this gateway when they hear this door close upon "them,"

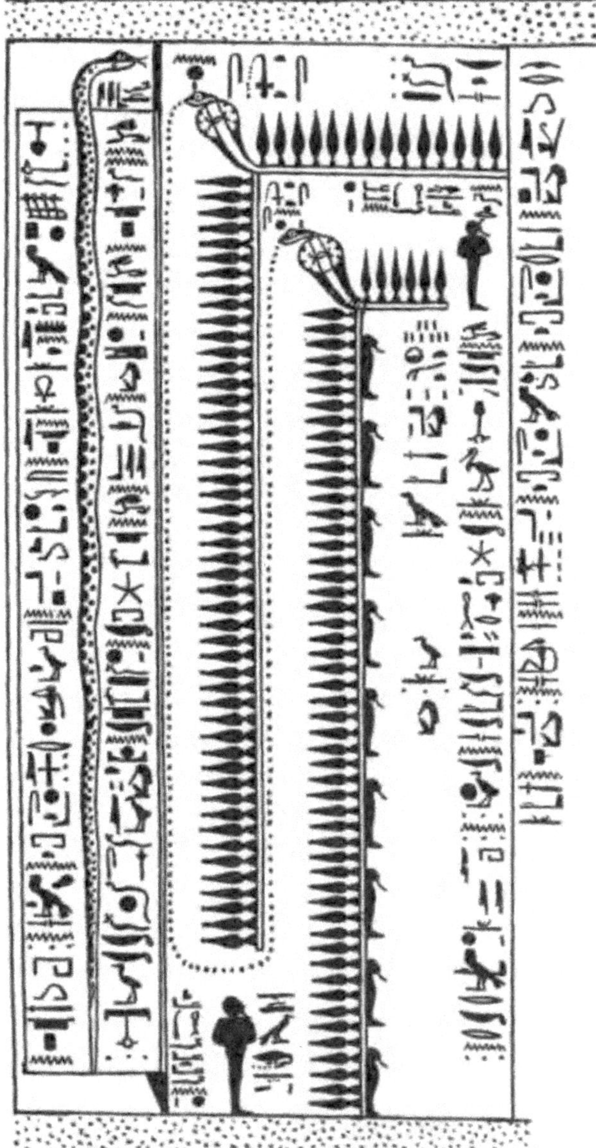

The Gate of the Serpent Tcheṭbi.

In the middle of this Division we see the boat of Rā being towed on its way by four gods of the Ṭuat; the god is in the same form as before, and stands in a shrine enveloped by MEḤEN. SA stands in the bows, and ḤEKA at the stern. The boat advances to a long, low building with a heavy cornice, which contains nine small shrines or chapels; in each of these is a god in mummied form lying on his back. The nine gods are described as the "gods who follow Osiris, who are in their abodes" (literally, "holes"), . Immediately in front of the nine shrines are two groups, each containing six women, who stand upon a slope, one half of which appears to be land and the other half water; these women are called "the hour goddesses which are in the Ṭuat," . Each group is separated from the other by a monster serpent of many folds called ḤERERET, , and of him it is said that he "spawneth twelve serpents to be devoured by the hours," .

The Gods of the Fourth Division of the Ṭuat towing the Boat of Rā.

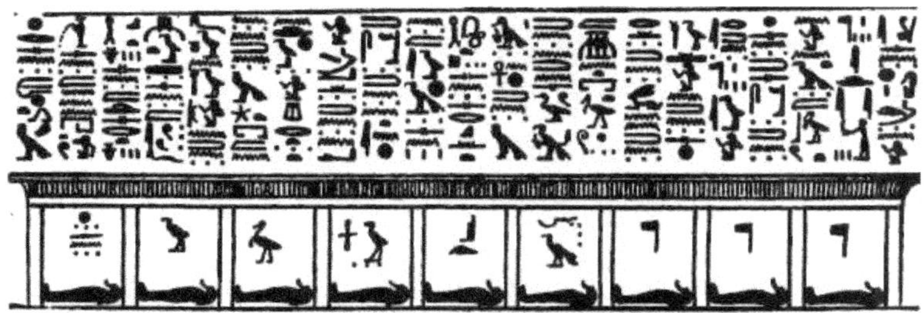

The Nine Gods who follow Osiris.

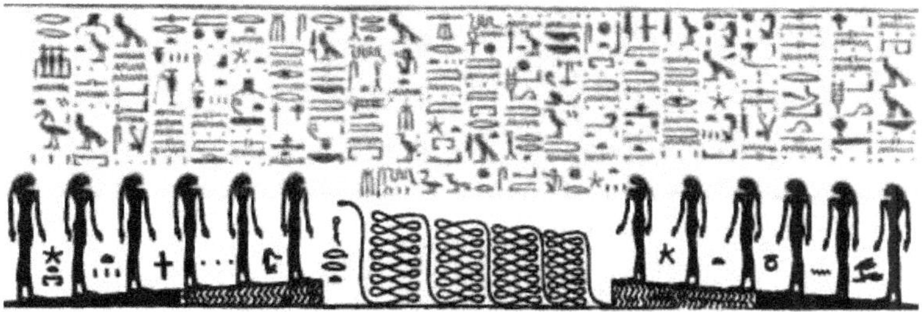

The Serpent Ḥereret and the Goddesses of the Hours.

The text relating to the passage of the boat of the sun reads :—

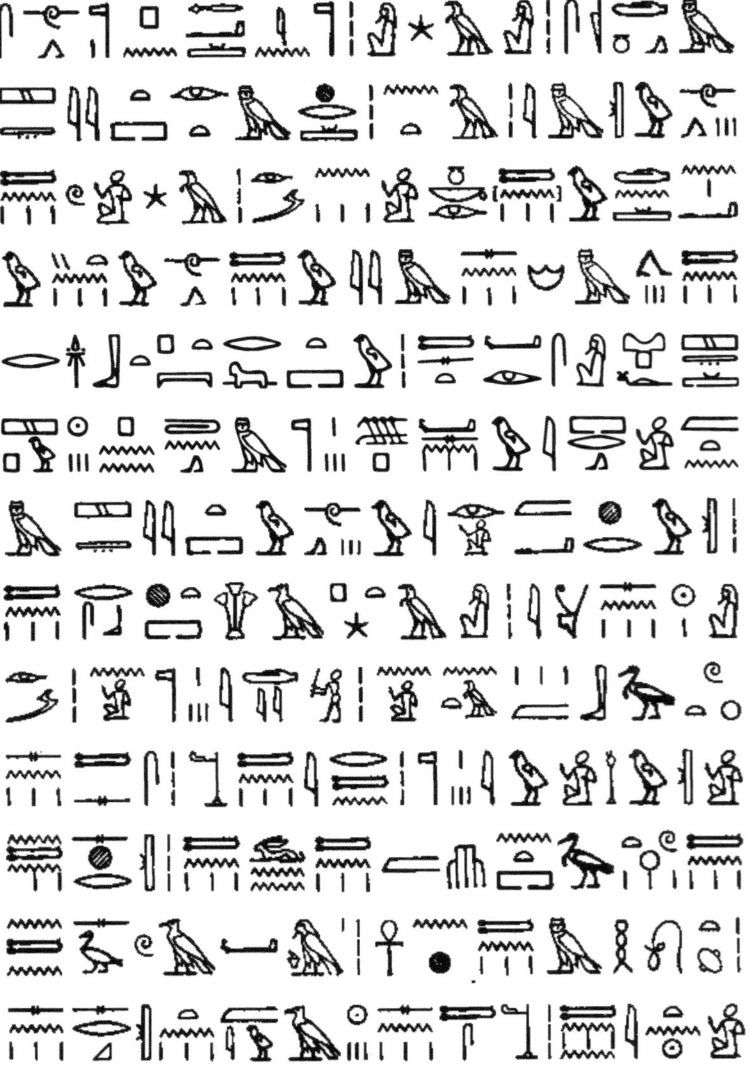

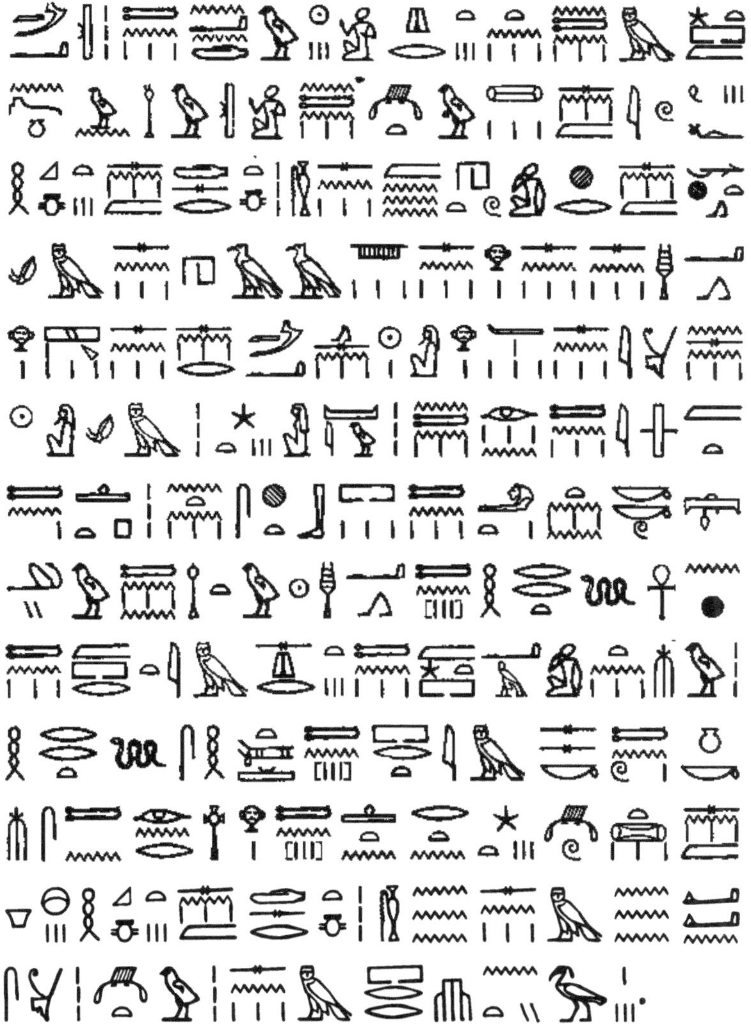

"This great god is drawn along by the gods of the "Ṭuat, and he journeyeth in the hidden place, and "worketh in respect of the things which are there.

"[He saith:—] 'Draw ye me along, O ye beings of the "Ṭuat, look ye upon me, [for] I have created you. "Pull ye with your arms and draw ye me therewith, "and turn ye aside to the eastern part of heaven, to "the habitations which surround ĀRES (or, SĀR) [and "to] that hidden mountain, the light (or, radiance) of "which goeth round about among the gods who receive "me as I come forth among you into the hidden place. "Draw ye me along, [for] I work on your behalf in the "gateway which covereth over the gods of the Ṭuat.'"

"And Rā saith unto them:—'Look ye upon me, O "gods, for I strike those who are in their sepulchres, "[saying], Arise, O ye gods! I have ordered for you the "plan and manner of your existence, O ye who are in 'your sepulchres, whose souls are broken, who live "upon your own filth and feed upon your own offal, "rise up before my Disk, and put ye yourselves in a "right state by means of my beams. The duties which "ye shall have in the Ṭuat are in conformity with the "things which I have decreed for you.' Their food "consisteth of flesh, and their ale is [made] of the red "[barley], and their libations are of cool water. There "is lamentation to them after they have heard their "doors close upon them."

In respect of the twelve goddesses of the hours it is said:—"[These are] they who stand upon their lake, "and it is they who guide Rā in a straight line by "means of their instruments. To them Rā saith:— "'Hearken, O ye goddesses of the hours of the night "sky. Work ye, and eat ye, and rest ye in your "gateways, with your breasts towards the darkness, "and your hind-parts towards the light. Make to "stand up the serpent ḤERERET, and live ye upon that "which cometh forth from it. It is your duty in the "Ṭuat to eat up the spawn of ḤERERET, and ye shall "destroy that which cometh forth from it. Draw ye "me, for I have begotten you in order that ye may pay "homage [to me]. Take ye your rest (or, be at peace), "O ye Hours!' Their food consisteth of cakes of "bread, and their ale is [made] of the red [barley], and "their draughts are of cool water, and there is given "unto them as their food that which cometh forth with "the *khu* (i.e., the beatified dead)."

On the right hand of the path of the boat of the Sun in the Fourth Division we see:—1. Twelve gods, bearded and standing upright, who are called "the gods who carry along their doubles," . 2. Twelve jackal-headed gods, who stand round the "Lake of Life," , who are called the "jackals in the lake of life," . 3. Ten uraei, which stand round the "Lake of the Uraei," , and are called the "Living Uraei," . The texts which refer to these three groups of beings read:—

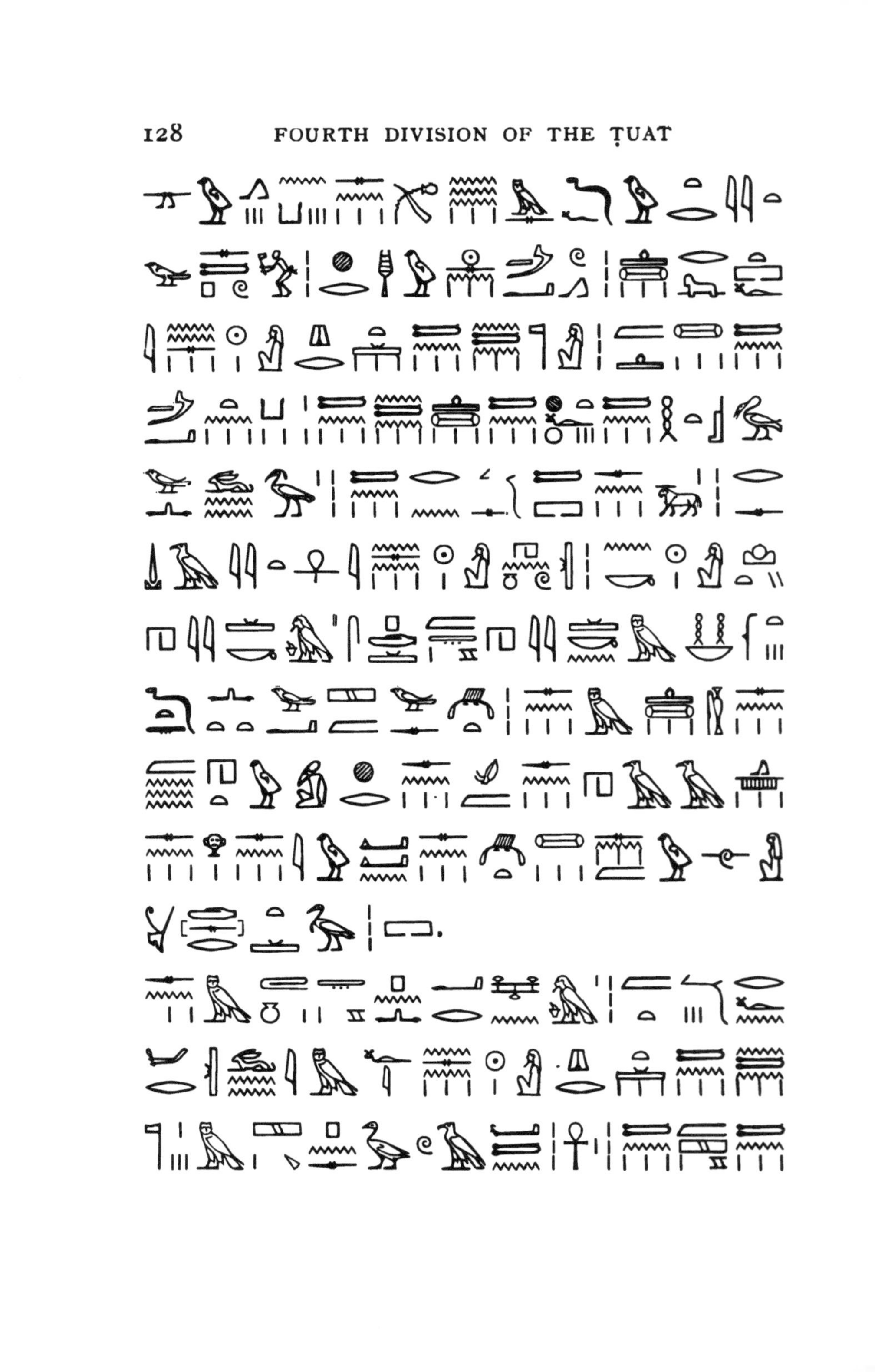

The paragraph which refers to the first twelve gods reads:—

"[These are] they who bear along their doubles, "who immerse themselves in that which floweth in "abundance from the slaughtered ones during the time "of their existence, and who carry the offerings which "are rightly due [to the god] to his abode. Unto them "saith Rā:—'That which belongeth to you [to do], O "ye gods who are among your offerings, is to offer as "an obligatory offering your doubles. Ye have your "own offerings, your enemies are destroyed, and they "are not. Your spirits are on their thrones, [and your] "souls are on their places.' They say unto Rā, 'Adora-"tions be unto thee, O RĀ-KHUTI! Hail to thee, O "thou Soul who art protected in the earth! Hail to "thee, as being eternity, the lord of the years and of "the everlastingness which hath no diminution.' Their "food consisteth of offerings, their drink is of cool "water, and there is lamentation to them when they "hear their doors close upon them. Their food is given "to them from the goddess Mu-sta (?) by ṬESERT-BAIU."

The paragraph which refers to the jackal-headed gods reads:—

"[These are] they who come forth from this lake "whereunto the souls of the dead cannot approach by "reason of the sanctity which is therein. Unto them "saith Rā:—'That which belongeth to you [to do], O ye "gods who are in this lake, is to keep guard upon your "lives in your lake; your offerings are under the guard "of the jackals which have set themselves on the edge "of your lake.' They say unto Rā:—'Immerse thyself, "O Rā, in thy holy lake, wherein the lord of the gods "immersed himself, whereunto the souls of the dead "approach not; this is what thou thyself hast com-"manded, O KHUTI.' Their food consisteth of bread, "their drink is [made] of the red [barley], and their

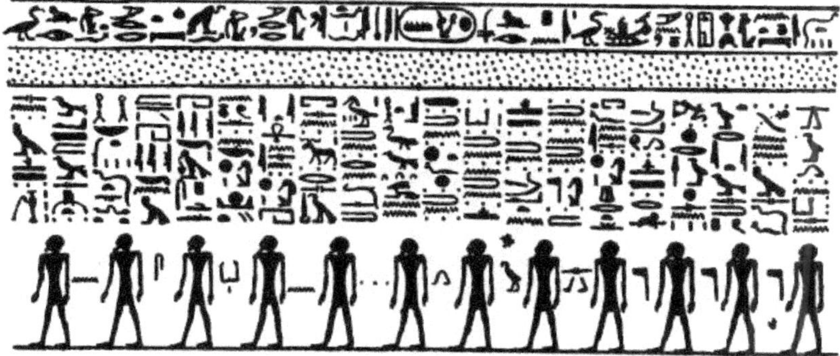

The Twelve Gods who carry their Doubles.

The Twelve Gods of the Lake of Life.

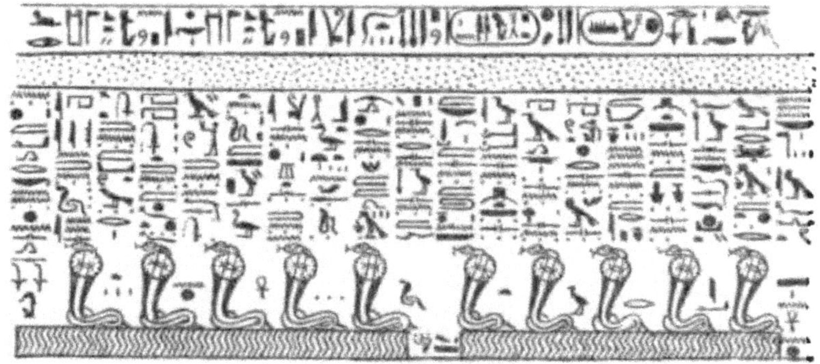

The Ten Living Uraei of the Lake of the Uraei.

"vessels of drink are filled with wine. There is lamen- "tation among them when they hear their doors close "upon them. Their food is given unto them as lord[s] "of their sceptres round about this lake."

The paragraph which refers to the uraei reads:—

"[These are] they who have their speech after Rā "cometh to them, and souls are turned backwards, and "shadows are destroyed at the hearing of the words "(or, voices) of the uraei. Unto them saith Rā:—'That "which belongeth to you [to do], O ye URAEI who are "in this lake, is to guard your flames and your fires [so "that ye may hurl them] against my (literally, his) "enemies, and your burning heat against those whose "mouths are evil. Hail to you, O URAEI.' They "say unto Rā:—'Come thou to us, stride thou over "TANEN.'"

On the left of the path of the boat of the sun through the Fourth Division we see the god Osiris, in mummied form, and wearing on his head the crown of the South, standing on a serpent, and partially covered by the earth of a mountain; his head only is above the ground, and he stands in a naos with a vaulted dome. His name or title, KHENT ÅMENTI, , is written by his side. Before the shrine is a Flame-goddess in the form of a uraeus, and behind her are twelve gods, who stand in front of ḤERU-UR (or, Horus the Aged), the Haroeris of the later Greek writers. Ḥeru-ur is in the form of a hawk-headed man, who leans on a staff. Behind the shrine which contains Osiris stand twelve gods, who are described as "the gods who are behind the shrine," [hieroglyphs]. Behind, or by the side of these, are four pits or hollows in the ground, by the side of each of which stands a god, with his body bent forward in adoration before a bearded god, who holds the symbol of life in the right hand and a sceptre in the left. The four gods are called "Masters of their pits," [hieroglyphs], and their lord is called the "Master of Earths (?)," [hieroglyphs].

The texts referring to these gods read:—

The text referring to Horus reads:—

"Horus worketh on behalf of his father Osiris, he "performeth magical ceremonies for him, and restoreth "to him the crown [, saying], 'My heart goeth out to "thee, O my father, thou who art avenged on those "who would work against thee, and in all the matters "which concern thee thou art guided by magical "ceremonies. Thou hast the mastery, O Osiris, thou "hast the sovereignty, O KHENTI ÅMENTI, thou hast "whatsoever is thine as Governor of the Ṭuat, O thou "whose forms (or, attributes) are exalted in the hidden "place; the beatified spirits hold thee in fear, and "the dead are terrified at thee. Thy crown hath been "restored unto thee, and I, thy son Horus, have "reckoned thy weakness there.'"

The twelve gods who are in front of the shrine of Khenti Åmenti say:—

"Let Him of the Ṭuat be exalted! Let Khenti "Åmenti be adored! Thy son Horus hath restored to "thee thy crown, he hath protected thee by means of "magical ceremonies, he hath crushed for thee thine "enemies, he hath brought to thee vigour for thy arms, "O Osiris, Khenti Ȧmenṭi."

In reply to this address of the twelve gods Khenti Ȧmenti saith unto his son Horus:—

"Come to me, O my son Horus, and avenge me on "those who work against me, and cast them to him "that is over the things which destroy, [for] it is he "who guardeth the pits [of destruction]."

Then saith Horus unto those gods who are behind the shrine:—

"Make inquisition for me, O gods who are in the "following of Khenti Ȧmenti, stand ye up, and with-"draw ye not yourselves, and be ye masters over "yourselves, and come, and live delicately on the bread "of Ḥu, and drink ye of the ale of Maāt, and live ye "upon that whereon my father liveth there. That "which belongeth to you in the hidden place is to be "behind the shrine, according to the commandment of "Rā. I call unto you, and behold, it is for you to do "what it is your duty [to do].' Their meat consisteth "of cakes of bread, and their ale is of the *tchesert* "drink, and their libations are [made with] cool water. "Their food is given unto them by the guardian of "the things which are in the shrine. And Horus "saith unto these gods:—'Smite ye the enemies of my "father, and hurl ye them down into your pits because "of that deadly evil which they have done against the

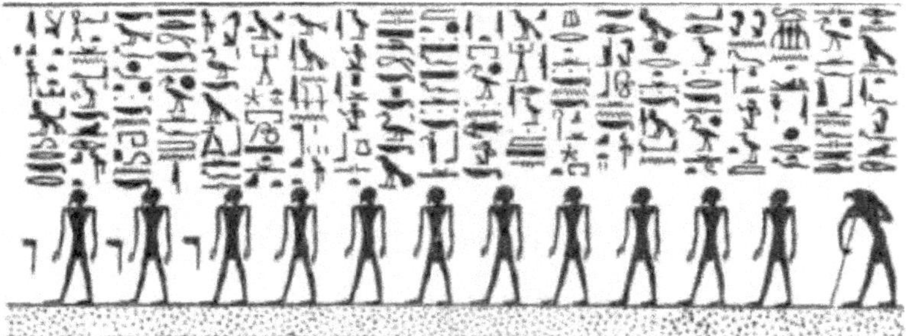

The Twelve Gods before the Shrine. Ḥeru-ur.

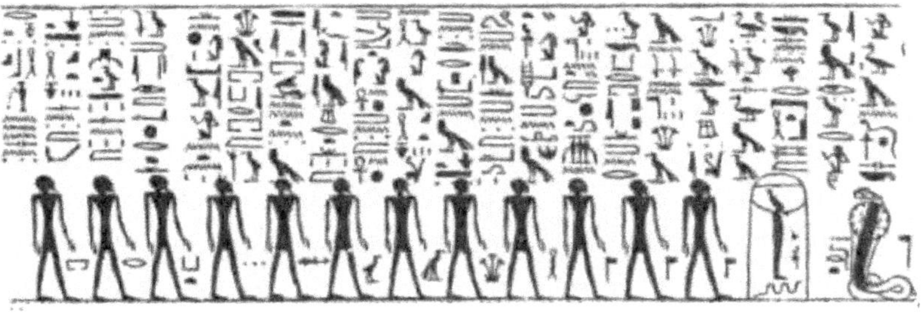

The Twelve Gods behind the Shrine. Osiris Khent-Ȧmenti. The goddess of Flame (Nesert).

The Master of Earths. The Four Masters of their Pits.

"Great One, [which] found(?) him that begot me. "That which belongeth to you to do in the Ṭuat is to "guard the pits of fire according as Rā hath commanded, "and I set [this] before you so that, behold, ye may do "according to what belongeth to you [to do].' This "god standeth over (or, by) the pits."

CHAPTER VI.

THE GATE OF TEKA-ḤRÅ.

THE FIFTH DIVISION OF THE ṬUAT.

THE boat of the sun having passed through the Fourth Division of the Ṭuat arrives at the gateway which leads to the FIFTH DIVISION. This gateway is similar to that which guards the Fourth Division, and is guarded by nine gods, who are described as the "Fourth Company," ; at the entrance to the corridor and at its exit stands a jackal-headed god, the former being called ĀAU, , and the latter TEKMI, ; each is said to "extend his arms and hands to Rā." The corridor is swept by flames of fire, as before. The gateway is called ÅRIT, , and the text says, "This great god cometh to this "gateway, and entereth in through it, and the gods "who are therein acclaim him," . The nine gods say to

Rā, "Rā-Ḥeru-khuti unfoldeth our doors, and openeth "our gateways. Hail, Rā, come thou to us, O great "god, lord of hidden nature," . The monster serpent which stands on his tail and guards the gateway is called Teka-ḥrȧ, , and the two lines of text which refer to his admission of Rā read:—"He who is over this door openeth to Rā. "Sa saith to Teka-ḥrȧ:—'Open thy gate to Rā, unfold "thy doors to Khuti, that he may send light into the "thick darkness, and may make his radiance illumine "the hidden habitation.' This door is shut after the "great god hath passed through it, and there is "lamentation to those who are in this gateway when "they hear this door close upon them." As the hieroglyphic text is identical with that given above on p. 120 it is not repeated here.

In the middle of this Division we see the boat of Rā being towed on its way by four gods of the Ṭuat; the god is in the same form as before, and stands in a shrine enveloped by Meḥen. Sa stands in the bows, and Ḥeka at the stern. In front of those who tow the boat are nine shrouded gods, with projecting elbows; each of these holds in his hands a part of the body of a long, slender serpent, and the group is called "those who hold Ennutchi," . In front of these are

The Gate of the Serpent Teka-ḥrȧ.

twelve bearded beings, who are advancing towards a god, who is styled [the god] "of his angle," ; the twelve gods are described as BAIU RETH-ÅMMU-ṬUAT, i.e., "the souls of the men who are in the Ṭuat," . The texts read:—

The Boat of Râ being towed by the Gods of the Fifth Division of the Ṭuat.

"The gods of the Ṭuạt draw along this great god, "and he journeyeth through the hidden place. [Rā "saith:—] 'Draw ye me along, O ye gods of the Ṭuat, "and sing praises unto me, O ye who are at the head "of the stars; let your cords be strong (or, vigorous), "and draw ye me along by means of them, and let "your hands and arms be steady, let there be speed in "your legs, let there be strong intent in your souls, "and let your hearts be glad. Open ye a prosperous "way into the chambers (*qerti*) of hidden things.'"

The Nine Gods who hold Ennutchi.

The text relating to the bearers of the serpent reads:—

"Those who are in this scene carry this serpent. "Rā striketh them and advanceth towards them to "make himself to rest in [the gateway called] Nebt-"Āḥāu. This serpent travelleth as far as it (i.e., this "gateway), but he passeth not beyond it. Rā saith "unto them:—'Strike ye the serpent Ennutchi there, "give him no way [whereby to escape], so that I may "pass by you. Hide your arms, destroy that which "you guard, protect that which cometh into being "from my forms, and tie ye up (or, fetter) that which "cometh into being from my strength.' Their food "consisteth of the hearing of the word of this god, and "offerings are made to them from the hearing of the "word of Rā in the Ṭuat."

"Unto those who have spoken what is right and "true upon earth, and who have magnified the forms "of the god, Rā saith:—'Praises shall be [sung] to

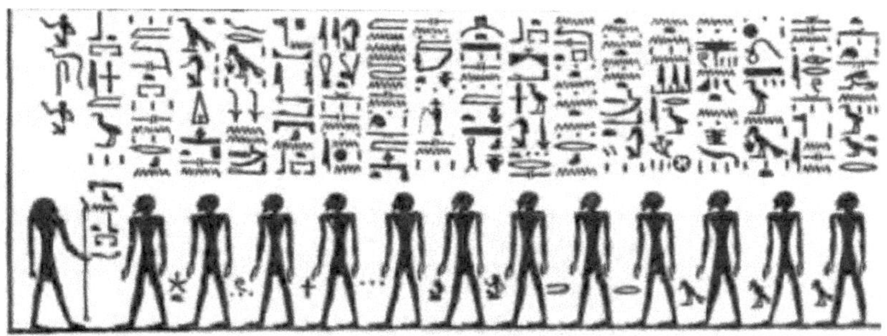

Ḥeri-qenbet-f. The souls of men who are in the Ṭuat.

"your souls, and there shall be breath to your nostrils, "and there shall be to you joints in SEKHET-ÅRU. "That which shall be indeed yours is what belongeth "to the MAĀTI GODS. The habitations which shall be "yours shall be (or, are) at the corner where [live] "those who are with me who weigh words for them.' "Their food is of bread-cakes, and their drink of "*tchesert* drink, and their libations are of cool water. "Offerings are made unto them upon earth as to the "god Ḥetepi, according to what should be offered unto "them."

Rā saith unto this god:—"Let him that is over his "Corner (Ḥeri-qenbet-f) cry out to those souls who "are right, and true, and divine, and make them to sit "at peace in their habitations at the Corner of those "who are with myself."

On the right hand of the path of Rā in the Fifth Division of the Ṭuat are:—1. Twelve male beings bowing in adoration; they are described as "those who make adorations in the Ṭuat," . 2. Twelve male beings who bear in their hands a cord for measuring plots of ground and estates; these are called "Holders of the cord in the Ṭuat," . 3. Four gods, standing upright, each holding the symbol of life in his right hand, and a sceptre in the left. The hieroglyphic texts which relate to these groups read:—

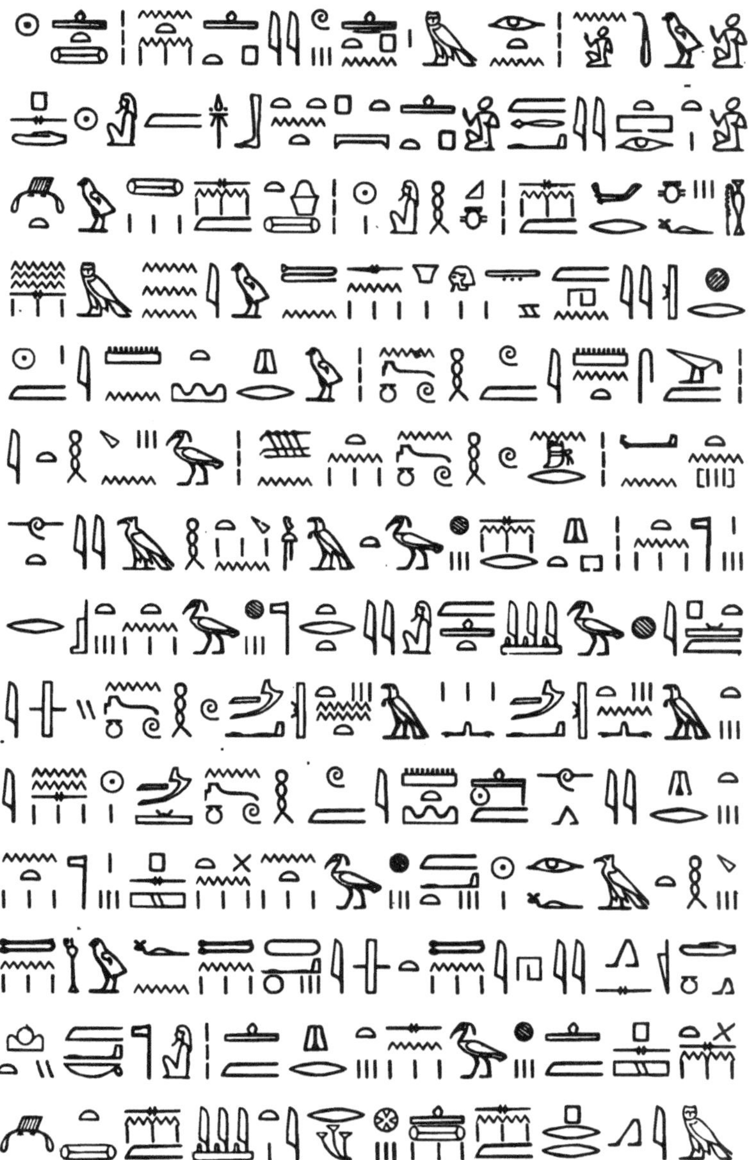

The Twelve Gods who make adoration in the Ṭuat.

The passage in the text which refers to the adorers reads:—

"[These are] they who make songs to Rā in Ȧmentet "and exalt Ḥeru-khuti. [These are they who] knew "Rā upon earth, and who made offerings unto him. "Their offerings are in their place, and their glory "is in the holy place of Åment. They say unto "Rā:—'Come thou, O Rā, progress through the Ṭuat. "Praise be to thee! Enter thou among the holy "[places] with the serpent Meḥen.' Rā saith unto "them:—'There are offerings for you, O ye who made "offerings. I am content with what ye did for me, "both when I used to shine in the eastern part of "heaven, and when I was sinking to rest in the "chamber of my Eye.' Their food is of the bread-

The Twelve Gods who hold the cord for measuring land.

"cakes of Rā, and their drink is of his *tcheser* drink, "and their libations are made of cool water, and "offerings are made unto them on the earth in [return] "for the praisings which they make unto Rā in Åment."

The passage in the text which refers to the holders of the measuring cord reads:—

"[These are they who] hold the measuring cord in "Åment, and they go over therewith the fields of "the KHU (i.e., the beatified spirits). [Rā saith to "them]:—'Take ye the cord, draw it tight, and mark "out the limit (or, passage) of the fields of Ȧmentet, "the KHU whereof are in your abodes, and the gods "whereof are on your thrones.' The KHU of NETERTI "are in the Field of Peace, [and] each KHU hath been "judged by him that is in the cord. Righteousness "is to those who are (i.e., who exist), and unrighteous-"ness to those who are not. Rā saith unto them:—"'What is right is the cord in Ȧment, and Rā is "content with the stretching (or, "drawing) of the same. Your "possessions are yours, O ye gods, "your homesteads are yours, O ye "KHU. Behold ye, Rā maketh "(or, worketh) your fields, and "he commandeth on your behalf "that there may be sand (?) with "you.'"

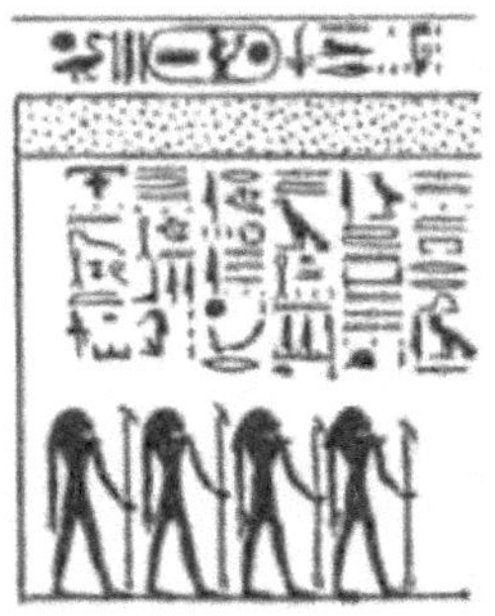

The Four Ḥenbi Gods.

"Hail, journey on, O KHUTI, for "verily the gods are content with "that which they possess, and the KHU are content "with their homesteads. Their food [cometh] from "Sekhet-Ȧru, and their offerings from that which "springeth up therein. Offerings are made unto them "upon earth from the estate of Sekhet-Ȧru."

To the four bearded gods Rā saith:—"Holy are ye, "O ḤENBI gods, ye overseers of the cords in Ȧmentet. "[O stablish ye fields and give [them] to the gods and "to the KHU (i.e., spirits) [after] they have been "measured in Sekhet-Åaru. Let them give fields and "sand to the gods and to the souls who are in the Ṭuat. "Their food shall be from Sekhet-Åaru, and their "offerings from the things which spring forth therein]."

On the left of the path of the boat of Rā are:—
1. A hawk-headed god, leaning upon a staff; he is called Horus, . 2. Four groups, each group containing four men. The first are RETH, , the second are ĀAMU, , the third are NEḤESU, , and the fourth are THEMEḤU, . The RETH are Egyptians, the ĀAMU are dwellers in the deserts to the east and north-east of Egypt, the NEḤESU are the black races and NEGROES, and the THEMEḤU are the fair-skinned Libyans. 3. Twelve bearded beings, each of whom grasps with both hands the body of a long serpent; these are called the "Holders of the period of time in Ament," , . 4. Eight bearded gods, who are called the "Sovereign chiefs of the Ṭuat," . The hieroglyphic text which relates to these groups reads:—

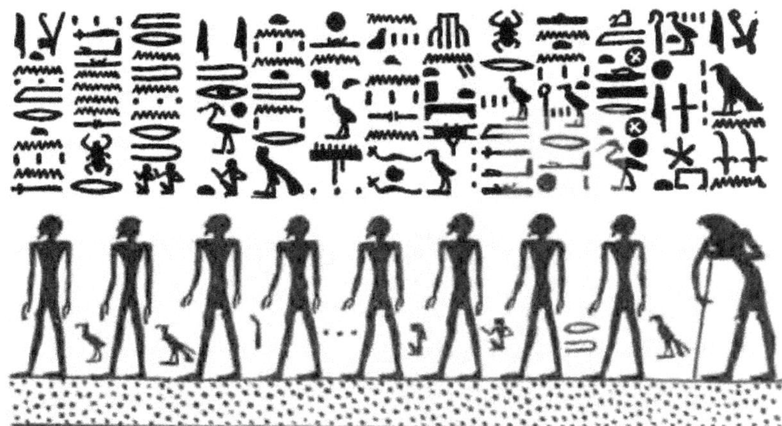

The Āamu, i.e., Asiatics. The Reth, i.e., Egyptians. Horus.

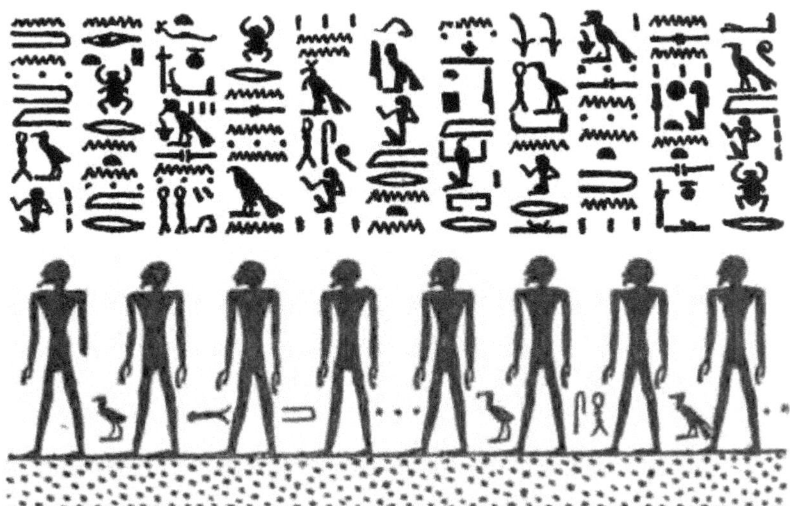

The Themeḥu, i.e., Libyans. The Neḥesu, i.e., Negroes.

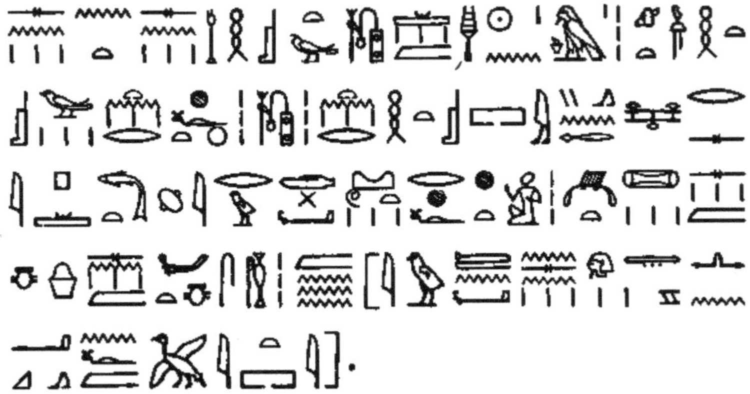

The passage which refers to the four groups, each containing four men, reads:—

Horus saith unto the creatures of Rā who dwell in the Black Land (Qemt, i.e., Egypt) and in the Red Land (i.e., the deserts which lie on each side of the Black Land formed of the mud of the Nile):—"Magical "protection be unto you, O ye creatures of Rā, who "have come into being from the Great One who is at "the head of heaven! Let there be breath to your "nostrils, and let your linen swathings be unloosed! "Ye are the tears[1] of the eye of my splendour in your "name of RETH (i.e., men). Mighty of issue (ĀA-MU) "ye have come into being in your name of ĀAMU; "Sekhet hath created them, and it is she who delivereth "(or, avengeth) their souls. I masturbated [to produce "you], and I was content with the hundreds of thou-"sands [of beings] who came forth from me in your

[1] Or, the weeping.

"name of NEḤESU (i.e., Negroes); Horus made them to "come into being, and it is he who avengeth their "souls. I sought out mine Eye, and ye came into being in your name of THEMEḤU; Sekhet hath created "them, and she avengeth their souls."

The passage which refers to the gods who make stable the period of life (KHERU-ĀḤĀU-EM-ÅMENT) reads:—

Those who make firm (or, permanent) the duration

The Twelve Gods of Life in Åment.

of life stablish the days of the souls [in] Åmenti and possess the word (or, command) of the place of destruction. Rā saith unto them:—"Inasmuch as ye "are the gods who dwell in the Ṭuat, and who have "possession of [the serpent] METERUI, by means of "whom ye mete out the duration of life of the souls "who are in Åmenti who are condemned to destruc-"tion, destroy ye the souls of the enemies according "to the place of destruction which ye are commanded "to appoint, and let them not see the hidden "place."

The passage in the text which refers to the divine sovereign chiefs reads:—

"[Here are] the divine sovereign chiefs who shall "destroy the enemies. They shall have their offerings

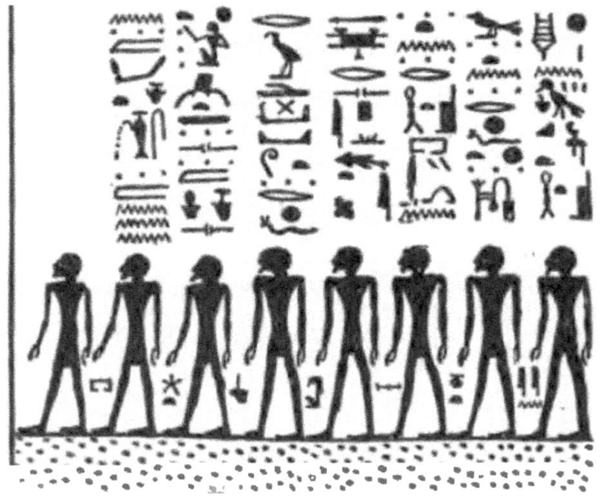

The Eight Sovereign Chiefs in the Ṭuat.

"by means of the word [which becometh] Maāt; they "shall have their oblations upon earth by means of the "word [which becometh] Maāt, and it is they who "destroy and who pass the edict concerning (literally, "write) the duration of the life of the souls who dwell "in Åmenti. The destruction which is yours shall be "[directed] against the enemies, and the power to write "which ye possess shall be for the place of destruction. "I have come, even I the great one Horus, that I may "make a reckoning with my body, and that I may "shoot forth evils against my enemies. Their food is "bread, and their drink is the *tchesert* wine, and they "have cool water wherewith to refresh (or, bathe) "themselves. [Offerings are made to them upon earth. "One doth not enter into the place of destruction.][1]

[1] Supplied from Champollion, *Notices*, p. 772.

CHAPTER VII.

THE JUDGMENT HALL OF OSIRIS.

THE SIXTH DIVISION OF THE ṬUAT.

THE boat of Rā having passed through the Fifth Division of the Ṭuat arrives at the gateway which leads to the SIXTH DIVISION, or, as the text says: "This god "cometh forth to this pylon, and he passeth in through "it, and those gods who are in the secret place acclaim "him." The gateway is guarded by twelve bearded mummy forms, who are described as the "gods and goddesses who are in this pylon," and it is called NEBT-ĀḤĀ. The gate which admits to the Sixth Division resembles those already described; at the entrance to the corridor and at its exit stands a bearded mummied form, the former being called MAĀ-ÅB, , and the latter SHETA-ÅB, . These names mean "Right (or, true) of heart" and

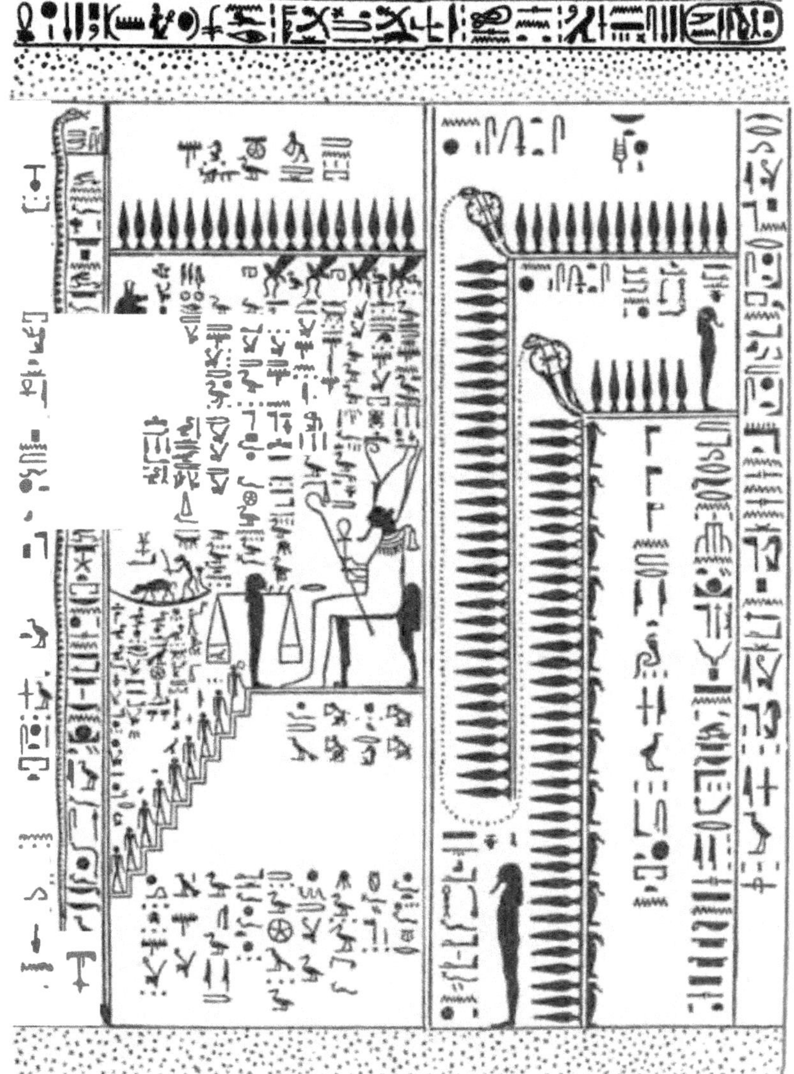

The Judgment Hall of Osiris. The Gate of the Serpent Set-em-maa-f.

"Hidden of heart" respectively, and each is said to extend his hands and arms to Rā. The corridor is swept by flames. The gods who acclaim the god say, "Come thou to us, O thou who art at the head of the "horizon, O great god, who dost open the hidden place. "Open thou the holy doors, and unfold the portals of "the hidden place,"

Between the gate which leads into the SIXTH DIVISION and the Division itself we find inserted a remarkable scene, which may be thus described:—In the upper part, from one side to another, a line is drawn, which is intended to represent the roof of the shrine or canopy in which the god is seated, and on it rests a row of *kakheru* , i.e., spear-head ornaments. From the inside of the roof hang, upside down, four heads of some kind of horned animal. These are called *Hahaiu* , and are supposed to be heads of gazelle[1] or oxen. In the space between the spear-head ornaments and the side of the Ṭuat is written

The transliteration of these characters appears to be *Ser ḥer Ṭuat sath then;* the meaning of the first three

[1] "Têtes de gazelles" (Champollion, *Monuments*, tom. ii., p. 495).

words is tolerably clear, i.e., "Osiris, governor of the Ṭuat," but the signification of the last signs is doubtful. M. Lefébure translates the inscription, "Osiris, master of Hades, Earth, and Tanen." Osiris, who wears the double crown of the South and North, and holds in his right hand the symbol of "life," and in his left a sceptre, , is seated on a chair of state, which is set on the top of a platform with nine steps. On each step stands a god, and the nine gods are described as the "company which is with SAR, i.e., Osiris," . On the topmost step is a Balance, in which the actions of the deceased are weighed; the beam of the Balance is supported either by the deceased, or by a stand which is made in the form of a bearded mummy. One pan of the Balance contains some rectangular object, and the other a figure of the bird which is symbolic of evil and wickedness. Behind the Balance is a boat, which is sailing away from the presence of Osiris; in it is a pig being driven along by a dog-headed ape which flourishes a stick. In the top left-hand corner is a figure of Anubis, jackal-headed, and under the floor of the platform on which Osiris is seated are figures of the enemy of SAR, or Osiris. From the variant of this scene which is found on the sarcophagus of Tcheḥrá at Paris,[1] as well as from the sarcophagus of Seti I., we may see that the pig in the

[1] Sharp, *Inscriptions*, part ii., pl. 9.

boat is called ÅM-Ā, [hieroglyphs], i.e., "Eater of the Arm," and the boat is piloted by a second ape which stands in the bows. On the Paris monument we see a man wielding a hatchet in a threatening manner and standing near the Scales, probably with the view of destroying the deceased if the judgment of Osiris prove adverse to him.

The nine short lines of text at the foot of the scene read:—

This inscription is in the so-called "enigmatic" writing,[1] a fact which was first noticed by Champollion, but a transcript of it exists on the sarcophagus of Tcheḥrå in characters which have the ordinary values,[2] and this reads as follows:—

[1] See Goodwin, *Aeg. Zeit.*, 1873, p. 138; Renouf, *ibid.*, 1874, p. 101; and Champollion, *Monuments*, pl. 272.

[2] Lefébure renders, "O ye who bring the word just or false to me, he, Thoth, examines the words" (*Records of the Past*, vol. x., p. 114).

, i.e., "His enemies are under his "feet, the gods and the spirits are before him; he is "the enemy of the dead (i.e., the damned) among the "beings of the Ṭuat, Osiris putteth under restraint "[his] enemies, he destroyeth them, and he performeth "the slaughter of them."

The text which refers to Anubis reads:—

,

and this Mr. Goodwin transcribed:—

, i.e., "Hail, O ye who make to be *maāt* "the word of your little one, may Thoth weigh the "words, may he make to eat his father."

Immediately over the boat is the short inscription:—

.

This Goodwin renders by, "[When] this god entereth, "he (i.e., the Ape) riseth and putteth under restraint "ĀM-Ā (i.e., the Eater of the Arm)."[1]

1 "The díver [when] this god rises, he gives up [the pig] to the plagues" (Lefébure, *op. cit.*, p. 114).

Behind the pair of scales is the following legend[1]:—

This Mr. Goodwin transcribes by:—

, and renders, "The balance-bearer does homage; the blessed spirits "in Ȧmenti follow after him; the morning star "disperses the thick darkness; there is good will "above, justice below. The god reposes himself, he "gives bread to the blessed, who throng towards him." The translation by M. Lefébure reads, "The bearer of "the hatchet and the bearer of the scales protect the "inhabitant of Ȧmenti, [who] takes his repose in "Hades, and traverses the darkness and the shadows. "Happiness is above, and justice below. The god "reposes and sheds light produced by truth which he "has produced."

[1] See also Champollion, *Monuments*, tom. ii., p. 490.

The upper part of the space between the roof and the platform on which Osiris sits is occupied by two short inscriptions, which are full of difficulty; they read:—

I.

II.

The meaning of these texts has puzzled several workers, and even the order in which the characters are to be read has given rise to differences of opinion. One of the chief difficulties in the matter is caused by the way in which the two legends are written on the sarcophagus of Seti I. Looking at the hieroglyphics as they stand, they seem to form one continuous inscription, but, if we examine the scene as it appears in the tomb of Rameses II., we see that we must divide them as above. Mr. Goodwin made an attempt to transcribe and translate a part of the texts, but as he considered them to form only one inscription we cannot accept his rendering. M. Lefébure has made translations of both texts, and they read [1]:—

I. "They, they hide those which are in the state of "the elect. They the country [belonging] to them, is "Ameh in the land. Behold, these are they whose "heads issue. What a mystery is their appearance, "[the appearance] of your images!"

II. "The examination of the words takes place, and "he strikes down wickedness, he who has a just heart, "he who bears the words in the scales, in the divine "place of the examination of the mystery of mysteries "of the spirits. The god who rises has made his "infernal [companions] all."

For purposes of comparison, the versions of the texts from the tomb of Rameses VI., as given by Champollion (*Monuments*, pl. 252) are given. It will be noted that a part of the line immediately over the head of Osiris, , is given in different places in the latter scene, for is immediately in front of the double crown of Osiris, and is immediately in front of the sceptre of the god. The other lines read:—

I. 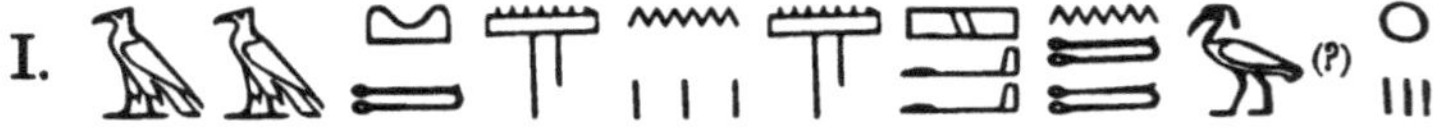

[1] *Records of the Past*, vol. x., p. 114.

CHAPTER VIII.

THE GATE OF SET-EM-MAAT-F.

THE SIXTH DIVISION OF THE ṬUAT—*continued.*

THE pylon which gives access to the SIXTH DIVISION of the Ṭuat has already been described. The monster serpent which stands on his tail and guards the gateway is called SET-EM-MAAT-F, , and the two lines of text which refer to his admission of Rā read:—

"He who is over this door openeth to Rā. SA "saith to SET-EM-MAAT-F:—'Open thy gate to Rā, "unfold thy doors to KHUTI, that he may send light "into the thick darkness, and may make his radiance "illumine the hidden habitation.' This door is shut "after this great god hath passed through it, and there "is lamentation to those who are in this gateway when "they hear this door close upon them" (see p. 169).

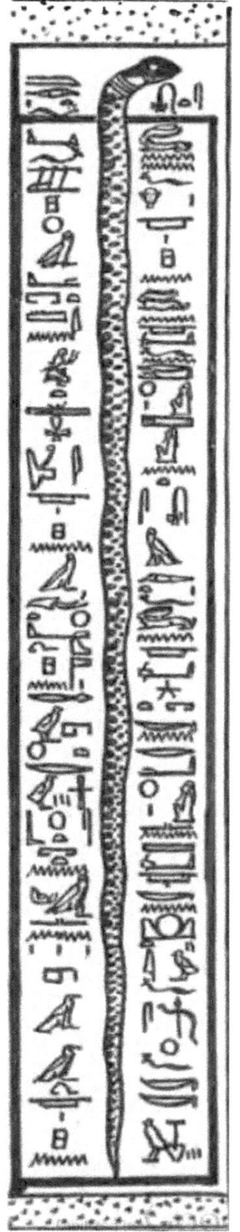

The Serpent Set-em-maat-f.

The scenes and texts which illustrate the Sixth Division of the Ṭuat cannot be obtained in a complete state from the sarcophagus of Seti I., and recourse must therefore be had to other documents. In the following pages, however, the fragments of the texts and scenes from the sarcophagus are first given, and these are followed by the complete texts as they are found in the tomb of Rameses VI., as published by Monsieur E. Lefébure in the third volume of the *Mémoires* of the French Archæological Mission at Cairo.

The fragmentary texts and scenes from the sarcophagus of Seti I. may be thus described:—

In the middle register are:—

1. Two of the four gods of the Ṭuat whose duty it is to tow along the boat of the Sun through this Division.

2. The god TEM, [hieroglyphs], in the form of an aged man, with bent shoulders, and leaning on a staff.

3. The jackal-headed standard called RĀ, [hieroglyphs], to which are tied two "enemies," who probably represent the damned.

4. The two UTCHATS, [hieroglyphs], which appear to be keeping watch on the "enemies."

5. The jackal-headed standard called TEM, [hieroglyphs], with two "enemies" tied to it.

6. A mummied form, with projecting elbows, called AFAT, [hieroglyphs].

7. The jackal-headed standard called KHEPER, [hieroglyphs] (?), with two "enemies" tied to it.

8. A mummied form, with projecting elbows, called Ṭ . . . . Ȧ, [hieroglyphs], or MEṬ, [hieroglyphs].[1]

9. The jackal-headed standard called SHU, [hieroglyphs], with two "enemies" tied to it.

10. A mummied form, with projecting elbows, called SENṬ, [hieroglyphs].

11. The jackal-headed standard called SEB, [hieroglyphs], with two "enemies" tied to it.

12. A mummied form, with projecting elbows, called AQA-SA, [hieroglyphs].

[1] The names are supplied from Champollion, *Notices*, p. 502.

13. The jackal-headed standard called SAR, (Osiris).[1]

14. A mummied form, with projecting elbows, called ĀĀ-KHER (?), (?).[1]

15. The jackal-headed standard called ḤERU, .[1]

16. A god holding a sceptre called SHEF-ḤRÅ, .[1]

The text which refers to the above-mentioned gods reads:—

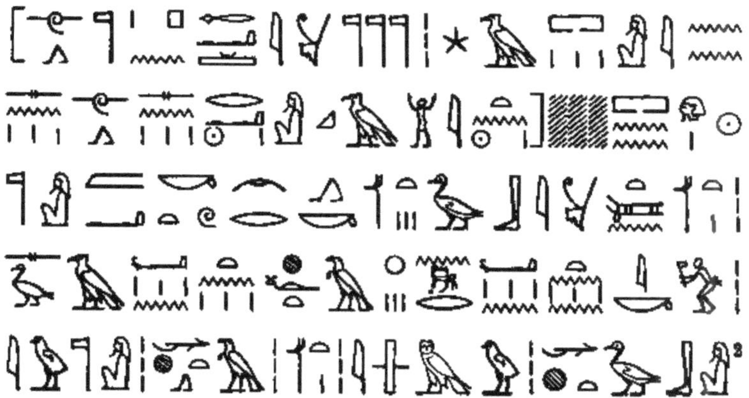

[1] The names are supplied from Champollion, *Notices*, p. 502.

[2] Champollion's text reads: (*Notices*, tom. ii., p. 503).

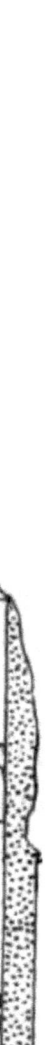

Fragment of the Division of Ṭuat, from the Cover of the Sarcophagus of Seti I.

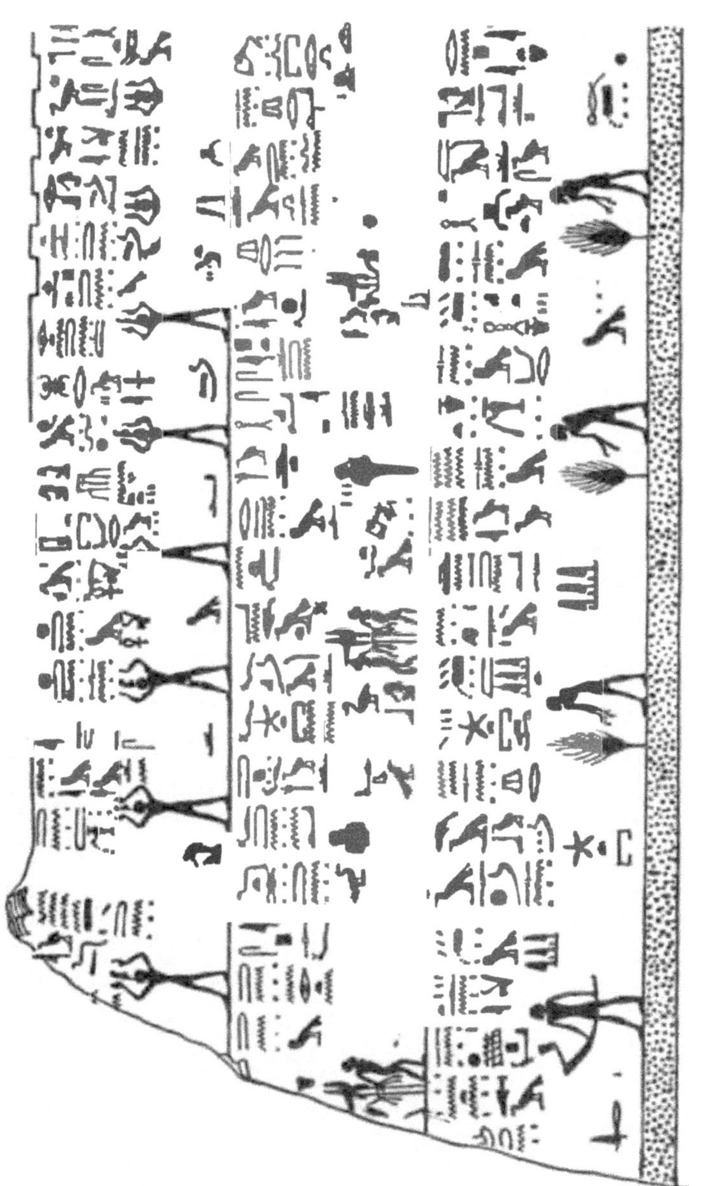

Fragment of the Sixth Division of the Ṭuat, from the Cover of the Sarcophagus of Seti I.

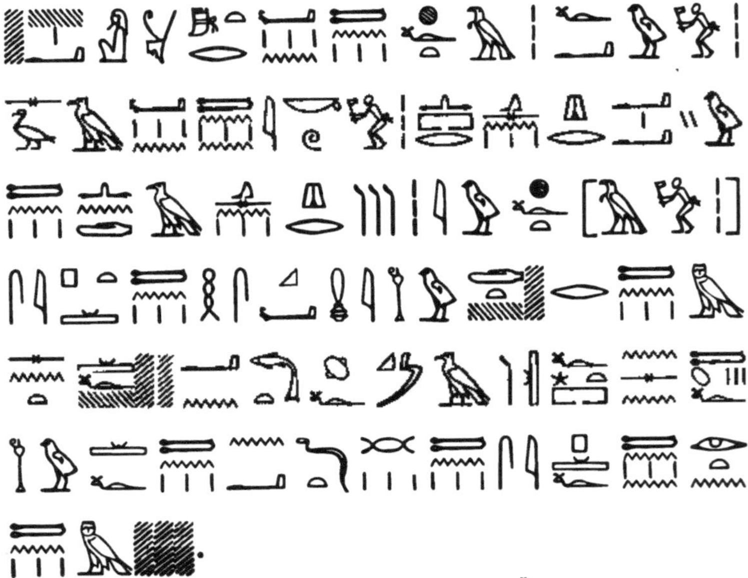

"[This great god is towed along by the gods in the "Ṭuat, and those who tow Rā along say, 'Rise up, O "disk,] . . . . god, verily get thee forth to "the standards of Seb.' Tem saith unto the standards:— "'Keep ward over the enemies, and bind ye fast those "who shall be smitten. O ye gods who are behind the "standards, and who are in the following of Seb, I give "ye the power to bind fast the enemies and to keep "ward over the wicked. Let them not go forth from "under your hands, let them not slip through your "fingers. O enemies, ye are reckoned for slaughter "according to the decree which [was given] to you by "him that . . . . . . with his body, and created the Ṭuat "by his members (?). He hath passed the decree for "you to be punished, and he taketh count of you and "what ye do . . . .'"

The upper register is much mutilated on the cover of the sarcophagus of Seti I.; on it we see:—

1. Five upright male figures, each of whom holds a large loaf of bread, , with both hands on his head; when the scene was complete these figures were twelve in number, as we learn from the variants published by Champollion,[1] and they are called ḤETEPTI-KHEPERU, .

2. Six upright male figures, each of whom holds the feather of Maāt with both hands on his head; when the scene was complete these figures were twelve in number, and they are called ĀUTU-MAĀMU-KHERU-MAĀT, [ ].[2]

The text which remains reads:—

[1] *Notices*, ii., p. 501.

[2] Supplied from Champollion, *Notices*, ii., p. 502.

"[These are they who have offered up incense to the

Fragment of the Cover of the Sarcophagus of Seti I. in the British Museum.

"gods, and whose doubles have been washed,

"maāt, they have been reckoned up and they are maāt

"in the presence of the great god, who destroyeth "iniquities. Osiris saith unto them:—'Ye are *maāt* of "*maāt*. Be ye at peace [because of what] ye have "done, O ye who are in the forms of those who are "in my following, and who dwell in the house of him "whose souls are holy. Live ye on what ye live . . . . . . "there, and have the mastery "over the cool waters which "are in your Lake . . . . .'"

A few years ago I purchased from a native at Luxor a fragment of the cover of the sarcophagus of Seti I. (see p. 176); this is now in the British Museum (No. 29,948), and it gives the following:—

1. Three male figures, each of which bears a loaf on his head.

2. The following fragmentary text:

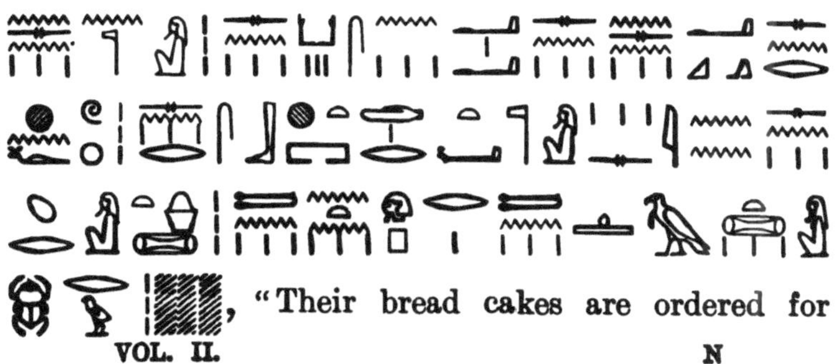

, "Their bread cakes are ordered for

"them by their gods; their *kau* are in their hands, "and they enter into their abodes at the pylon which "destroyeth its gods. The god SAR (Osiris) saith unto "them:—'Your bread shall be to you from that which "cometh forth from your mouths, O ye ḤETEPTI-"KHEPERU . . . . . .'"

In the lower register are:—

1. Five male figures, who are occupied in tending very large ears of corn; when the scene was complete these figures were twelve in number, and they were called, "Those who work about the plants of grain in "the fields of the Ṭuat,"

2. A man holding a sickle; he is one of the seven "reapers," , of which this section of the scene originally consisted.

The text which relates to those who tend the grain reads:—

[1] The passage in brackets is from Champollion, *Notices*, ii., p. 503.

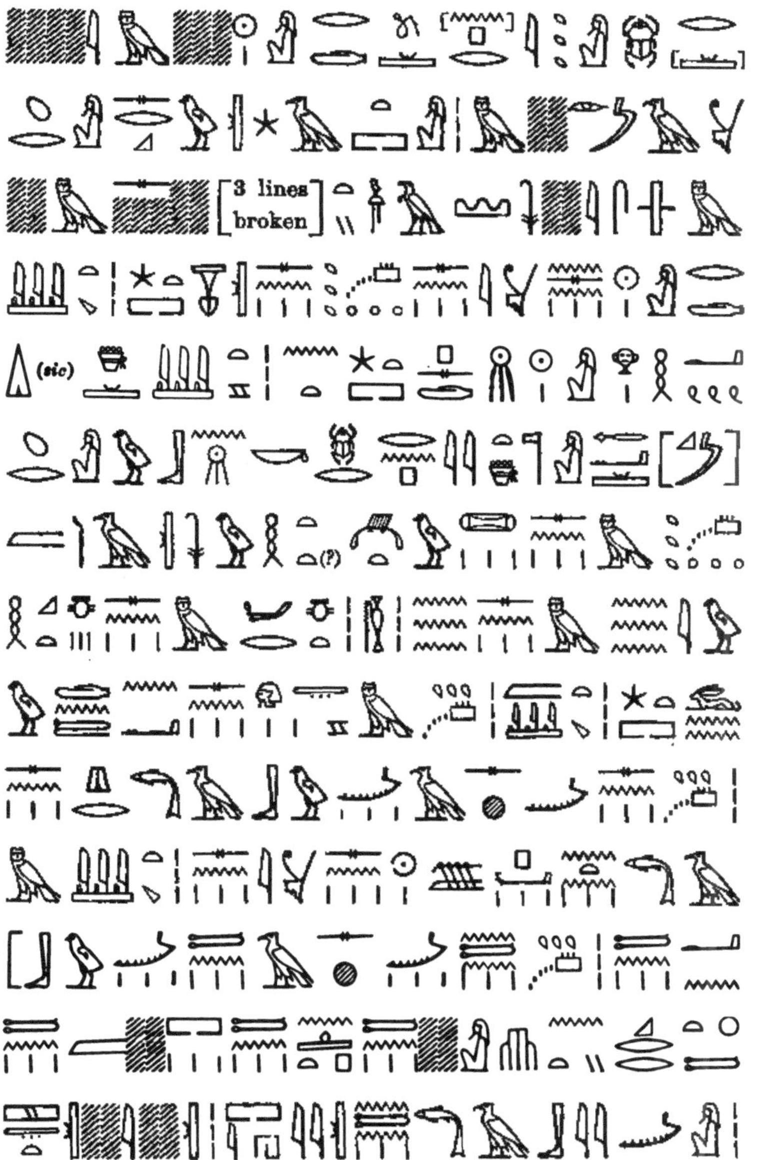
3 lines
broken
(sic)
(?)

].[1]

"[They perform the works in connection with the "grain, and they embrace the god of wheat (NEPRÅ) "which is eaten (?). Their grain becometh glorious in "the land through the light of Rā, when he appeareth, "and sendeth forth heat, and maketh his way by them. "The lord of joy of heart saith unto them:—'Let your "grain be glorious, and let the young shoots of your "grain germinate, and let your offerings be for Rā] ". . . . there . . . . Rā. Let NEPER germinate, and "let SAR (Osiris) be the source of food of the gods in "the Ṭuat . . . . ÅMENTI . . . . behold, in the "fields of the Ṭuat.' They gather together their grain, "and they say unto Rā:—'Let the fields of the Ṭuat be "green with young plants. May Rā shine upon the "members of SAR (Osiris). When thou dost shine the "young plants come into being, O great god, thou "creator of the grain.' Their offerings of food are of "grain, and their drink offerings are of *tcheser*, and "their libations are made with cool water. Offerings "are made unto them on the earth of the grain of the "fields of the Ṭuat."

[1] The words in brackets are supplied from Champollion, *Notices*, ii., p. 503.

Of the reapers it is said:—

"These are they who have their scythes, and who "reap the grain in their fields. Rā saith to them:— "'Take ye your scythes, and reap ye your grain, for it "is granted to you . . . . . . your habitations, and to "join yourselves [to] me in the Circle of the Hidden "Forms. Hail to you, O ye reapers!' Their food is of "bread, and their drink is of *tcheser*, and their libations "are made with cool water. Offerings are made unto "them upon earth as being those who hold scythes in "the fields of the Ṭuat."

The text which describes the middle register of the Sixth Division as it appears in the tomb of Rameses VI. reads:—

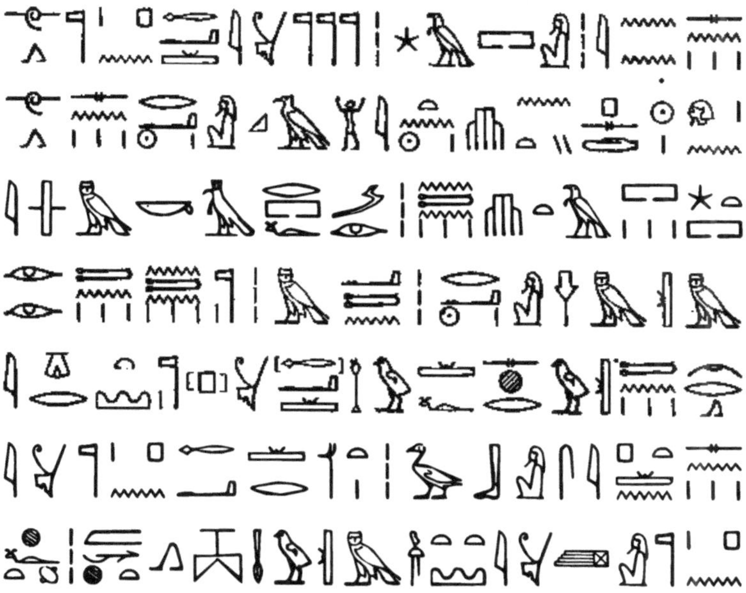

"This great god is being towed along by the gods of "the Ṭuat, and those who tow Rā along say:—'Be "exalted, O Åten (i.e., Disk), who art at the head of ". . . . . the Light, the head . . . . Look ye at the "abodes of the Ṭuat. Your eyes are to you, O gods, "observe ye Rā, the Power in Åḳert. This great god "decreeth your destinies. This great god cometh forth "to the standards of Seb, which reckon up the enemies "after the weighing of words in Åmentet. Behold, Sa "saith unto this god [when] he cometh forth to the "standards of Seb . . . . . . the head of Rā, the great "god . . . . verily, get thee forth to the standards of "Seb. Tem saith unto the standards:—'Keep ward "over the enemies, and bind ye fast those who are to "be smitten. O ye gods who are in the following of "the standards, and who are in the following of Seb, I "give ye power to bind fast the enemies, and to keep "ward over the wicked (or, those who are to be "smitten). Let them not come forth from under your "hands, let them not slip through your fingers. O ye "enemies, ye are doomed to slaughter, according to the "decree of Rā concerning you. His person is the body "of Åḳert, and he hath created the Ṭuat of his frame-"work. He hath issued the decree for you to be put "into restraint, he hath ordered your doom which shall "be wrought upon you in the great hall of Rā . . . . "the gods weep [and] lament, he setteth the gods "to ward you, and the enemies and those who are to "be smitten in the Ṭuat are condemned to these "standards.'"

In the upper register are twelve gods, each of whom

stands upright, and has the feather of Maāt on his head, and twelve gods, each of whom stands upright, and has a large loaf on his head. These gods are described as "Maāti gods bearing Maāt," , and the "Ḥetepṭiu gods bearing provisions," . The text reads:—

"Offerings of incense to their gods, libations of cool "water to their doubles, and fillings of the mouth ". . . . . . by his sustenance afterwards by their offer- "ings of drink and their offerings of bread. Come "forth to them their gods and their doubles. Their "hands are to them, and they go to their cakes "through the pylon of . . . . . and to its gods. SAR "saith unto them:—'Your bread is to you, [according "to] your utterances, and the peace cakes of Kheper, "and loaves of bread. Ye shall have the mastery over "your legs, and ye shall have satisfaction in your "hearts, and your gods shall present unto you your *khenfu* cakes and unto your doubles their provisions, "which consist of bread, and their drink, which shall "be of *tcheser* ale, and their libations shall be of cool "water, and offerings shall be made unto them upon "earth as the lord[s] of offerings in Åmentet. For "they have done what was right whilst they were "upon earth, and they have fought on behalf of their "god, and they shall be called to the enjoyment of the "land of the House of Life with *maāt*. That which "is theirs by right shall be allotted to them in the "presence of the Great God, who doeth away iniquity.' "Then shall Osiris say unto them:—'*Maāt* be to you, "O ye MAĀT gods, and peace be unto you by reason of "what ye have done in following after me, O dwellers "in the House, the soul of which is holy. Ye shall "live your life upon that whereupon those who live "there feed, and ye shall have dominion over the cool "waters of your land. I have decreed for you that ye "shall have your being in all of it with *maāt*, and "without sin (or, defects).' Their bread shall be *maāt* "cakes, their drink shall be of wine, and their libations "shall be of cool water. And there shall be offered "unto them upon earth the offerings which must be "made from their land."

In the lower register are the figures of twelve men, each of whom tends a monster ear of corn (?), or a tree, under the superintendence of a god who leans on a staff, and a group of reapers, each holding a sickle. The text, which is mutilated in places, reads:—

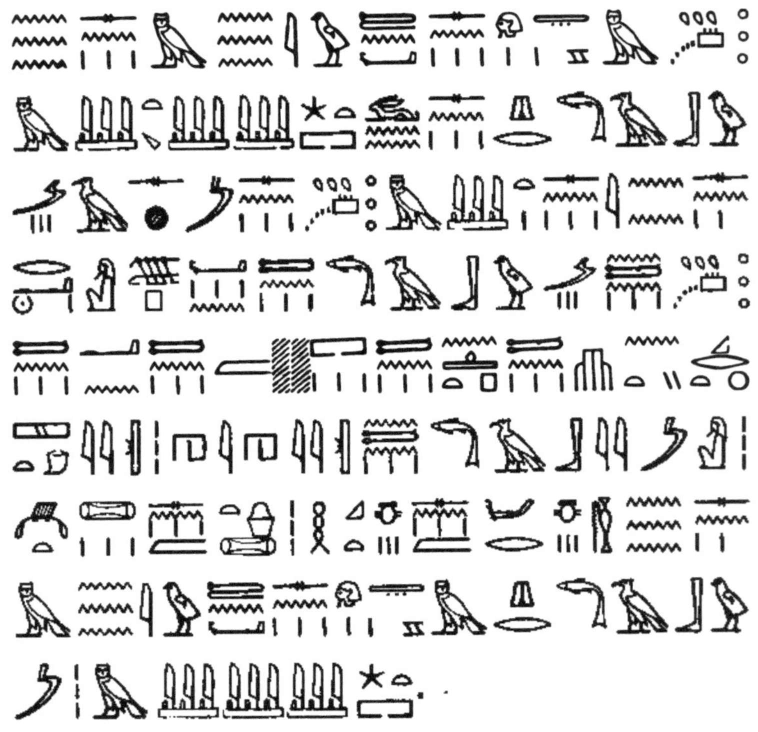

"They perform their work in connection with the "grain, and they embrace (i.e., cultivate) the divine "grain (or, NEPRÅ), and the spirits feed upon their "grain in the land of the god of light (KHU), who "cometh forth and passeth by them, and [NEB-ĀUT-ÅB, " , i.e., the Lord of joy of heart, saith unto "them:—'Let your grain be glorious], and let your ears "of wheat germinate, and let your offerings be for Rā. "Your *khenfu* cakes are in the Ṭuat, your offerings are "to you, the offerings which are yours by *maāt* are "decreed (?) for you. Herbs . . . . . . among you. "SAR . . . . . germinate . . . . . .' and they say unto "Rā :—'Let plants spring up in the Fields of the Ṭuat, "and let Rā shine upon the members of SAR. When "thou dost shine the young plants come into being, "O great god, thou creator of the Egg.' Their food "offerings are of grain, their drink is of *tcheser* ale, and "their libations are made with cool water. Offerings "are made unto them upon earth of the grain from the "Fields of the Ṭuat."

Of the reapers it is said :—

"These are they who have their sickles and who "reap the grain in their Field. Rā saith unto them :— "'Take ye your sickles, and reap ye your grain, for it is "granted unto you . . . . . . your habitations, and to "join yourselves to the Circle of the Hidden of Forms. "Hail to you, O ye reapers!' Their food is of bread-"cakes, and their drink is of *tcheser* ale, and their "libations are made with cool water. Offerings are "made unto them upon earth as being those who reap "the grain in the Fields of the Ṭuat."

CHAPTER IX.

THE GATE OF ĀKHA-EN-MAAT.

THE SEVENTH DIVISION OF THE ṬUAT.

THE boat of the Sun having passed through the Sixth Division of the Ṭuat arrives at the gateway which leads to the SEVENTH DIVISION. This gateway is similar to that which guards the Sixth Division, and is guarded by nine gods, who are described as the "Seventh Company," ; at the entrance to the corridor, and at its exit, stands a bearded god, with arms hidden, the former being called SHEPI, , and the latter HEQES (?), , and each is said to extend his arms and hands to Rā. The corridor is swept by flames of fire as before. The gateway is called PESṬIT, , and the text says, "This "great god cometh to this gateway, and entereth in "through it, and the gods who are therein acclaim him,"

. Part of the text of the speech which the nine gods make to Rā is broken away, but what remains reads, "Open the secret places, open the holy pylons, "and unfold the hidden portals," . The monster serpent which stands on his tail and guards the gateway is called ĀKHA-EN-MAAT, , and the two lines of text which refer to his admission of Rā read, "He who is over this door openeth to Rā. SA saith to "ĀKHA-EN-MAAT[1]:—'Open thy gate to Rā, unfold thy "doors to KHUTI, that he may send light into the "thick darkness and may make his radiance illumine "the hidden habitation.' This door is shut after the great "god hath passed through it, and there is lamentation "to those who are in this gateway when they hear this "door close upon them." A portion of the text is mutilated, but it can be restored with certainty.[2]

In the middle of this Division we see the boat of Rā being towed on its way by four gods of the Ṭuat; the god is in the same form as before, and stands in a shrine enveloped by MEḤEN. SA stands in the bows and ḤEKA at the stern. The text relating to the god reads:—

[1] Var., , ĀKHA-ḤRÀ.

[2] See Lefébure, *Mémoires*, tom. ii., part ii., pl. 11 ff.

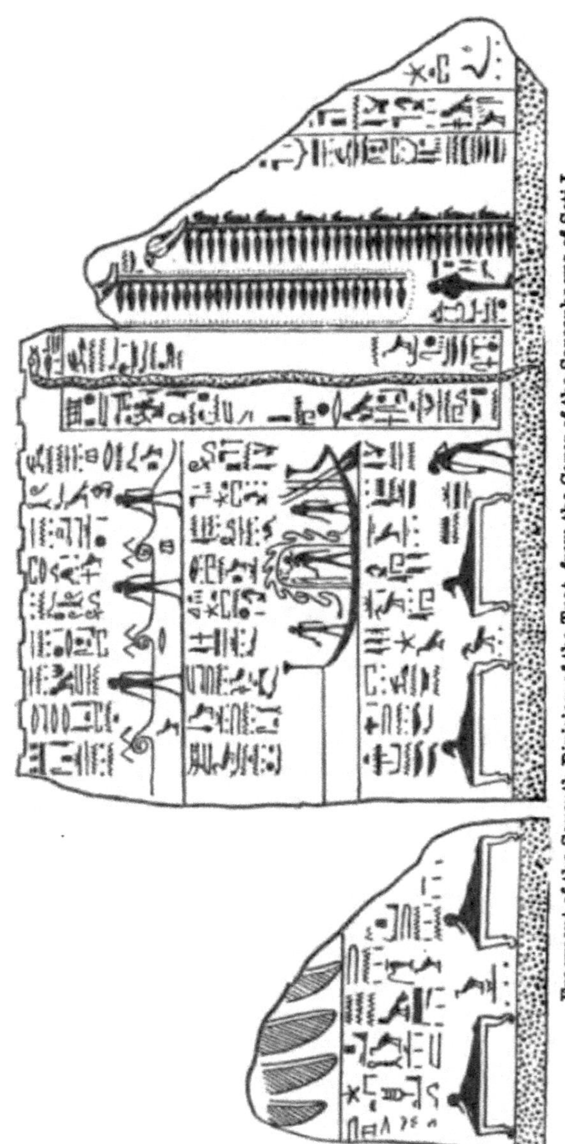

Fragment of the Seventh Division of the Ṭuat, from the Cover of the Sarcophagus of Seti I.

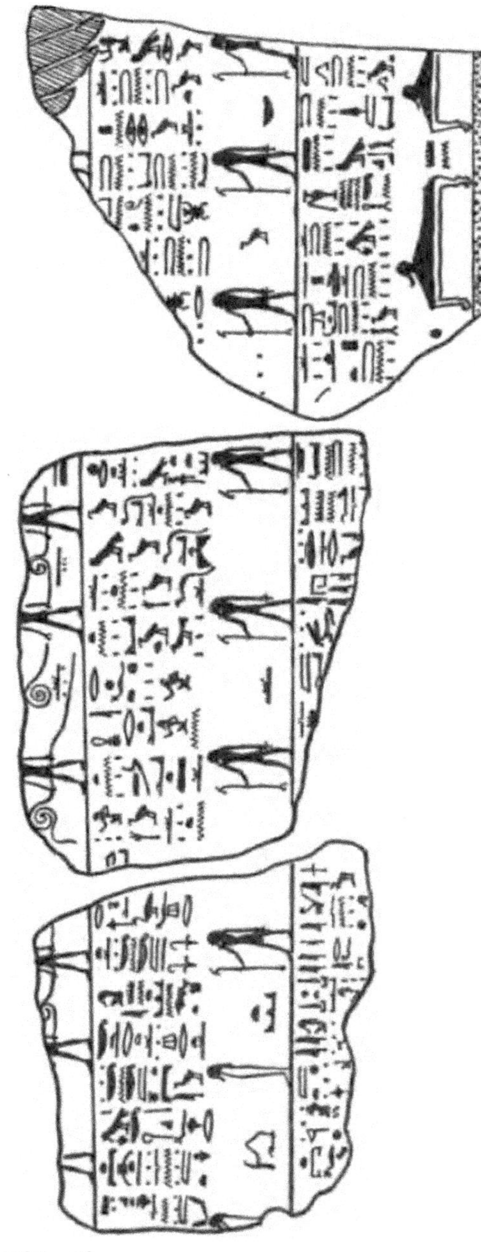

Scenes and Texts of the Seventh Division of the Ṭuat, from the Sarcophagus of Seti I.

The Boat of Rā being towed through the Seventh Division of the Ṭuat by the gods thereof.

"The gods of the Ṭuat tow along this great god, and "they say unto Rā:—'Thou art towed along, O great "god, lord of the hours, who dost work on behalf of "those who are under the earth.' The gods have life "in his attributes, and the spirits look upon his forms. "And Rā saith unto them:—'There is magical protec-"tion to you, O ye who tow, and there is holiness to "you, O ye who tow and bring me into the nethermost "parts of the Ṭuat, tow ye me along until [ye arrive] "at the chambers (?), and take ye your stand upon the "hidden mountain of the horizon."

In front of the divine towers of the boat march:—

1. Twelve bearded gods, the ÅMENNU-ĀĀIU-KHERU-SHETAU, whose hands and arms are hidden; they are described as "hidden of hands and arms and possessing hiddenness," [hieroglyphs].

The text relating to them reads:—

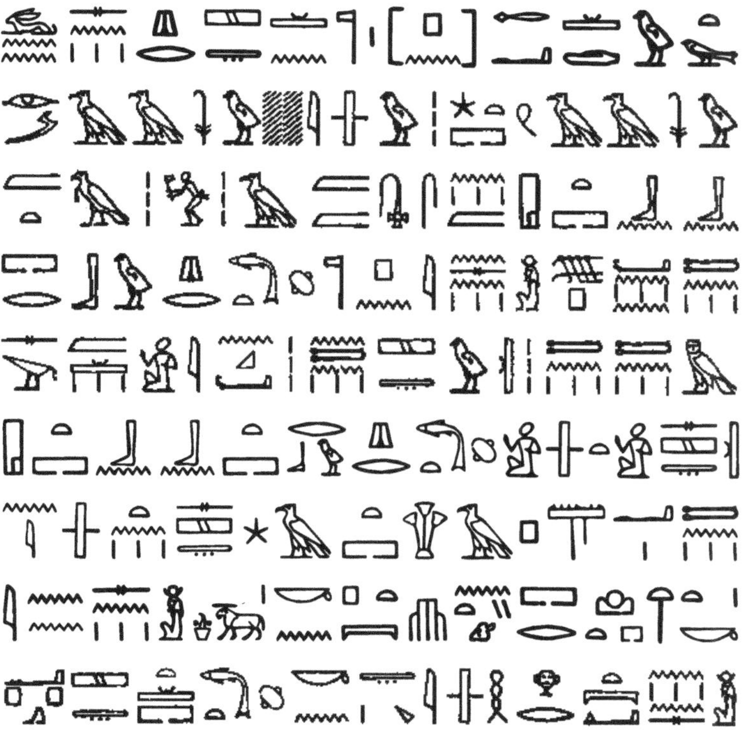

"These are they who possess the hiddenness (or, who "hold the mystery) of this great god. Verily those "who are in the Ṭuat see him, and the dead see him, "who burn in Ḥet-Benben (or, the temple of Rā), and "they come forth to the place where is the body of this "god. Rā saith unto them:—'Receive ye my forms, "and embrace ye your hidden forms (or, mysteries). "Ye shall be in Ḥet-Benben, the place where my body "is. The hiddenness which is in you is the hiddenness "of the Ṭuat, and cover ye your arms therewith.' And "they say unto Rā:—'Let thy soul be in heaven, at "the head of the horizon, let thy shadow penetrate "the hidden place, and let thy body be to the earth; "as for the upper regions of the sky we ascribe Rā "thereto . . . . . Fulfil thou thyself, and take thou "thy place [with] thy body in the Ṭuat.' Their food "consisteth of offerings of every kind whereby souls "become content, and offerings are made unto them "upon earth by reason of the sight of the light in the "Ṭuat."

2. Eight bearded gods, the NETERU-ḤETI, who stand

The Twelve Gods whose hands and arms are hidden.

upright, with their hands hanging by their sides, and are described as "the gods of the temples,"; and eight gods, the SENNU, who stand upright, with their arms held straight together in front of them, at a little distance from their bodies. The text which refers to them reads:—

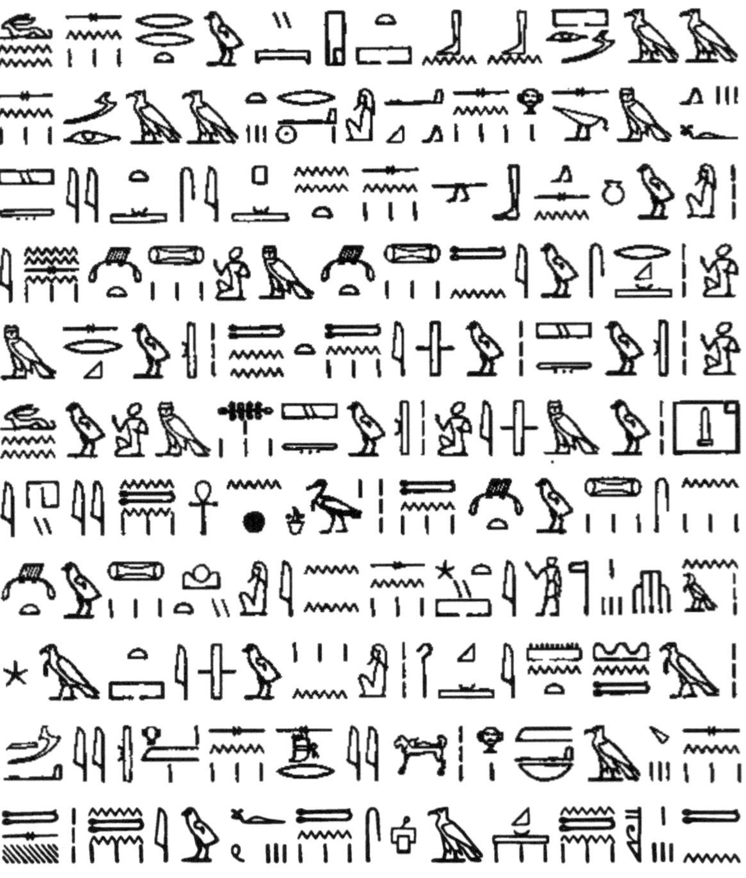

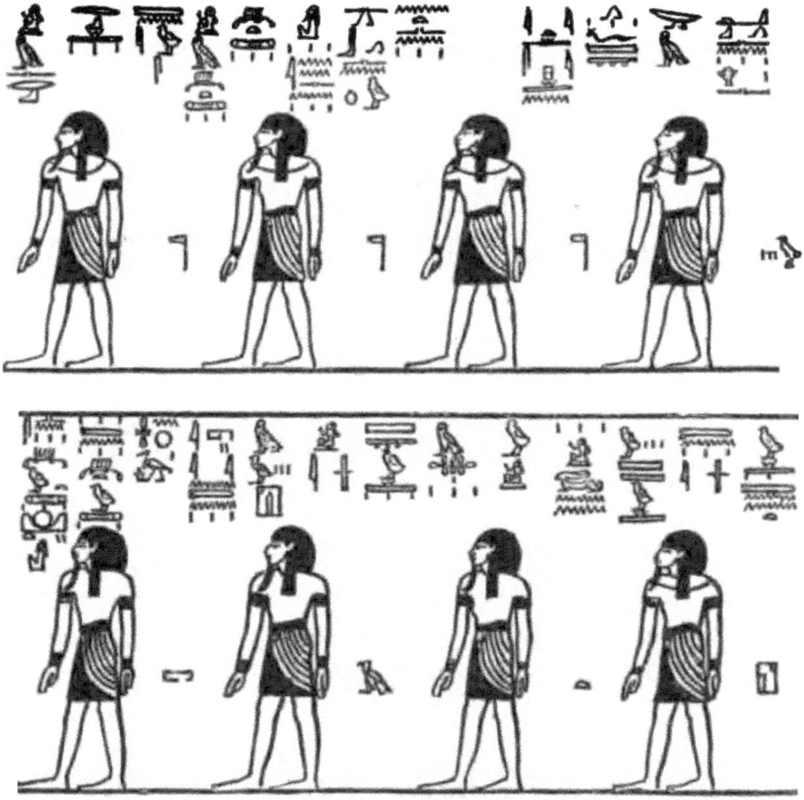

The Eight Neteru-ḥeti.

Four of the Sennu Gods.

"These are they who are outside Ḥet-Benben, and "they see Rā with their eyes, and they enter into his "secret (or, hidden) images; that which is theirs is "apportioned, and the SENNU gods bring it. [And Rā] "saith unto them:—'My offerings (or, provisions) are "from your offerings, and my nourishment is from "your nourishment which is to you, O ye who are in "my secret places. I protect my secret things which "are in Ḥet-Benben. Hail to you! Your souls live, "and their offerings are the offerings of KHUTI.' ṬUATI "saith unto them:—'O ye gods who dwell in the Ṭuat, "who are in the divine [places] of the governor of "Ȧment, to whom what is their due is given upon "their ground, who lie down upon their own lands, "your own flesh is to you, ye have gathered together "your bones, ye have knit together your members, and "ye have collected your flesh. There are, moreover, "sweet winds to your nostrils, ye have girded on your "apparel, and ye have put on your wigs.'"

In the upper register are:—

1. Twelve gods, the KHERU-METAU[Ḥ], each of whom holds a stake or weapon, forked at one end; they are described as "those who hold the *metau* weapons,"

The text relating to these reads :—

"Rā saith unto them :—'Receive ye your *metauḥ* "weapons, and take ye them with you. Hail to you, "[go against] the serpent fiend MĀMU; hail to you, "make ye gashes in him when the heads appear from "out of him, and turn ye him backwards.' They say "unto Rā:—'Our *metauḥ* weapons in our hands are for "Rā [and against] Māmu, and we will make gashes in "the great and evil Worm. O Rā, do away the heads "when they come forth from the windings of the "serpent Kheti.' These are the gods who are in the "[Boat of Rā], and they repulse Āpep in the sky, and "they travel through the Ṭuat. It is their duty to

The Kheru-Metanḥ Gods.

"turn back Āpep on behalf of Rā in Āmentet and the "places of the Ṭuat. And this god allotteth to them "their provisions of bread, and their beer is the *tchesert* "drink, and their libations are of cool water, and "offerings are made to them upon earth because they "repulse the Enemy of Rā in Āmentet."

2. The gods Kheru-Āmu-pereru-ṭepu-em-qebu-f, and the monster serpent Sebȧ-Āpep, the body of which is held

The Kheru-Metauḥ Gods.

up above the ground by twelve bearded gods, who are described as "those who have food when the heads appear from his folds," [hieroglyphs]. Twelve human heads grow out from his body,

The Kheru-Metauḥ Gods.

the first appearing from his head, and the other eleven from his back. The text which relates to them reads :—

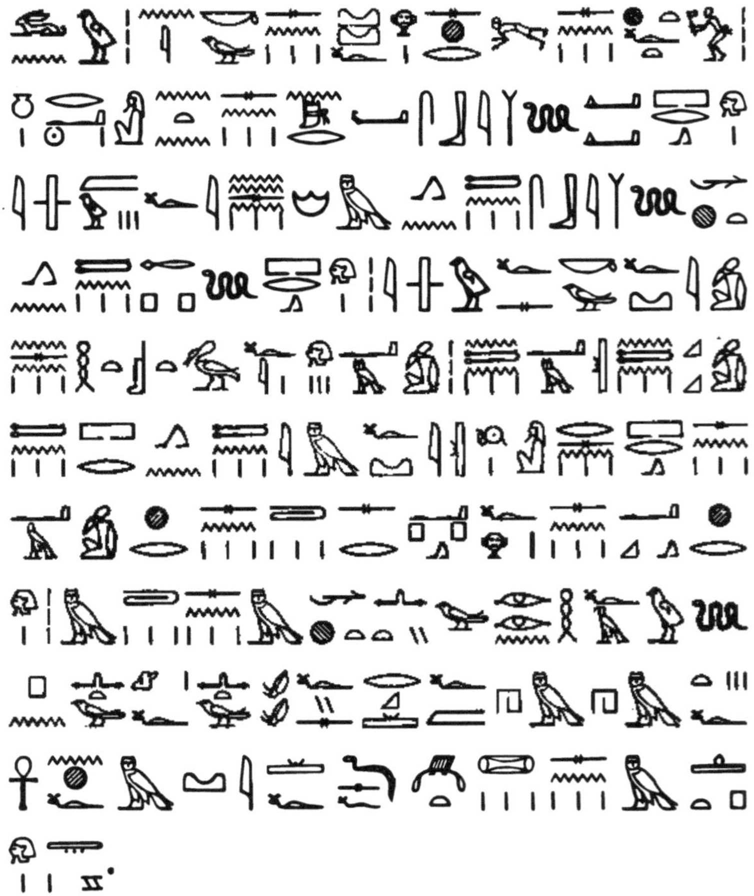

"These are they who are the adversaries of his "two-fold evil, and who overthrow the enemies of Rā, "and it is their duty to seize the SEBȦ-Fiend when he "maketh heads to come forth from him. [Rā] saith to "them:—'Turn ye back SEBÅ, make ye to go back-"wards ĀPEP when the heads appear from out of him, "and let him perish.' [Rā] ordereth for him his "destruction. 'O heads, ye shall be eaten, ye shall be "eaten, ye shall be consumed, when ye come forth from "him.' Rā ordereth for them when they come forth "that they shall be consumed (or, swallowed up) [in] "their folds when he journeyeth to them, and that the "heads shall retreat within their folds. The WORM "ḤEFAU shall be without eyes, and he shall be without "his nose, and he shall be without his ears, and he "shall exist upon his roarings, and he shall live upon "that which he himself uttereth. The food [of these "gods] consisteth of the offerings [which are made to "them] upon earth."

3. An upright, bearded mummied form called QĀN, [hieroglyphs]. To the neck of this figure are attached two ropes, which are twisted together symmetrically, and are grasped by twelve bearded men with both hands. Each god stands within a loop formed by the two ropes, and has a star before him. The gods are described as "those who hold the rope which cometh forth . . . . . ." [hieroglyphs]. Before the figure are the words [hieroglyphs]. The text reads:—

[hieroglyphs]

The Serpent Sebȧ-Āpep, with the twelve human heads which grow out of his body and his twelve attendant gods.

The Serpent Sebȧ-Āpep, with the twelve human heads which grow out of his body and his twelve attendant gods.

The god Qenā, and the gods who hold the rope.

"The Enemy of Rā cometh forth from the Ṭuat.
"Offerings shall be made unto the gods of that whereby
"I exist under the trees. Seize ye the rope, and tie ye

The gods who hold the rope.

"therewith the mouth of ĀQEN. Your hours come "forth, and there is benefit to you therein. Rest ye "upon your throne[s], and let the rope enter into the "mouth of the god ĀQEN when he cometh to the place

The gods who hold the rope.

"where the hours are born; Rā crieth out, and it "resteth in its place, and it maketh an end of ĀNEQ. "They say unto Rā:—'The god NĀQ is tied up with "the rope, the hours of the gods (?) are to thee, O Rā, "with light. Rest thou and thy hidden body . . . . .' "Their provisions of loaves of bread are to them, their "beer is *tchesert*, and their libations are of cool water, "and offerings are made to them upon earth."

The god Ṭuati.

In the lower register are:—

1. A god, standing, and leaning upon a long staff; his name is ṬUATI, .

2. The serpent NEHEP, , the long body of which is made to serve as biers for twelve gods in mummied form; the serpent's body is provided with twenty-four legs of lions, and a mummied god rests over each pair of them. These gods are described as "those who are in the body of Osiris asleep," , and "those who are in inactivity," .

3. Four gods, each with his arms stretched straight together before him at an acute angle with his body. The legend reads, *khast-ta-rut* .

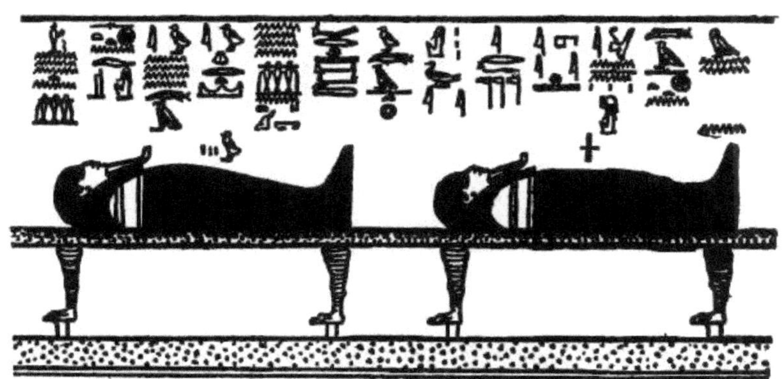

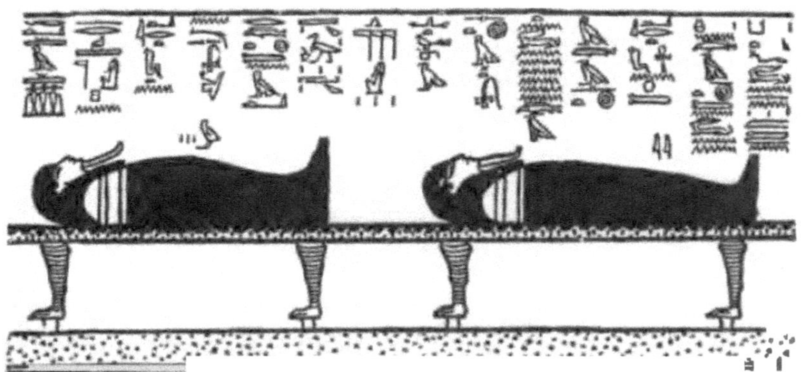

The gods who are asleep in the body of Osiris.

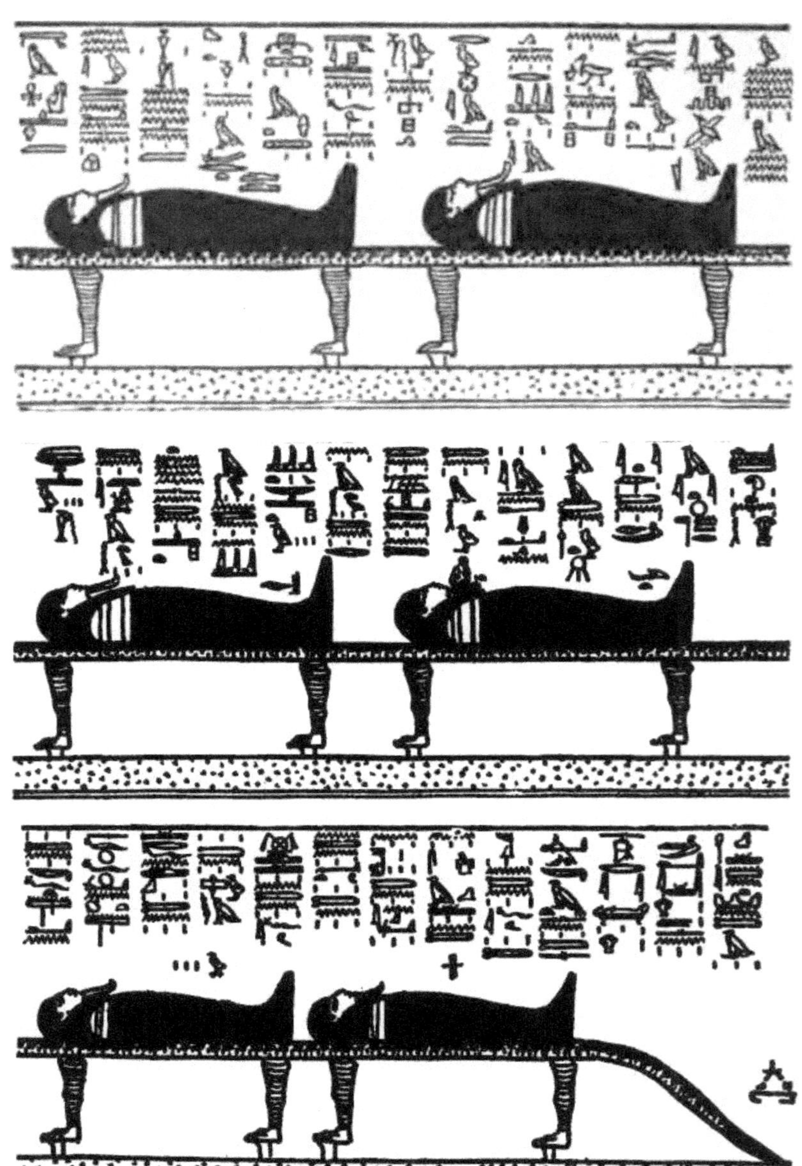

The gods who are asleep in the body of Osiris.

Four Khast-ta-ruṭ Gods.

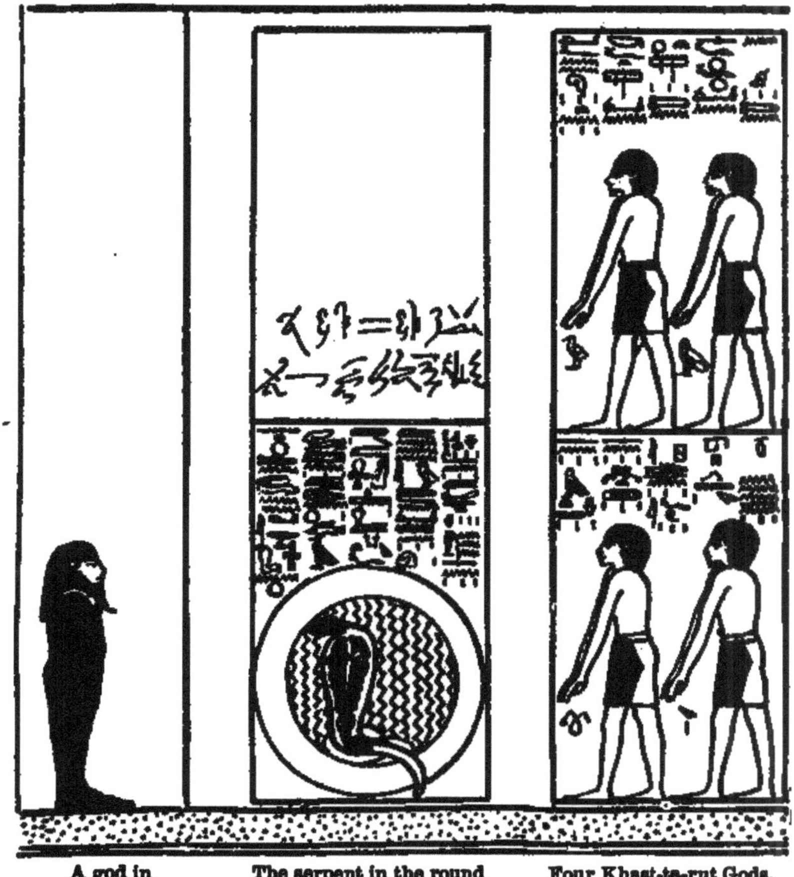

A god in mummied form.

The serpent in the round pool of fire.

Four Khast-ta-ruṭ Gods.

4. Four gods.
5. A serpent within a circle filled with water.
6. A god in mummied form.

The text relating to these reads:—

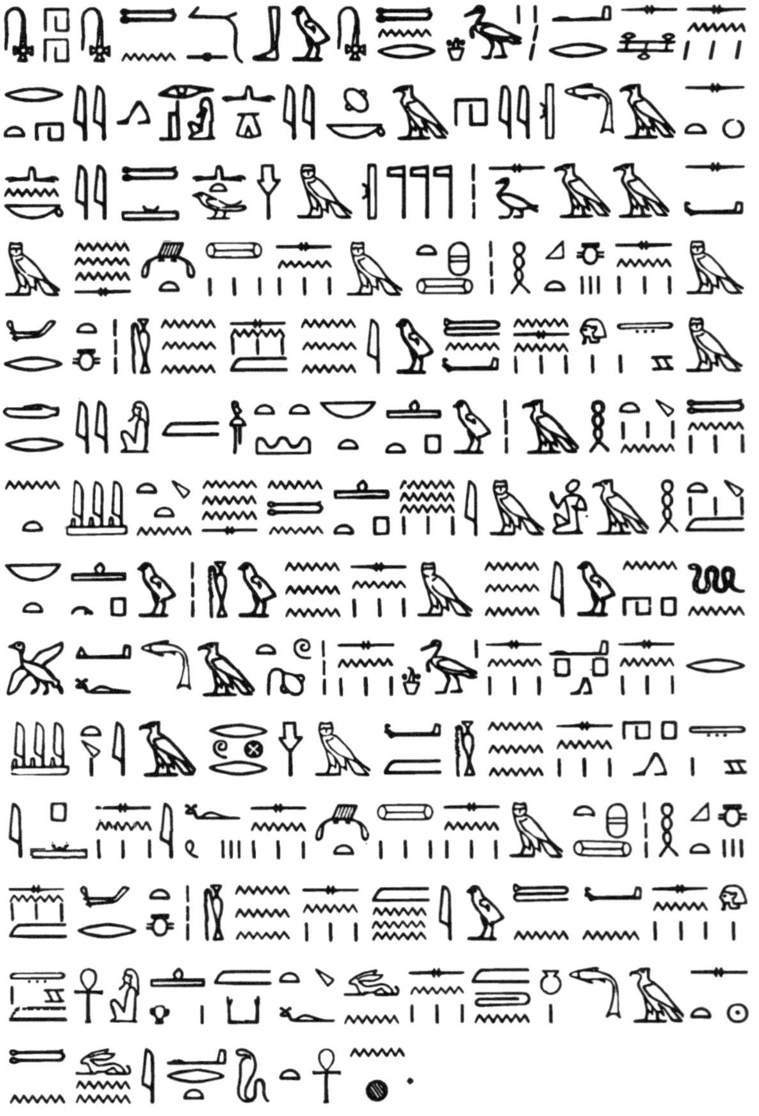

"The god Ṭuati saith unto them:—'Hail, O ye gods

"who are over the Ṭuat, ye gods who dwell in this "[place] of the governor of Ȧment, who abide permanently on your places, and who lie down upon "your couches, lift up the flesh of your bodies, and "gather together your bones, and gird up your "members, and bring ye into one place your flesh! "There is sweet (or, fresh) air for your nostrils. Loose "and take off your funeral swathings, untie and remove "your wigs, unclose your eyes and look ye at the light "therewith, rise ye up from out of your inert and "helpless state, and take possession yourselves of your "fields in Sekhet-nebt-ḥetepu (i.e., Field, lord of offerings). There are fields for you in this Field, and the "waters thereof are for you. Let your offering be "there, [and] fields from Nebt-ḥetepu.' Their libations "shall be of water. It is the serpent NEHEP who "giveth their bodies [and] their souls, and they journey "on to SEKHET-ȦARU to have dominion over their "libations, and to walk over the earth. They count "up their flesh, their food is of bread-cakes, and "their drink is of *tchesert* ale, and their libations "are of water. Offerings are made unto them upon "earth as [unto] the god SĀḤ, who resteth upon his "ground."

"These are they who are in the circuit of this pool. "There is a serpent living in this pool, and the water "of the pool is of fire, and the gods of the earth and "the souls of the earth cannot descend thereto by "reason of the flames of fire of this serpent. This "great god who is the governor of the Ṭuat liveth "in the water of this pool."

And Rā saith unto them:—"Hail to you, O ye gods "who guard this holy pool, give ye yourselves to him "that is the Governor of Åuḳert. The water of this "pool is Osiris, and this water is KHENTI-ṬUAT. This "flame consumeth and destroyeth the souls which dare "to approach Osiris, and the awe of this pool cannot "be done away, or made an end of, or overcome. As "for the gods who keep ward over its waters, their "food is bread, and their drink is *tchesert* ale, and "their libations are of water. Offerings are made unto "them upon earth as unto ṬERI in Åmentet, lord of "offerings. There are fields for you in this Field, "and the waters thereof are for you. Let your offer-"ings be there [and] fields from Nebt-ḥetepu. Their "libations shall be of water. It is the serpent NEHEP "who giveth their bodies [and] their souls, and they "journey into SEKHET-ÅARU to have dominion over "their libations, and to walk on the earth. They "count up their limbs, their food is of bread-cakes, and "their drink is of *tchesert* ale, and their libations are "of water. Offerings are made unto them upon earth "as unto SĀḤ, who resteth upon his ground.

"These are they who are in the circuit of this pool. "There is a serpent living . . . . . ."

CHAPTER X.

THE GATE OF SET-ḤRÅ.

THE EIGHTH DIVISION OF THE ṬUAT.

HAVING passed through the Seventh Division of the Ṭuat, the boat of the Sun arrives at the gateway called BEKHKHI, , which leads to the EIGHTH DIVISION, or, as the opening text reads: , "This great god "cometh forth to this gate, and entereth through it, "and the gods who are therein acclaim this great god." The gateway is like that through which the god passed into the previous Division, and its outwork is guarded by nine gods in the form of mummies, who are described as the PAUT, i.e., the company of the nine gods, . At the entrance to the gate proper stands a bearded, mummied form, with his hands folded on his breast, called BENEN, , and at its exit stands a similar form called ḤEPTTI, ; each of these is said to "extend his arms and hands to Rā," . The corridor is swept by flames of fire, which proceed from the mouths of two uraei, as before. The company of the gods who guard the outwork address Rā, and say, "Come thou to us, O thou who "art at the head of the horizon, O thou great god "who openest hidden places, open for thyself the holy "pylons, and unfold the doors thereof," . The monster serpent, which stands on his tail and guards the door, is called SET-ḤRÅ, , and the two lines of text which refer to his admission of Rā read, "He who is over this door "openeth to Rā. SA saith unto SET-ḤRÅ:—Open thy "gate to Rā, unfold thy portal to KHUTI, so that he "may illumine the thick darkness, and may send light "into the hidden abode. This gate closeth after the "great god hath passed through it, and the souls who "are on the other side of it wail when they hear the "door closing upon them,"

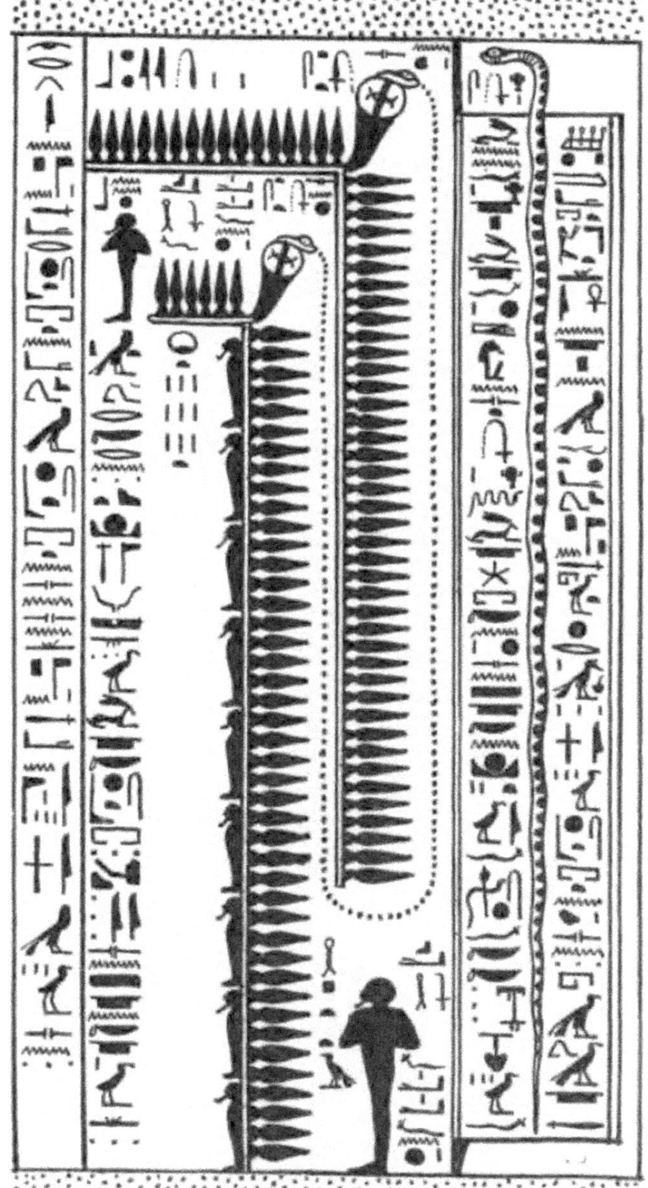

The gate of the Serpent Set-ḥrȧ.

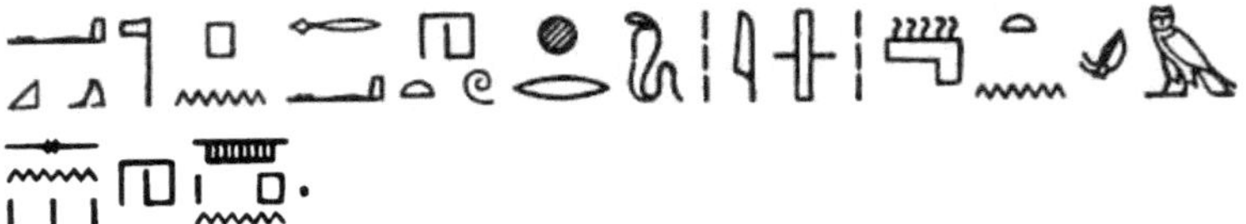

In the middle of the Division we see the boat of Rā being towed on its way by four gods of the Ṭuat, ; the god is in the same form as before, and SA stands on the look-out, and Ḥeka obeys his instructions as to the steering. At the head of the

The Boat of Rā being towed through the Eighth Division of the Ṭuat by the gods thereof.

four gods who tow the boat stands an aged god, who leans on a long staff, and is called "He who dwelleth in Nu," . Immediately in front of the divine procession is a long tank, wherein we see four groups, each containing four beings, who are represented in the act of performing various evolutions in the water. These are called HERPIU, , ĀḲIU, , NUBIU, , and KHEPAU, [hieroglyphs], which names may be translated "Bathers, Floaters, Swimmers, and Divers." The text which refers to this section reads:—

[hieroglyphic text]

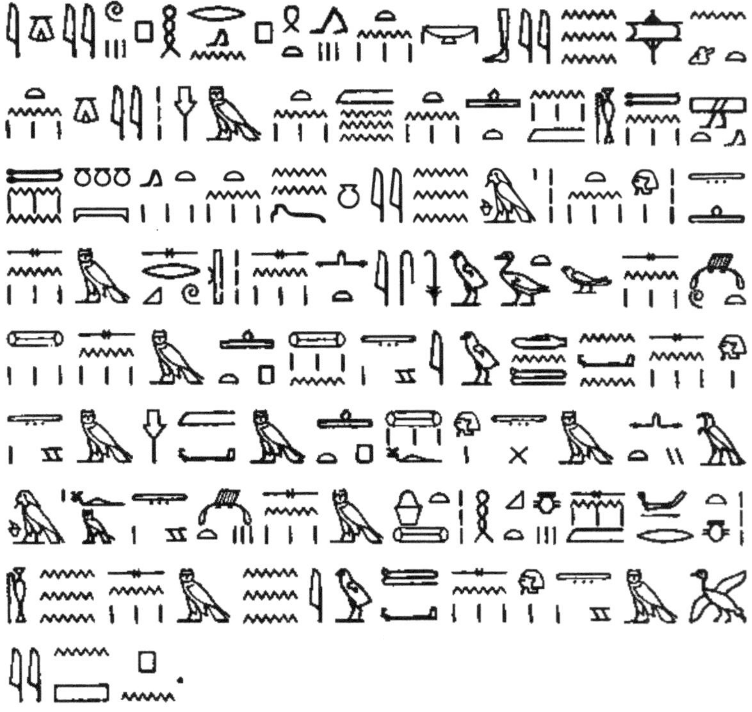

The first section of this text reads:—

This great god is towed along by gods of the Ṭuat, and behold, those who tow Rā along say, "Let there be "praise in heaven to the soul of Rā, and let there be "praise on earth to his body, for heaven is made young "by means of his soul, and earth is made young by "means of his body. Hail! We open for thee the "hidden place, and we make straight for thee the roads "of Åkert. Be thou at peace, O Rā, with thy hidden "things, O thou who art praised [by] thy secret things "in thy forms (or, attributes). Hail! We tow thee "along, O Rā, we guide thee, O thou who art at the "head of heaven, and thou comest forth to those who "are immersed in the waters, and thou shalt make thy "way over them."

The passage which refers to the aged god reads :—

"He (literally, those) who is in Nu saith to those "who are immersed in the water, and to those who are "swimming in the pools of water, 'Look ye at Rā, who "journeyeth in his boat, [for he is] Great of Mystery.

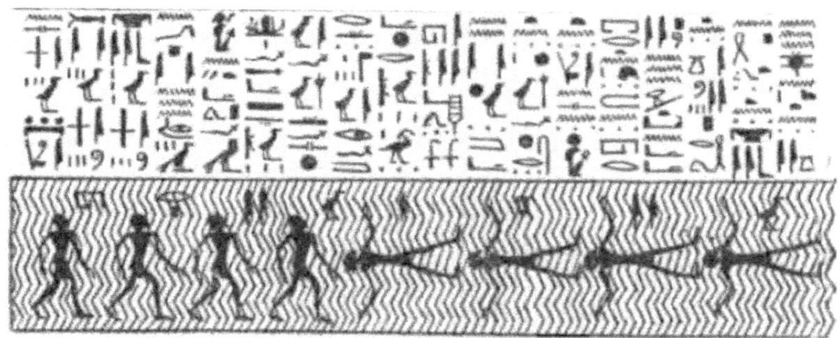

The Four Herpiu Gods, and the Four Āḳiu Gods.

"It is he who ordereth the destinies (or, affairs) of the "gods, it is he who performeth (or, maketh) the plans "of the Khu (i.e., the spirits). Hail! Rise up, O ye "beings of time, pay ye heed to Rā, for it is he who "ordereth your destinies.'"

The speech of Rā reads :—

"Put forth your heads, O ye who are immersed in "the water, thrust out your arms, O ye who are under "the waters, stretch out your legs, O ye who swim, let "there be breath to your nostrils, O ye who are deep "in the waters. Ye shall have dominion over your "waters, ye shall be at peace in your tanks of cool "waters, ye shall pass through the waters of Nu, and ye "shall make a way through your cisterns. Your souls "are upon earth, and they shall be satisfied with their "means of subsistence, and they shall not suffer destruc- "tion. Their food shall consist of the offerings of the "earth, and meat and drink shall be given unto them "upon earth, even as to him that hath obtained dominion

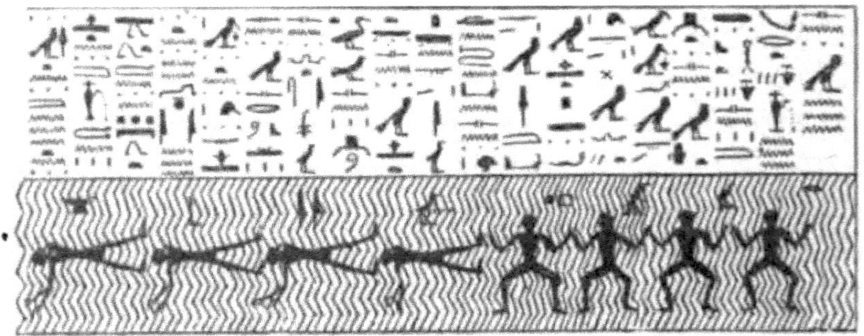

The Four Nubiu Gods, and the Four Khepau Gods.

"over his offerings upon earth, and whose soul is not "upon the earth. Their food shall consist of bread, "and their drink shall be *tchesert* wine, and their "cisterns shall be full of cool water, and there shall be "offered unto them upon earth of that which this lake "produceth."

In the upper register are the following:—

1. Twelve bearded gods, who stand with their arms hanging by their sides, and are described as the "divine "sovereign chiefs who give the bread which hath been

"allotted and green herbs to the souls who are in the "Lake of SERSER (i.e., blazing fire)," [hieroglyphs]

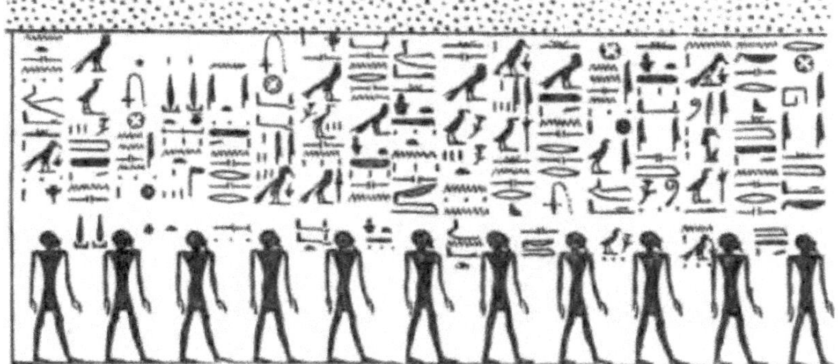

The Tchatchau who give the bread of Maāt.

Souls who are in the Lake of Serser.

2. Nine bearded, human-headed and human-handed hawks, which stand with their hands raised in adoration; before each is a loaf of bread, [hieroglyph], and a few

green herbs, [hieroglyph]. These are described as the "souls "who are in the Lake of Serser," [hieroglyphs].

3. A god, who holds a sceptre in his right hand, and [hieroglyph] in his left.

The texts which relate to these read:—

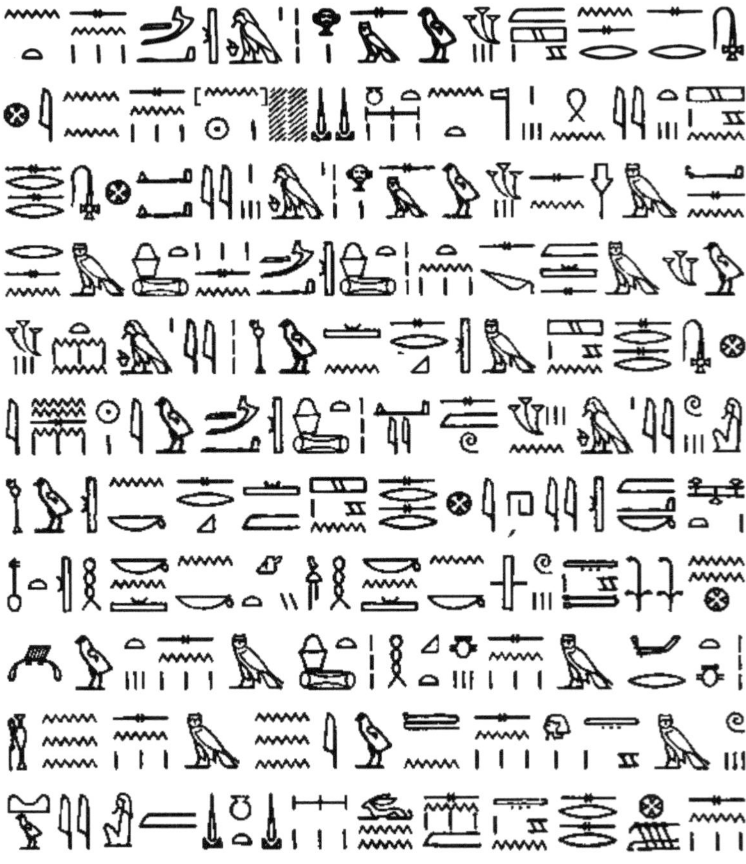

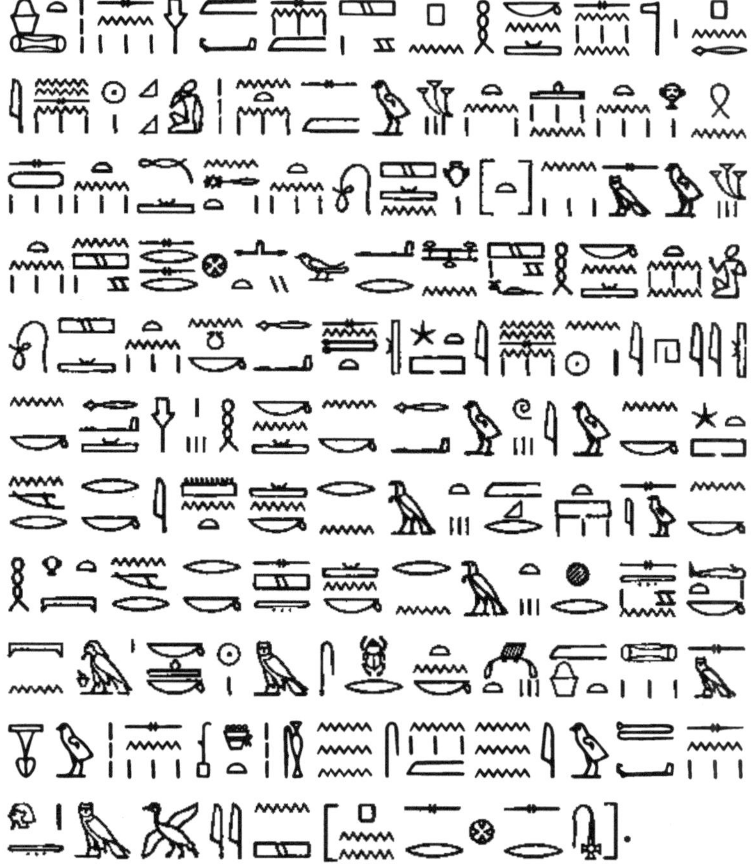

The portion of the text which refers to the twelve sovereign chiefs reads:—

"These are they who make souls to have a right to "the green herbs in the Lake of Serser. Rā saith "unto them:—'[Hail, ye] divine sovereign princes of "the gods, and ye chiefs of the Lake of Serser, who "place souls over their green herbs, let them have "dominion themselves over their bread; give ye your "bread which is appointed, and bring ye your green "herbs to the souls who have been ordered to exist "in the Lake of Serser.' They say unto Rā:—'The "bread appointed hath been and the green herbs have "been brought to the divine souls whom thou hast "ordered to exist in the Lake of Serser. Hail! Verily, "the way is fair; for KHENTI-ÅMENTI praiseth thee, "and those who dwell in TA-THENEN praise thee.' Their "food is of bread-cakes, and their beer is the *tchesert* "beer, and their libations are of cool water; and "offerings are made unto them upon earth by those "who are with (?) ṬUI by the divine sovereign princes."

The passage which refers to the souls in the Lake of Serser reads:—

"These are they who are in the Land of Serser; "they have received their bread, and they have gained "the mastery over this Lake, and they praise this "great god. Rā saith unto them:—'Eat ye your "green herbs, and satisfy ye yourselves with your "cakes; let there be fulness to your bellies, and satis-"faction to your hearts. Your green herbs are of "the Lake of Serser, the Lake which may not be "approached. Praise ye me, glorify ye me, for I am "the Great One of terror of the Ṭuat.' They say "unto Rā:—'Hail to thee, O thou Great One of the "SEKHEMU (i.e., Powers)! Praise is thine, and majesty "is thine. The Ṭuat is thine, and [is subservient] to "thy will; it is a hidden place [made] by thee for "those who are in its Circles. The height of Heaven "is thine, and [is subservient] to thy will; it is a "secret place [made] by thee for those who belong "thereto. The Earth is for thy dead Body, and the "Sky is for thy Soul. O Rā, be thou at peace (or, be "content) with that which thou hast made to come "into being.' Their food consisteth of bread-cakes, "their green herbs are the plants of the spring, and "the waters wherein they refresh themselves are cool.

Souls who are in the Lake of Serser. A god with a sceptre.

"Offerings are made unto them upon the earth as "[being] the product of this Lake of Serser."

In the lower register are:—

1. Horus [the Aged], in the form of a bearded man, leaning upon a staff.

2. Twelve bearded beings, who are described as the "burnt enemies of Osiris," . The first four have their arms tied

behind their back in such a way that the right hand projects at the left side, and the left hand at the right side. The second four have their hands tied together at the elbows, and the upper parts of the arms are at right angles to their shoulders. The third four have their arms tied together at the elbows, and their elbows are on a lower level than their shoulders.

3. A monster speckled serpent, which lies in undulations immediately in front of the enemies of Osiris,

Horus the Aged. The Burnt Enemies of Osiris.

and belches fire into the face of their leader; the name of this serpent is KHETI, . In each undulation stands a bearded god in mummied form, and the hieroglyphics written above describe them as "the gods who are above KHETI," . The text reads:—

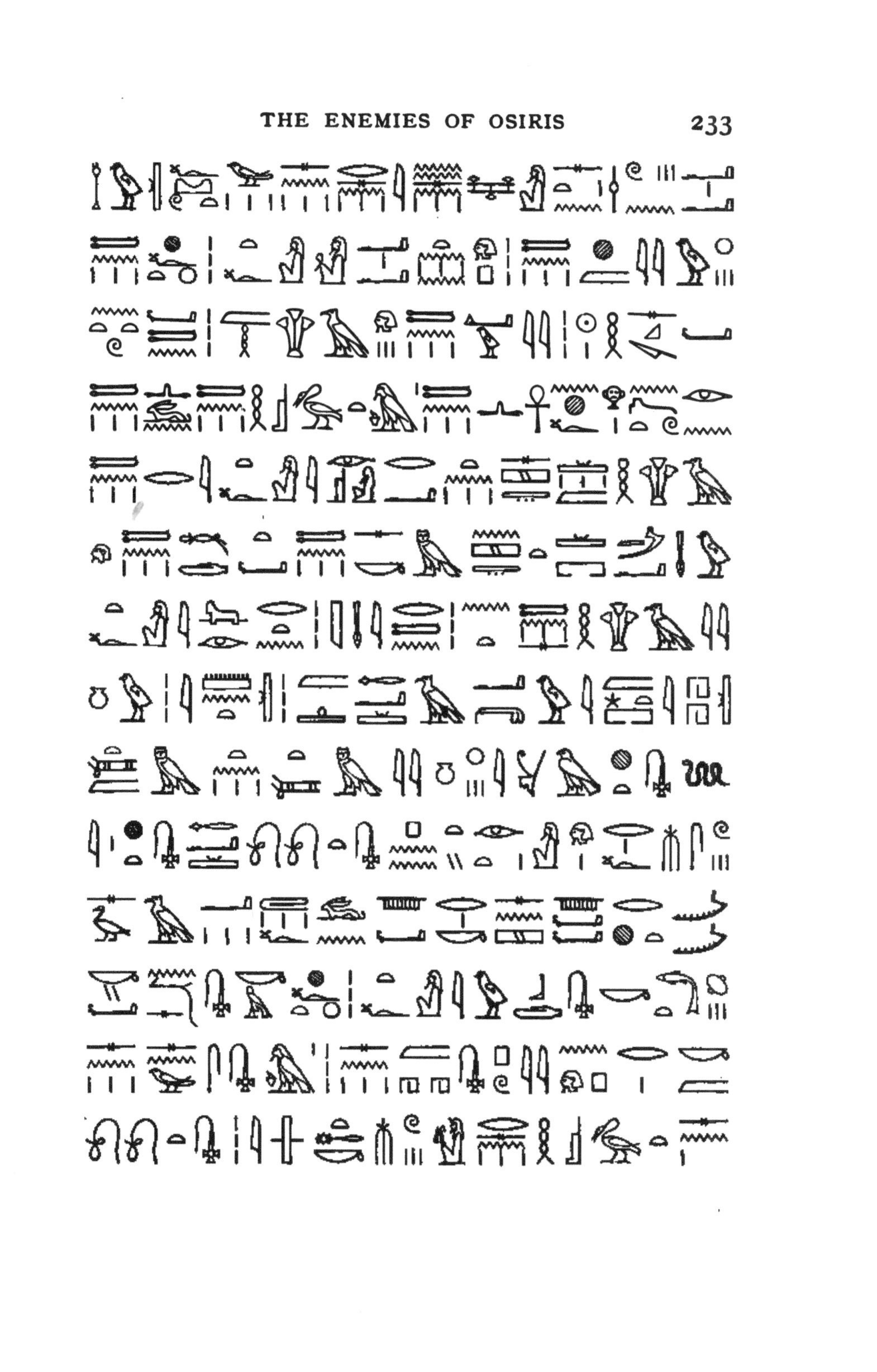

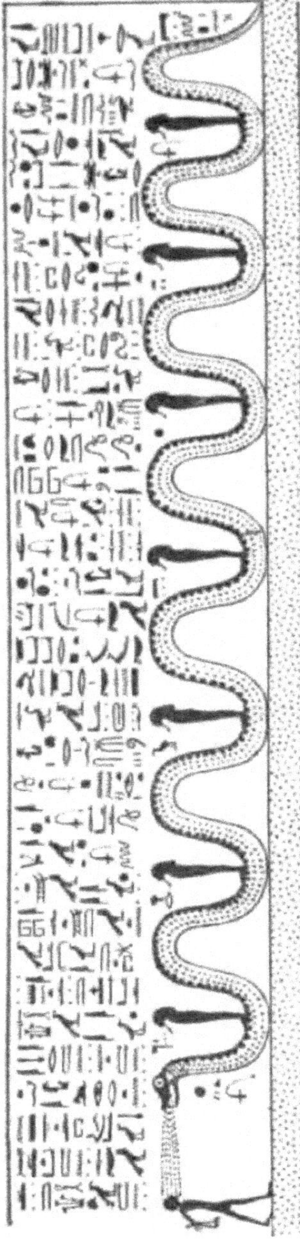

"[This scene representeth] "what Horus doeth for his "father Osiris. The enemies "who are in this scene have "their calamities ordered for "them by Horus, who saith "unto them:—'Let there be "fetters on your arms, O "enemies of my father, let "your arms be tied up towards "your heads, O ye who have "no [power], ye shall be fettered "[with your arms] behind you, "O ye who are hostile to Rā. "Ye shall be hacked in pieces, "ye shall nevermore have your being, your souls shall "be destroyed, and none [of you] shall live because of "what ye have done to my father Osiris; ye have "put [his] mysteries behind your backs, and ye have "dragged out the statue [of the god] from the secret "place. The word of my father Osiris is *maāt* against "you, and my word is *maāt* against you, O ye who "have desecrated (literally, laid bare) the hidden things "which concern the rest (or, resting-place) of the Great "One who begot me in the Ṭuat. O ye shall cease to "exist, ye shall come to an end.'"

"Horus saith:—'[O] my serpent KHET, thou Mighty "Fire, from whose mouth cometh forth this flame "which is in my Eye, whose undulations are guarded "by [my] children, open thy mouth, distend thy jaws, "and belch forth thy fires against the enemies of my "father, burn thou up their bodies, consume their "souls by the fire which issueth from thy mouth, "and by the flames which are in thy body. My "divine children are against them, they destroy "[their] spirits, and those who have come forth from "me are against them, and they shall never more "exist. The fire which is in this serpent shall come "forth, and shall blaze against these enemies whensoever "ever Horus decreeth that it shall do so.' Whosoever "knoweth how to use words of power [against] this "serpent shall be as one who doth not enter upon his "fiery path."

The end of this text on the sarcophagus of Seti I. is

defective, but from the tomb of Rameses VI. we see that it should end thus:—"Offerings shall be made "to these gods who are upon this great serpent. Their "food is of bread, their drink is of *ṭesher* beer, and the "waters of their libations are cool."

CHAPTER XI.

THE GATE OF ĀB-TA.

THE NINTH DIVISION OF THE ṬUAT.

HAVING passed through the Eighth Division of the Ṭuat, the boat of the sun arrives at the gateway called ĀAT-SHEFSHEFT, , which leads to the NINTH DIVISION, or, as the opening text reads: , "This great god cometh to this gate, and entereth "through it, and the gods who are therein acclaim this "great god." The gateway is like that through which the god passed into the previous Division, and its outwork is guarded by nine gods in the form of mummies, who are described as the PAUT, i.e., the company of the nine gods, . At the entrance to the gate proper stands a bearded, mummied form, with his hands folded on his breast, called ĀNḤEFTA, , and at its exit stands a similar form called Ermen-ta, ; each of these is said to "extend his arms and hands to Rā," , or . The corridor is swept by flames of fire, which proceed from the mouths of two uraei, as before. The company of the gods who guard the outwork address Rā, and say, "Come thou to us, O "thou who art the head of the horizon, O thou great "god who openest the secret places, open for thyself "the holy pylons, and unfold for thyself the holy doors "thereof," . The monster serpent which stands on his tail and guards the door is called Āb-ta, , and the two lines of text which refer to his admission of Rā read, "He "who is over this door openeth to Rā. Sa saith unto "Āb-ta, 'Open thy gate to Rā, unfold thy portal to "Khuti, so that he may illumine the thick darkness, "and may send light into the hidden abode.' This gate "closeth after this god hath passed through it, and the "souls who are on the other side of it wail when they "hear this door closing upon them,"

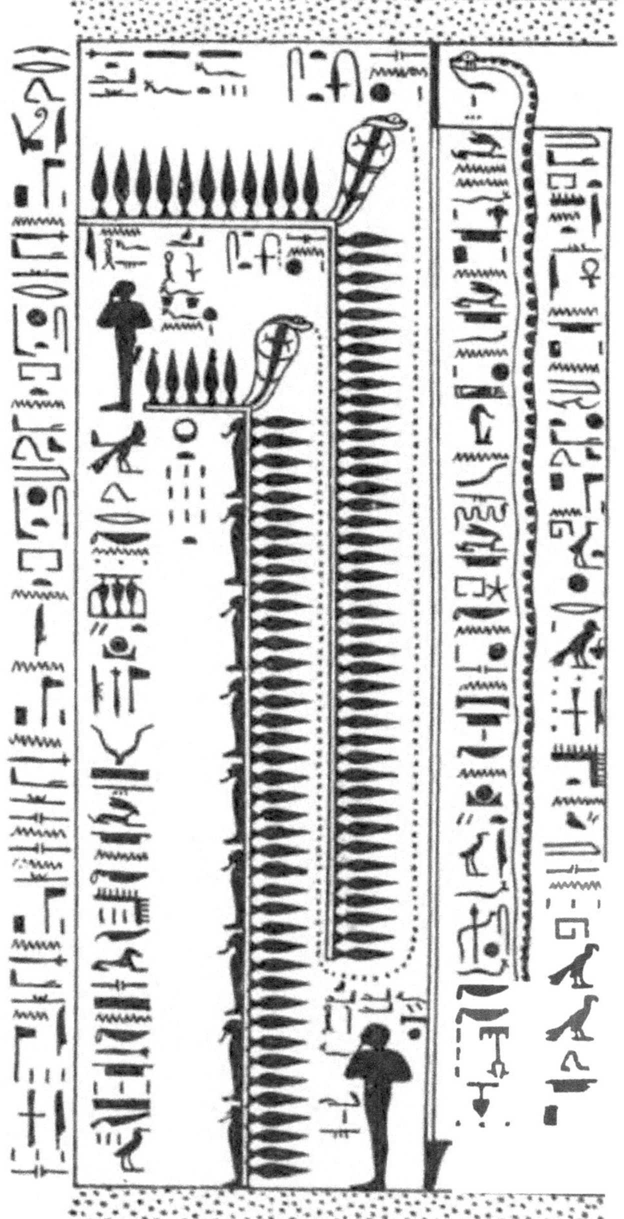

The Gate of Āb-ta.

In the middle of the Division we see the boat of Rā being towed on its way by four gods of the Ṭuat, ; the god is in the same form as before,

The Boat of Ȧf-Rā in the Ninth Division of the Ṭuat.

and Sa stands on the look-out, and Ḥeka obeys his instructions as to steering. The procession which marches in front of the boat consists of:—

1. Six bearded male figures, standing upright, who hold in their hands the ends of a rod, or rope, which is bent in the shape of a bow over their heads; these are described as "those who are over the words of magical power," .

2. Four dog-headed apes, which hold a rod bent as already described; these are described as "those who work magic by means of knots for Rā," [hieroglyphs].

3. Four women, who stand upright, and hold a bent

Gods, goddesses, and apes casting spells on Āpep.

The spearmen. Åai. Shesshes and Āpep.

rod, or rope, over their heads like the four apes and the six male figures; they are described as "those who work magic by means of knots for Rā," [hieroglyphs].

4. Three male figures, each holding a harpoon in

his right hand, and a cord in his left; they are called "spearmen," . Immediately in front of these is a bearded male figure, who has been lying prostrate on his face; he has upon his head a small solar disk and a pair of ass's ears, and his name is ȦAI, , i.e., the Ass. In his hands he grasps a rope, which passes over his head and along his back, and is held by each of the three spearmen in his left hand; from the knees upwards his body is raised in a diagonal position, and this attitude suggests that he has either raised himself by means of the rope, or has been pulled into this position by the spearmen. Facing the Ass are:—1. The monster serpent ĀPEP, , and 2. The crocodile SHESSHES, , with a tail ending in the head of a serpent.

The text, which refers to the whole of this section, reads:—

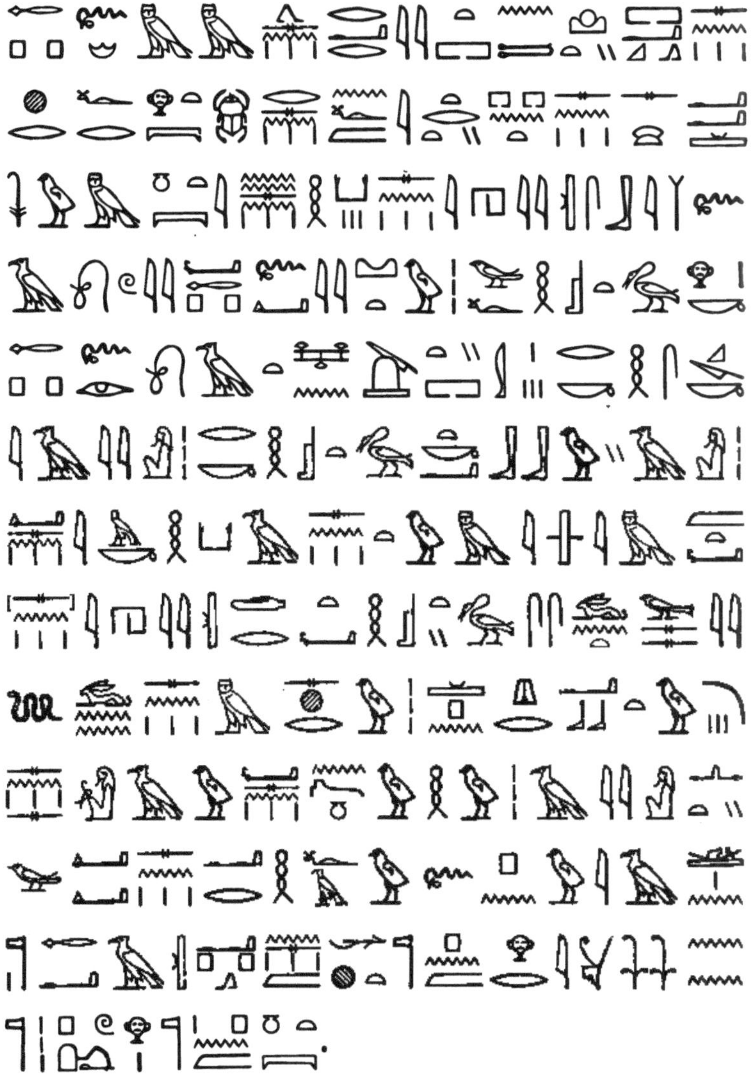

"This great god is towed along by the gods of the "Ṭuat, and those who tow Rā along say:—'The god "cometh to his body, and the god is towed along to his "shadow. O be thou at peace with thy body, and we "will tow thee along in thy integrity into thy (literally, "his) secret place. Come thou, O Rā, and be thou at "peace with thy body, for thou shalt be protected by "those who are over the curved ropes (?).'"

The text which refers to the six men, four apes, and four women, with nets over their heads, reads:—

"Those who are in this picture march before Rā, and "they utter words of power against Āpep, and [then] "return to the Ārit (or, Hall) of the horizon. They "journey onwards with him into the height of heaven, "and they come into being for him in the Āterti "(i.e., the two portions of the sky in which Rā rises "and sets), and they cause him to rise in Nut. And "they say their words of power which are these:—'Out "upon thee, O thou Rebel Serpent! Out upon thee, "thou monster that destroyest, thou Āpep that sendest "forth thy evil emanations (or, deeds)! Thy face shall "be destroyed, O Āpep. Thou shalt advance to the "block of execution. The Nemu are against thee, and "they shall hack thee in pieces. The Āaiu are against "thee, and they shall destroy thee. The Ābebuiti "(i.e., the three spearmen) shall drive [their harpoons] "into thee, and they shall enchant thee by means of "their Hail! Thou art destroyed, dashed in pieces, "and stabbed to death, O serpent Sessi.'"

"Those who are in this scene, and who have their

"spears, keep ward over the rope of Ai, and they do "not permit this Worm to approach the boat of the "great god. They pass behind this god upwards. "These gods who do battle on behalf of this god in "heaven say":—(The speech is wanting).

Gods of the South raising the Standard of the South.

In the upper register are the following:—

1. Four gods, who in the place of heads have each a crown of the South, to which is affixed a uraeus, upon his body, and who, aided by a bearded male figure, are engaged in raising up from the ground, by means of a rope, a pole or staff, which is surmounted by a bearded

human head wearing a crown of the South; the gods are called "gods of the South," [hieroglyphs], and the bearded male figure "he who is over the front end," [hieroglyphs].

2. Four gods, who in the place of heads have each a

Gods of the North raising the Standard of the North.

crown of the North, to which is affixed a uraeus, upon his body, and who, aided by a bearded male figure, are engaged in raising up from the ground, by means of a rope, a pole or staff, which is surmounted by a bearded human head wearing a crown of the North; the gods are called "gods of the North," [hieroglyphs], and the bearded male figure is "he who is over the hind part," [hieroglyphs].

3. Between the two groups described above is the hawk-headed sphinx which typifies "Horus in the Boat," [hieroglyphs]. Above its hind-quarters spring the head and shoulders of a bearded human figure called ĀNĀ, [hieroglyphs], and on the head of the hawk and that of Ānā is a crown of the South. Standing on the back of the sphinx is the figure of HORUS-SET with

Heru-àm-uàa with Set-Horus on his back.

characteristic heads, with his arms outstretched, and with each hand laid upon the upper part of the crowns of the South. The hawk head of this figure faces the back of the hawk head of the sphinx, and the animal's head, which is characteristic of Set, faces the back of the human head of Ānā. It is thus quite clear that

Horus was regarded as a form of the Sun-god of the South, and Set as a form of the Sun-god of the North.

4. The serpent SHEMTI, , which has four heads and necks at each end of its body, and each head and neck are supported on a pair of legs. A male figure called ÅPU, , stands and grasps the middle of the body of the serpent with both hands.

5. The serpent BÅTA, , with a bearded head at each end of his body; each head wears a crown of the South. Above the back of this serpent is another serpent, from each end of the body of which spring the upper portions of the bodies and heads of four bearded male figures; the first figure of each group has a pair of hands and arms which are raised in adoration, and each figure of the two groups has a pair of legs, which rest on the back of the serpent BÅTA. A male figure called ÅBETH stands and grasps the middle of the body of the serpent ṬEPI, , with both hands.

6. Two male beings, swinging over their heads a net, wherewith they are going to attack the serpent, or to resist him.

The text which refers to the above reads:—

The Shemti Serpent and his warder Åpu.

The passage which refers to the gods of the South reads:—

"Those who are in this scene rise up for Rā, who

"saith unto them:—'Receive ye your heads, O ye gods, "and draw tightly the front end of your rope. Hail, "O ye gods, come into being! Hail, possess ye the "power of light, O ye gods, and come ye into being, O "ye gods. Possess ye the power of light, O ye gods, by

The Serpents Bȧta and Țepi and the warder Ȧbeth.

"my coming into being in the secret place, and by my "power of light in the hidden place (Ȧment), in the "chambers of things.'"

The passage which refers to Horus-Set reads:—

"Rā maketh to arise this god. This god with his "two faces goeth in after Rā hath passed by him."

The passage which refers to the gods of the North reads:—

"Rā saith unto them:—'Let your heads be to "you, O ye gods! Receive ye your crowns of "the North, and pull ye tightly at the hinder "end of the boat of him that cometh into being "from me. Behold now Horus of the handsome "Face!'"

The passage which refers to the serpent SHEMTI reads:—

"He who is in this picture strideth through the secret "place, and he withdraweth to QA-ṬEMT, the Hall (or, "Court) of Ȧment. Those who are in it are the heads "which have been devoured, and they breathe the "odour of SHEMTI, of which ȦPU is the warder."

The passage which refers to the serpent BȦTA reads:—

"He who is in this picture maketh his rising up for "SAR, and he keepeth count of the souls which are "doomed in the Ṭuat. He strideth through the secret "place, and he withdraweth to ṬESERT-BAIU, to the "Hall (or, Court) of Ȧment; then ṬEPI entereth into "BȦTA. Those who are in it are they whose heads "have been devoured. They breathe the odour of "BȦTA, of which ȦBETH is the guardian."

The passage which refers to the two gods with nets reads:—

"These are the gods who make use of words of "power for Horus-Rā in Ȧment. [They have power] "over the net, and they make use of words of power on "those who are in the net[s] which are in their hands."

In the lower register are:—

1. Sixteen gods, who stand at one end of the scene, and grasp a rope with both hands. The first four are bearded, man-headed beings, and are said to be "the souls of Ȧment," ; the second four are ibis-headed, and are "the followers of Thoth," ; the third four are hawk-headed, and are "the followers of Horus," ; and the last four are ram-headed, and are "the followers of Rā," .

Two gods with nets.

2. Eight bearded, man-headed beings, who stand at the other end of the scene in two groups of four, and who are described as "Powers," ;

each grasps a rope with both hands. The rope which is held by these groups of beings is attached to the legs of the enormous serpent KHEPRI, 𓆣𓇌. This serpent has a head at each end of its body, the foremost part of which is supported on a pair of human legs; from each end of that portion of its body which lies flat on the ground springs a uraeus. On the centre fold of the body is seated a hawk, which wears on its head the double crown, 𓋖. This hawk is the symbol of "Horus of the Ṭuat," *Ḥeru ṭuati* 𓅃𓇼.

The text which refers to this section of the scene reads:—

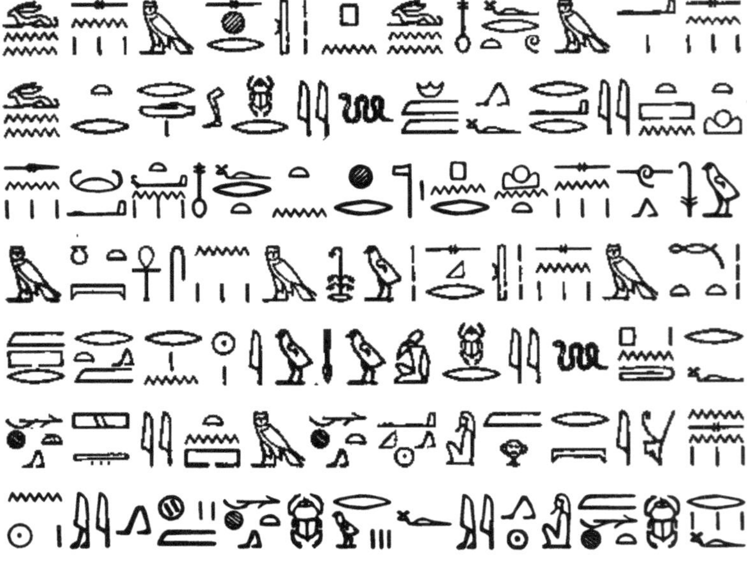

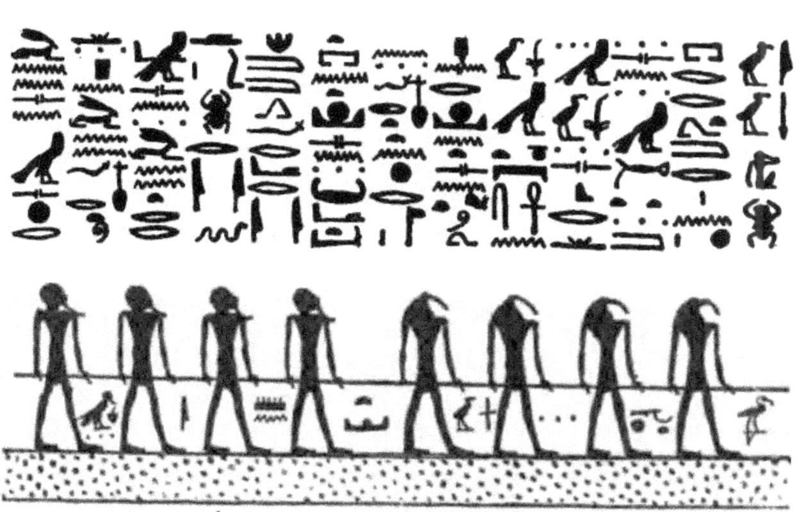

The Souls of Ȧment, and the Followers of Thoth who tow Khepri.

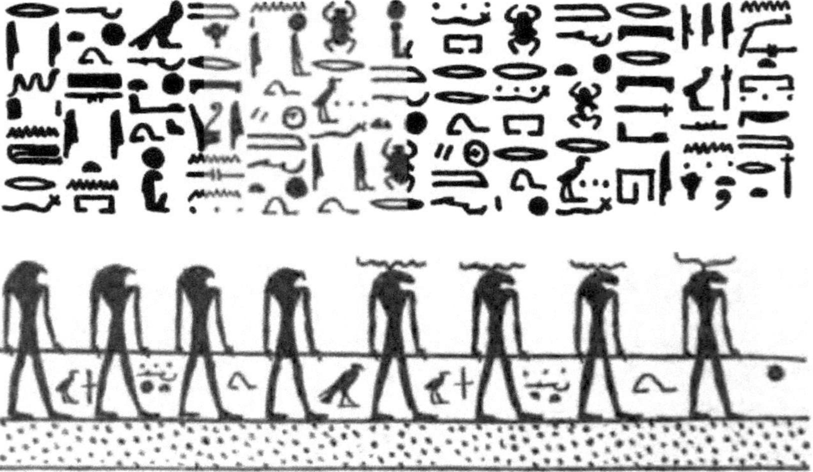

The Followers of Horus and the Followers of Rā who tow Khepri.

"Those who are in this scene have the rope in their "hands, and it is fastened to the leg[s] of KHEPRI, who "moveth backwards to the Hall of their horizon. They "draw this rope with the god into their horizon, and "they tow him along in the sky (NUT). They live upon "the things of the South, and their sustenance is from "the things of the North, [and they exist] on that which "cometh forth from the mouth of Rā. The voice of "this serpent KHEPRI goeth round about and travelleth "into the secret place after Rā hath entered into the "height of heaven."

The four groups, each containing four beings, "say "unto Rā:—'Come, O come, after thy transformations! "Come, O Rā, after thy transformations! Appear,

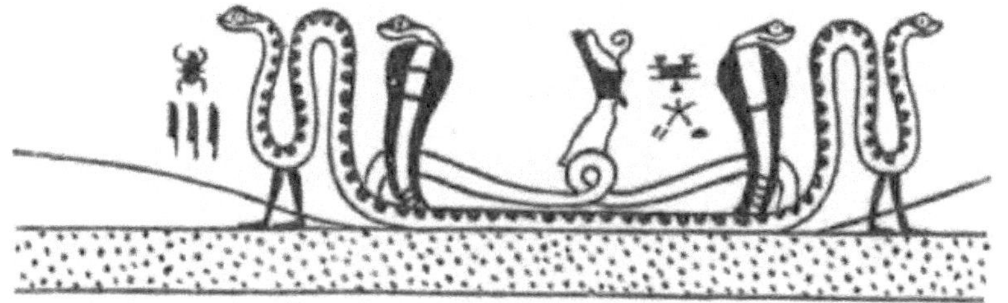

The Serpent Khepri and Horus of the Ṭuat.

"appear, after thy transformations! Appear, O Rā, "after thy transformations in heaven, in the great "heaven! Hail! We decree for thee thy habitations "by the excellence which is in the words of the Mighty "One of Forms in the secret (or, hidden) place.'"

The passage which refers to Horus reads:—

"He who is in this scene is ḤERU ṬUATI (i.e., Horus

"of the Ṭuat). The head cometh forth from him, "and the forms [in which he appeareth] from the "coiled [serpent]. Rā crieth unto this god to whom "the two divine URAEI unite themselves; he entereth "in upon the way into KHEPRI, who listeneth when Rā "crieth to him."

The two groups, each containing four beings, "have

The Eight Powers who tow Khepri.

"in their hands the rope which is fastened to the foot "of KHEPRI, and they say to Rā:—'The ways of the "hidden place are open to thee, and [the portals] which "are in the earth are unfolded for thee, the SOUL which "Nut loveth, and we will guide thy wings to the moun-"tain. Hail! Enter thou into the East, and make thou "thy passage from between the thighs of thy mother.'"

CHAPTER XII.

THE GATE OF SETHU.

THE TENTH DIVISION OF THE ṬUAT.

HAVING passed through the Ninth Division of the Ṭuat, the boat of the sun arrives at the gateway TCHESERIT, , which leads to the Tenth Division, or, as the opening text reads: , "This great god cometh "forth to this gate, and entereth through it, and the "gods who are therein acclaim the great god." The gateway is like that through which the god passed into the previous Division, and its outwork is guarded by sixteen uraei. At the entrance to the gate proper stands a bearded, mummied form called NEMI, , who holds a knife in his hands, and at its exit stands a similar mummied form called KEFI, . The corridor is swept by flames of fire, which proceed from the mouths of two uraei, as before. The uraei which guard the outwork address Rā, and say, "Come thou to "us, O thou who art at the head of the horizon, O thou "great god who openest the secret place, open thou "the holy pylons and unfold the portals of the earth," The monster serpent which

The Boat of Åf-Rā in the Tenth Division of the Ṭuat.

stands on his tail and guards the door is called SETHU, , and the two lines of text which refer to his admission of Rā read:—"He who is over this gate "openeth to Rā. SA saith unto SETHU, 'Open thy "gate, unfold thy portal, so that he may illumine the "thick darkness, and may send light into the hidden "abode.' This gate closeth after the great god hath

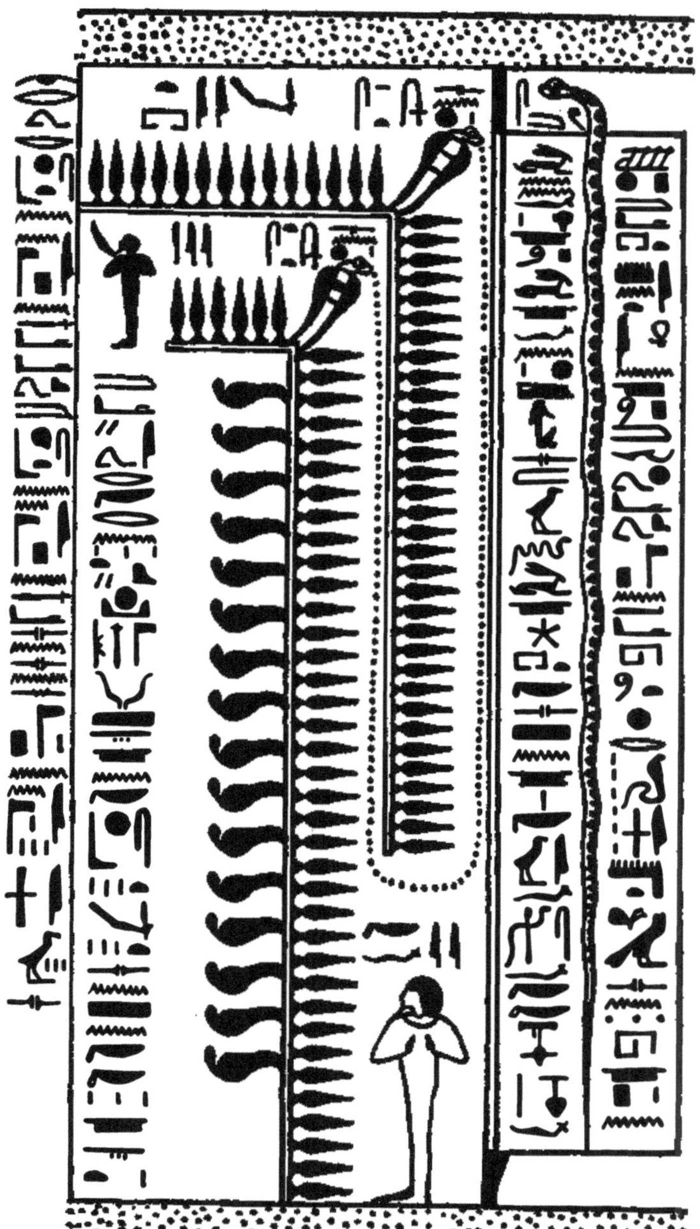

The Gate of the Serpent Sethu.

"passed through it, and the uraei who are on the other "side of it wail when they hear it closing upon them,"

In the middle of this Division we see the boat of the sun being towed on its way by four gods of the Ṭuat, ; the god is in the same form as before, and his boat is piloted by SA, who commands, and by ḤEKA, who steers according to his directions.

The procession in front of the boat of the sun consists of:—

1. A bearded male figure called UNTI, , i.e., the "god of the hour," who holds a star in each hand.

2. Four kneeling gods, each with a uraeus over his head. The first is HORUS, , hawk-headed; the second is SEREQ, , bearded, and wearing a wig; the third is ÅBESH, bearded and without a wig; and the fourth is SEKHET, , with the head of a lioness.

3. Three bearded beings, the "Star-gods," , each holding a star in his right hand, which is stretched aloft, and with his left towing a small boat containing the "Face of the Disk."

4. A small boat holding a uraeus, which has the latter part of its body bent upwards; within the curve is the "Face of the Disk," .

5. The winged serpent SEMI, standing on its tail, with its body in folds.

6. The bearded figure BESI, , receiving in his hand the flame which spouts up from the head of a horned animal, which forms the top of a staff, and is transfixed by a knife.

7. The serpent ÅNKHI, , from each side of the neck of which grows a bearded, mummy figure.

8. Four women, each with both hands raised in adoration; they are described as "Criers," .

9. Two bows, set end to end, , on each of which three uraei rear their heads. Standing over the place where the two ends of the bows meet, with a foot on the end of each, is the two-headed figure HORUS-SET, with two pairs of hands, one pair on each side of his body, raised in adoration. HORUS-SET is called "he of the two heads," , and the two bows are "the Crown of the Uraei," .

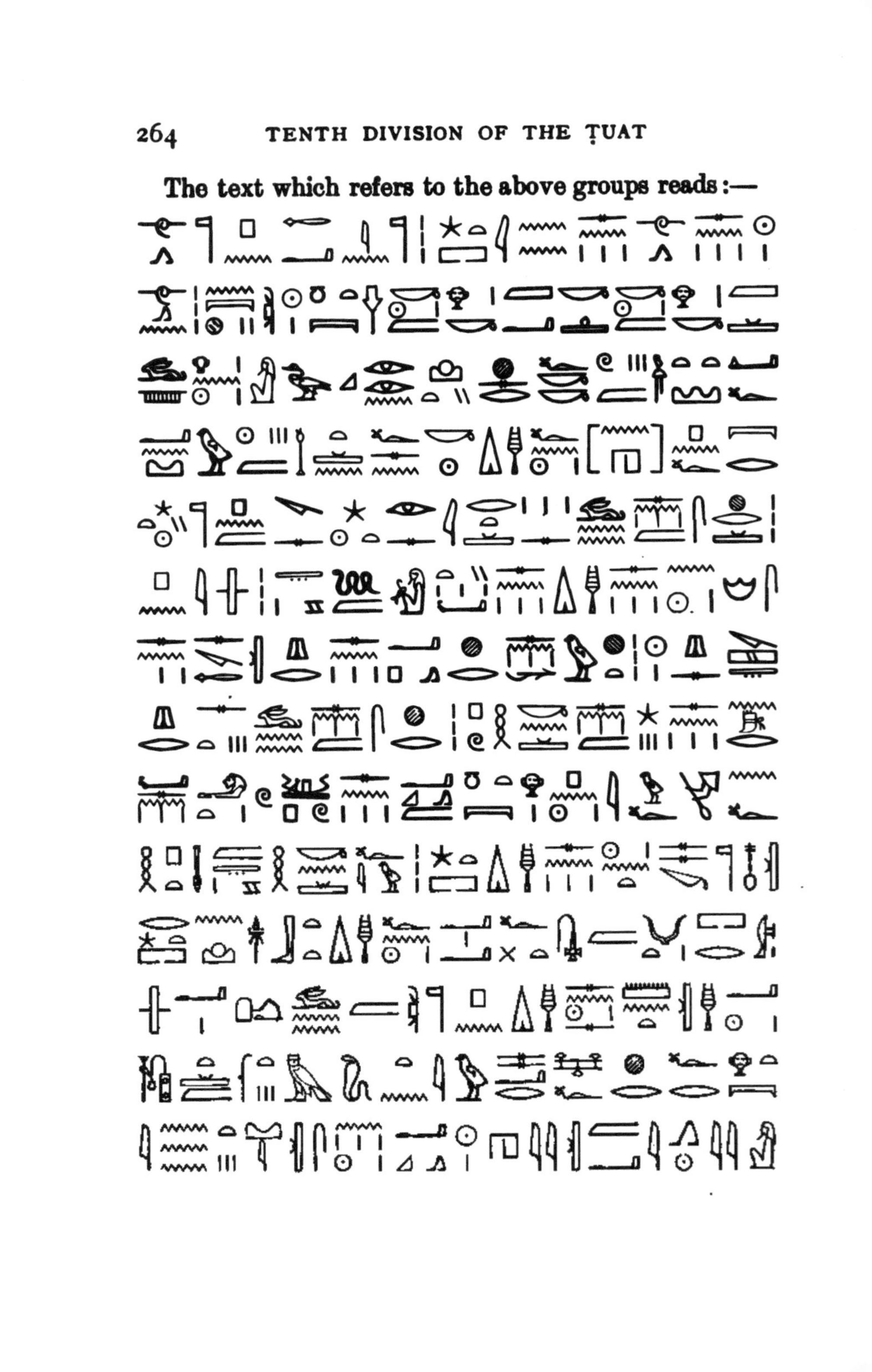

The text which refers to the above groups reads:—

"This great god is towed along by the gods of the "Ṭuat, and those who tow Rā along say:—'We are "towing Rā along, we are towing Rā along, and Rā "followeth [us] into Nut. O have the mastery over "thy Face, indeed thou shalt unite thyself to thy Face, "O Rā, [by] Maāt. Open, O thou Face of Rā, and let "the two Eyes of Khuti enter into thee; drive away "thou the darkness from Ȧmentet. Let him give light "by what he hath sent forth, the light.'"

Of the god with stars it is said:—

"He maketh a rising up for Rā (or, he stablisheth "Rā), UNTI maketh to be light the upper heaven; this "god leadeth the hour, which performeth that which "belongeth to it to do."

Of the four seated gods it is said:—

"The [four] serpents who are in the earth keep ward "over those who are in this picture. They make a "rising up for Rā, and they sit upon the great image[s "which are] under them, and they pass onwards with "them in the following of Rā, together with the hidden "images which belong to them."

Of the three gods who hold stars it is said:—

"Those who are in this picture sing hymns with "their stars, and they grasp firmly the bows of their "boat, [and it] entereth into Nut. And this Face of "Rā moveth onwards, and saileth over the land, and "those who are in the Ṭuat sing hymns to it, and make "Rā to stand up (i.e., establish Rā)."

Of the winged serpent SEMI it is said:—

"[It maketh a rising up for Rā], and it guideth the

Gods of Light and Fire. Star-gods. Face of the Disk. Semi.

"Well-doing god into the Ṭuat of the horizon of the "East."

Of the god BESI it is said:—

"He maketh a rising up for Rā, and he placeth fire "on the head and horns (or, [in] his hands is the fire "from the head and horns), and the weapon which is in "the hand of the Fighter is in the follower of this god."

Of the uraeus with the double male figure it is said:—

"It maketh a rising up for Rā. The stablishing of

"Time which is reckoned in writing by years is with "this uraeus, and it maketh it to go with him into the "heights of heaven."

Of the "Criers" it is said:—

"Those who cry unto Rā say, 'Enter in, O Rā! "Hail, come, O Rā! Hail, come, O thou who art born "of the Ṭuat! Come, O offspring of the heights of "heaven! Hail, come thou into being, O Rā!'"

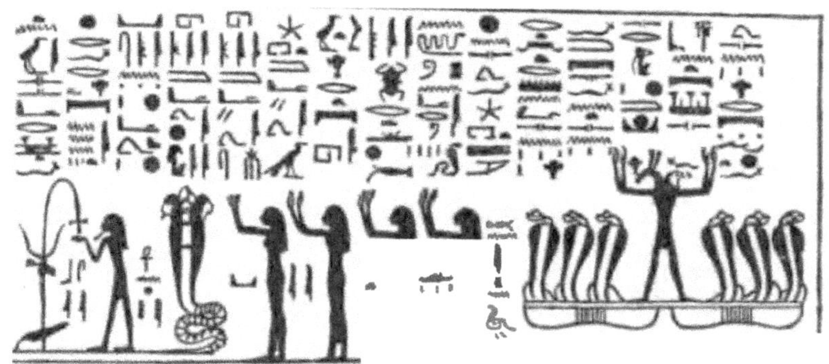

Besi. Ȧnkhi. The goddesses who hail the god. Meḥen and Horus-Set.

Of the double bow it is said:—

"This is the MEḤEN serpent of the uraei, which "strideth through the Ṭuat. The two bows are "stretched out, and they bear up on themselves him of "the Two-Faces (or, Two-Heads, i.e., Horus-Set) in his "mystery which [appertaineth] to them. They lead "the way for Rā in the horizon of the east of heaven, "and they pass on into the heights of heaven in his "train."

In the upper register are:—

1. The four ȦNTIU gods, , each of whom holds a knife in his right hand, and a short staff with one end curved and curled in his left.

2. The four ḤENĀTIU gods, , each having four uraei in the place of a head; they are armed with weapons similar to those of the ȦNTIU gods.

The Ȧntiu and Ḥenātiu Gods attacking Āpep.

3. The undulating length of the serpent ĀPEP, , of whom it is said, "his voice goeth round the Ṭuat," . Attached to the neck of the monster is a very long chain, which rises in an oval curve, and, passing along through the hands of sixteen male figures, is then grasped and held down by a large hand, from which it again rises in an oval curve, and passing on for some distance descends into the earth

immediately in front of Khenti-Åmenti. On the first curve of the chain, lying flat on her face, is the goddess Serq. Of the sixteen bearded figures who grasp the chain with both hands, four are called SEṬEFIU, and face to the left; the twelve are described as the "TCHAṬIU gods, strong of arm," . The right hand which grasps and pulls down the chain is called "HIDDEN BODY," . Lengthwise on the second curve of the great chain lean the upper portions of the figures of five gods, each of whom grasps the chain with his right hand, and holds in his left a sceptre and the end of a chain which fetters a serpent in coils. The name of the first serpent is UAMEMTI, , but of the remaining four no names are given. The five gods appear to grow out of the great chain, and are called SEB, , MEST, , ḤĀPI, , ṬUAMUTEF, , and QEBḤSENNUF, . At the end of this section of the scene stands the bearded mummied figure of KHENTI-ÅMENTI, wearing the White Crown and the *menàt*, and holding the sceptre in his two hands.

The text which refers to these groups reads:—

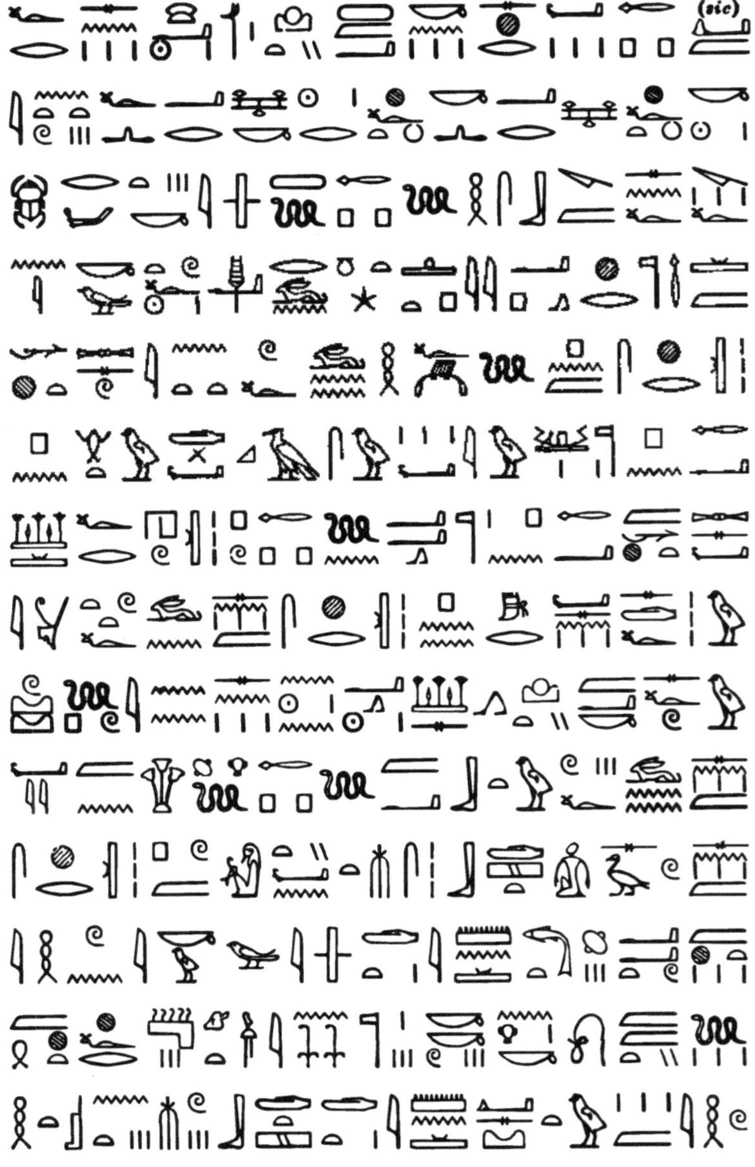
(sic)

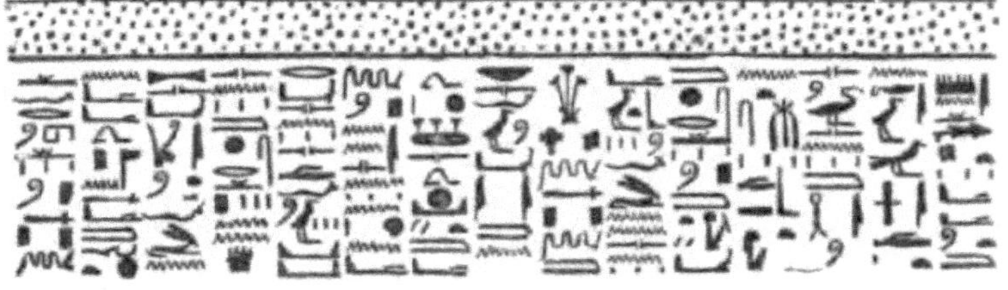

The Seṭefiu and other gods holding Āpep in restraint.

Of the eight gods (i.e., the ÅNTIU and ḤENĀTIU) it is said:—

"Those who are in this picture rise up (or, stand) for "Rā, and Rā riseth and cometh forth for them, [and "they say], 'Rise, Rā, be strong, Khuti; verily we will "overthrow Āpep in his fetters. Approach not thou, "O Rā, towards thine enemy, and thine enemy shall "not approach thee; may thy holy attributes come "into being within the serpent. The serpent Āpep is "stabbed with his knives, and gashes are inflicted on "him. Rā shall stand up in the hour wherein he is "content (or, the hour of peace), and the great god "shall pass on in strength when his chain (i.e., Āpep's) "is fixed.'"

"The reptile (literally, worm) who is in this picture "breaketh asunder the fetters, and the boat of this "great god beginneth [to move] towards the region

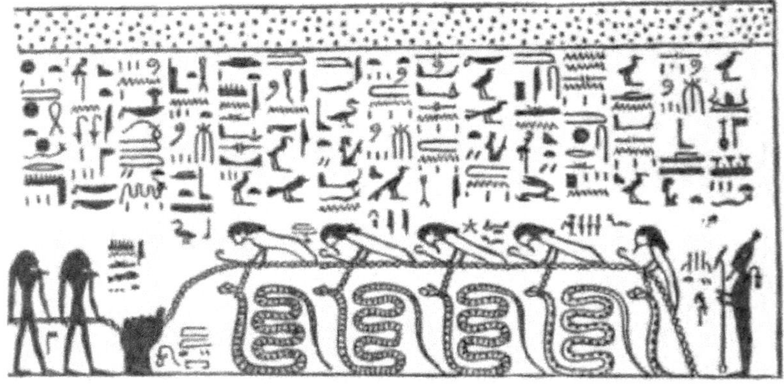

Seb and the Children of Horus holding Apep and his sons in restraint.

"of Āpep; this great god travelleth on after he (i.e., "Āpep) hath been put in restraint by means of his "fetters."

Of the four SEṬEFIU gods it is said:—

"These who are in this picture grasp the fetters of "the being of two-fold evil, and they say to Rā, 'Come "forward, Rā, pass onwards, Khuti. Verily fetters "have been laid upon NEḤA-ḤRÅ, and Āpep is in his "bonds.'"

Of the twelve other gods who grasp the chain it is said:—

"Those who are in this picture [act] as warders of "the sons of the helpless one, and they keep guard "over the deadly chain which is in the HIDDEN HAND, "for the dead bodies are placed with the things [which "belong to them] in the circuit of the battlements of "KHENTI-ÅMENTI. And these gods say, 'Let darkness "be upon thy face, O UAMEMTI, and ye shall be "destroyed, O ye sons of the helpless one, by the "HIDDEN HAND, which shall cause evils [to come upon "you] by the deadly chain which is in it. SEB keepeth "ward over your fetters, and the sons of the fetters "(i.e., Mest, Ḥāpi, Ṭuamutef, and Qebḥsennuf) put "upon you the deadly chain. Keep ye [your] ward "under the reckoning of KHENTI-ÅMENTI.'"

Of the children of Horus it is said:—

"Those who are in this picture make heavy the "fetters of the sons of the helpless one, and the boat of "the Well-doing God travelleth on its way."

In the lower register are:—

1. Twelve male beings, each of whom carries a paddle; they are called "gods who never diminish,"

2. Twelve female beings, each of whom grasps a rope with both hands; above the head of each is a star. They are called the "hours who tow along [the boat of Rā],"

3. The god BÅNTI, [hieroglyphs], with the head of a cynocephalus ape, holding a sceptre, [hieroglyph].

4. The god SESHSHÅ, [hieroglyphs], man-headed, with a star above him, holding a sceptre, [hieroglyph].

5. The god KA-ÅMENTI, [hieroglyphs], bull-headed, and holding a sceptre, [hieroglyph].

The Twelve Åkhemu-Seku Gods with their Paddles.

6. The god RENEN-SBAU, [hieroglyphs], man-headed, with a star above him, holding a sceptre, [hieroglyph].

7. A monkey, with a star over his head, standing on a bracket, [hieroglyph]; he is called the "god of Rethenu" (Syria), [hieroglyphs].

8. A bracket, whereon rests the Utchat, [hieroglyph].

9. A god called ḤER-NEST-F, 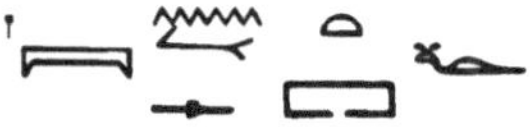, holding a sceptre.

The text which refers to the above reads:—

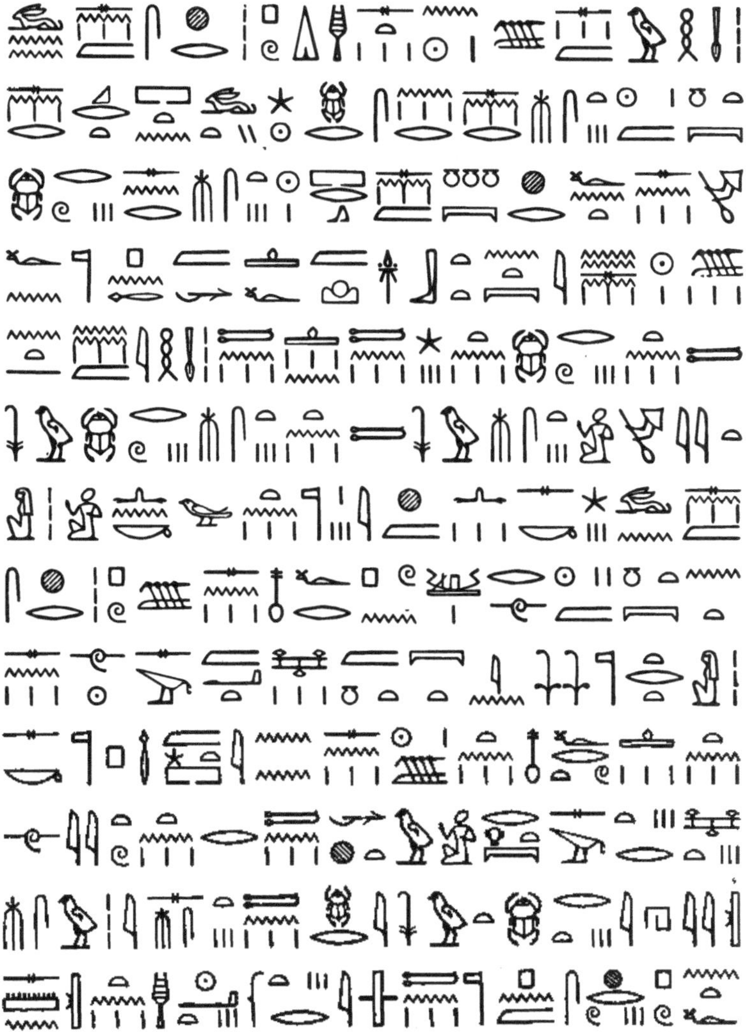

Of the twelve gods (the ÅKHEMU SEKU) it is said:—

"Those who are in this picture make a rising up for "Rā, and they take their paddles in this Circle of "UNTI. They come into being of their own accord at "the seasons when Rā is born in Nut; they come into "being for the births of Rā, and they make their "appearance in Nu along with him. It is they who "transport this great god after he hath taken his place "in the horizon of the East of heaven. Rā saith unto "them:—'Take ye your paddles and unite ye your-"selves to your stars. Your coming into being taketh "place when [I] come into being, and your births take "place when my births take place. O ye beings who "transport me, ye shall not suffer diminution, O ye "gods ÅKHEMU SEKU.'"

Of the twelve goddesses of the hours it is said:—

"Those who are in this scene take hold of the rope "of the boat of Rā to tow him along into the sky. It "is they who tow Rā along, and guide him along the "roads into the sky, and behold, they are the goddesses "who draw along the great god in the Ṭuat. Rā saith "unto them:—'Take ye the rope, set ye yourselves in "position, and pull ye me, O my followers, into the "height of heaven, and lead ye me along the ways. "My births make you to be born, and behold, my "coming into being maketh you to come into being. "O stablish ye the periods of time and years for him "who is among you.'"

1. "The god who is in this picture adjureth the

The Twelve Goddesses of the Hours.

"pylons to open to Rā, and he goeth on his way by his "side."

2. "The god who is in this picture crieth out to the "stars concerning the births of this great god, and he "goeth on his way with them."

3. "The god who is in this picture crieth to the gods "of the Boat of Rā, and he goeth on his way with "him."

4. "The god who is in this picture setteth the stars

"in their places (literally, towns), and he goeth on his "way with the great god."

The above f ur paragra hs must r fer to the four gods BĀNTI, SE I HÁ, KA-Á IENT, and RENEN-SBAU, and therefore th d f R thenu, the tchat, and the god ḤER-NEST- remain without de riptions. Fr m the toml f Rame V . M. Lefébure adds the two

Bānti. eshshá. Ka-Ámenti. Renen-sbau. N ter-Rethen. Eye of Rā. Ḥer-nest-f.

following paragraphs which concern the Utchat and ḤER-NEST-F, [hieroglyphs].

"This is the Eye of Rā, which the god uniteth to "himself, and it rejoiceth in it place in the boat."

"This is he who openeth the door of this Circle; he "remaineth in his position, and doth not go on his way "with Rā."

CHAPTER XIII.

THE GATE OF ÀM-NETU-F.

THE ELEVENTH DIVISION OF THE ṬUAT.

HAVING passed through the Tenth Division of the Ṭuat, the boat of the sun arrives at the gateway SHETAT-BESU, , which leads to the Eleventh Division, or, as the opening text reads: , "This "[great] god cometh forth to this gate, this great god "entereth through it, and the gods who are therein "acclaim the great god." The gateway is like that through which the god passed into the previous Division; at the entrance to the gate proper stands a bearded, mummied form called METES, , and at its exit stands a similar form called SHEṬĀU, . The corridor is swept by flames of fire, which proceed from the mouths of two uraei, as before. In the space which is usually guarded by a number

of gods stand two sceptres, , each of which is surmounted by a White Crown; the one on the right is the symbol of OSIRIS, (SAR), and the other of HORUS, . Between the sceptres is a line of text, which reads:—"They say to Rā, '[Come] in peace!
"[Come] in peace! [Come] in peace! [Come] in peace!
"O thou whose transformations are manifold, thy soul
"is in heaven, thy body is in the earth. It is thine
"own command, O great one,"

The monster serpent which stands on his tail and guards the door is called ÅM-NETU-F, , and the two lines of text which refer to his admission of Rā read:—"He who is over this door openeth to Rā.
"SAU saith to ÅM-NETU-F, 'Open thy gate to Rā, unfold
"thy portal to KHUTI, so that he may illumine the
"thick darkness, and may send light into the hidden
"abode.' This gate closeth after the great god hath
"passed through it, and the gods who are on the battle-
"ments wail when they hear it closing upon them,"

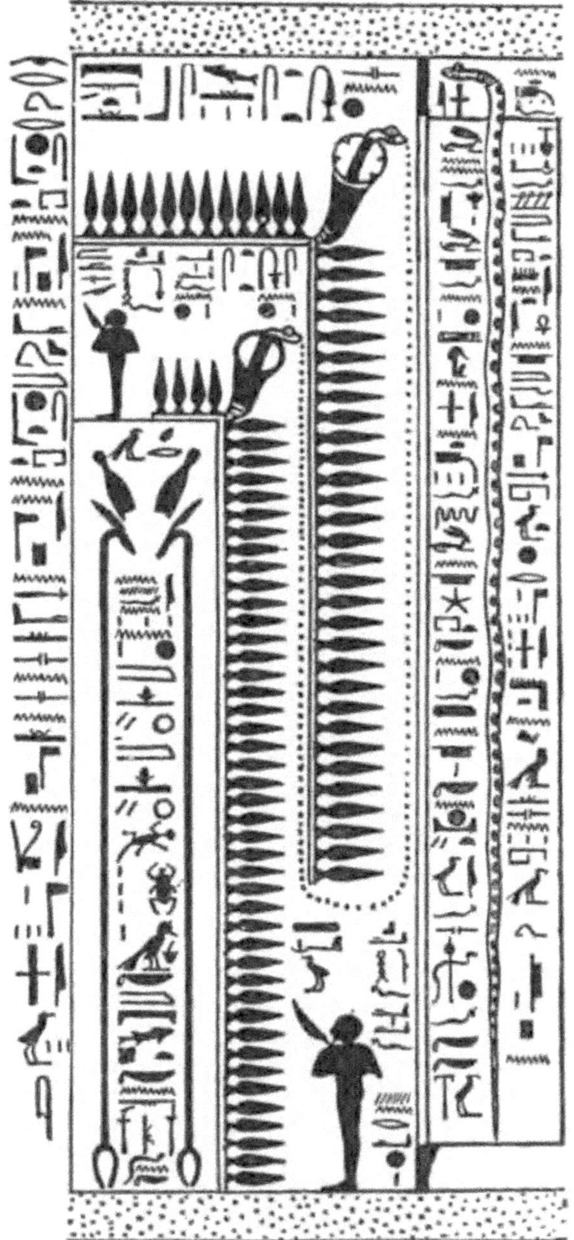

The Gate of the Serpent Ȧm-netu-f.

In the middle of this Division we see the boat of the sun being towed on its way by four gods of the Ṭuat, ; the god is in the same form as before, and his

The Boat of Åf-Rā in the Eleventh Division of the Ṭuat.

boat is piloted by SA, who commands, and by ḤEKA, who steers according to his directions.

The procession in front of the boat of the sun consists of:—

1. A company of nine gods, each holding a huge knife in his right hand, and a sceptre, , in his left; the first four have jackal heads, and the last five heads of bearded men. These nine beings represent the

"company of the gods who slay ĀPEP," [hieroglyphs].

2. The serpent ĀPEP, fettered by five chains which enter the ground; the fetters are further strengthened by small chains, which are linked to the larger ones, and are fastened to the ground by means of pegs with a hook at the top, [hieroglyph]. In an earlier picture we have

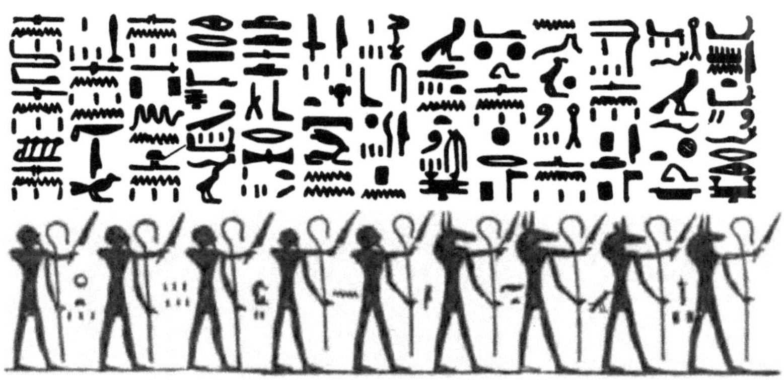

The Slaughterers of Āpep.

seen ĀPEP fettered by Seb, Mest, Ḥāpi, Ṭuamutef, and Qebḥsennuf, who were represented by five gods, but here the figures of the gods are wanting, and it is only the legend "Children of Horus," [hieroglyphs], that tells us the chains represent the gods.

3. Four Apes, [hieroglyphs], each holding up a huge hand and wrist.

4. The goddess of Upper Egypt, wearing the White Crown, and styled ÁMENTI, .

5. The goddess of Lower Egypt, wearing the Red Crown, and called ḤERIT, .

6. The bearded god SEBEKHTI, , who holds the emblem of "life" in his right hand, and a sceptre in his left.

The text which refers to the above gods reads :—

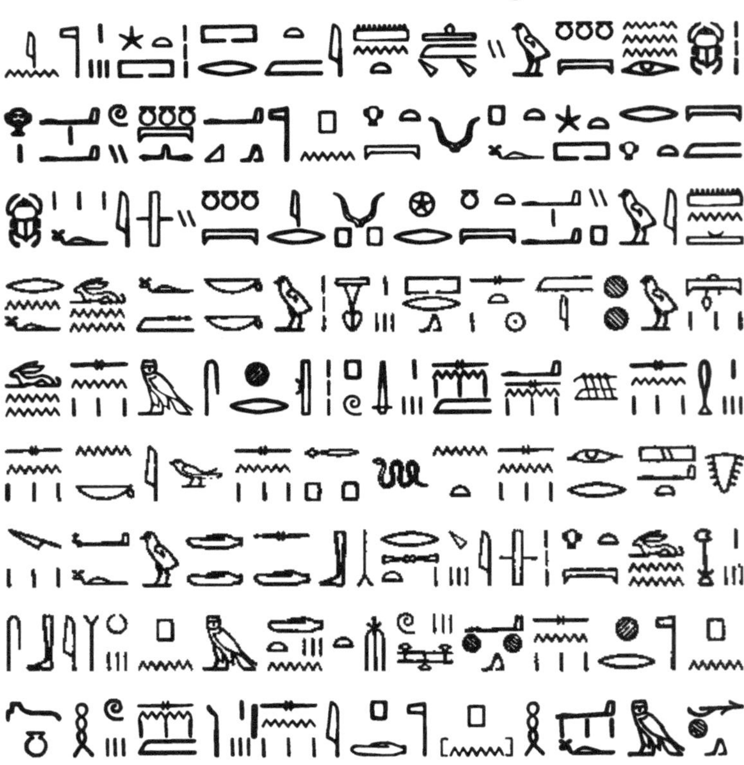

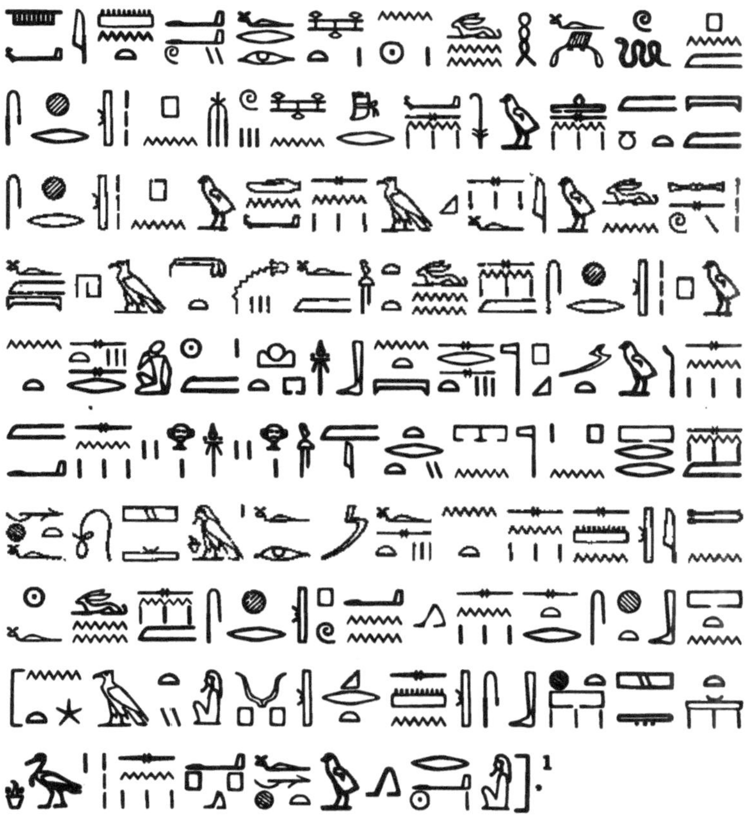

Of the gods of the Ṭuat who tow the boat of Rā it is said:—

"The gods of the Ṭuat say, 'Behold the coming "forth [of Rā] from Àment, and [his] taking up [his] "place in the two divisions of Nu, and [his] perform-"ance of [his] transformations on the two hands of Nu. "This god doth not enter into the height of heaven,

[1] Supplied from Champollion, *Monuments*, tom. ii., p. 537.

"[but] he openeth [a way through] the Ṭuat into the "height of heaven by his transformations which are in "Nu. Now, what openeth the Ṭuat into Nut (i.e., the "sky) are the two hands of ÅMEN-REN-F (i.e., he whose "name is hidden). He existeth in the thick darkness, "and light appeareth [there] from the starry night.'"

Of the nine gods with knives and sceptres it is said:—

"Those who are in this scene [with] their weapons "in their hand take their knives and hack [with them] "at Åpep; they make gashes in him and slaughter "him, and they drive stakes whereby to fetter him in "the regions which are in the upper height. The "fetters of the REBEL are in the hands of the Children "of Horus, who stand threateningly by this god "with their chains between their fingers. This god "reckoneth up his members after he whose arms are "hidden hath opened [the door] to make a way for Rā."

Of the serpent Åpep it is said:—

"The Children of Horus grasp firmly this serpent "which is in this picture, and in this picture they rest "in Nut (i.e., the sky). They heap their fetters upon "him, and whilst his folds (?) are in the sky his poison "drops down from him into Åmentet."

Of the four apes holding hands it is said:—

"It is those who are in this picture who make ready "for Rā a way into the eastern horizon of heaven, and "they lead the way for the god who hath created them "with their hands, [standing] two on the right hand

"and two on the left in the double *ātert* of this god; "then they come forth after him, and sing praises to "his soul when it looketh upon them, and they stablish "his Disk."

Of the three remaining deities it is said:—

"Those who are in this picture turn away SET from "this Gate [of the god ṮUATI. They open its cavern,

Āpep fettered by the chains of Seb and the Children of Horus.

"and stablish the hidden pylons, and their souls remain "in the following of Rā]."

In the upper register of this Division are:—

1. Four gods, each holding a disk in his right hand; these are "they who hold light-giving disks," [hieroglyphs].

2. Four gods, each holding a star in his right hand; these are "they who hold stars," .

3. Four gods, each holding a sceptre, , in his left hand; these are "they who come forth," .

4. Four ram-headed gods, each holding a sceptre in

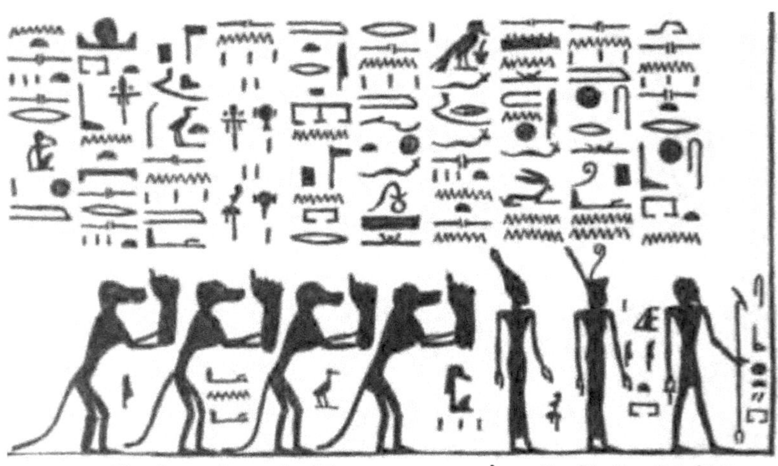

The Apes who praise Rā. Ȧmenti. Ḥerit. Sebekhti.

his left hand; their names are BA, , KHNEMU, , PENṬER, , and ṬENṬ, .

5. Four hawk-headed gods, each holding a sceptre in his left hand; these are called HORUS, , ȦSHEMTH, , SEPṬ, , and ȦMMI-UȦA-F, .

6. Eight female figures, each seated on a seat formed by a uraeus with its body coiled up, and holding a star in her left hand; these are called "the protecting hours," .

7. A crocodile-headed god called SEBEK-RĀ, who grasps a fold of a serpent that stands on its tail in his right hand, and a sceptre in his left.

The text which refers to these reads:—

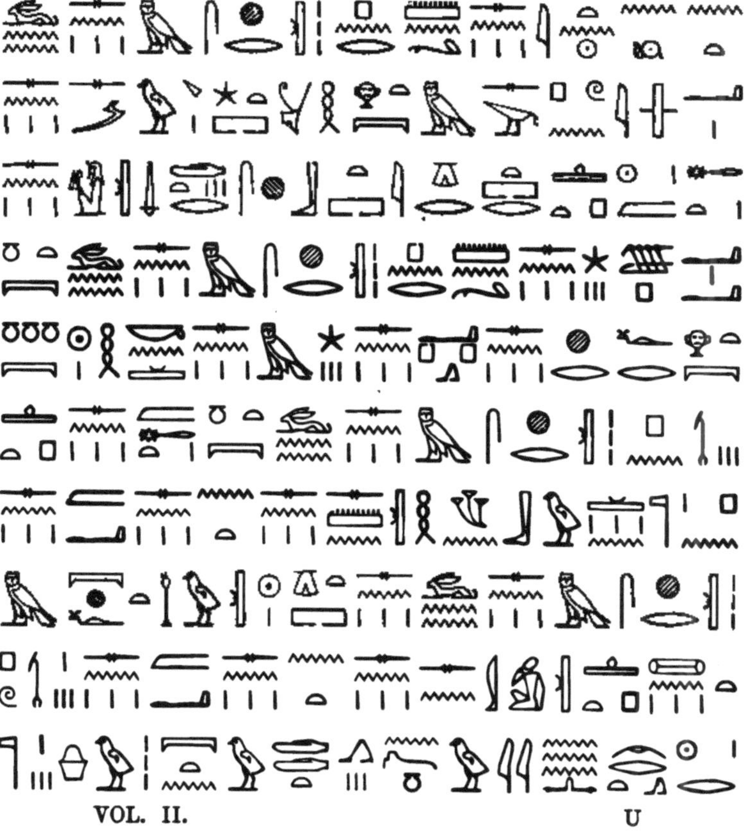

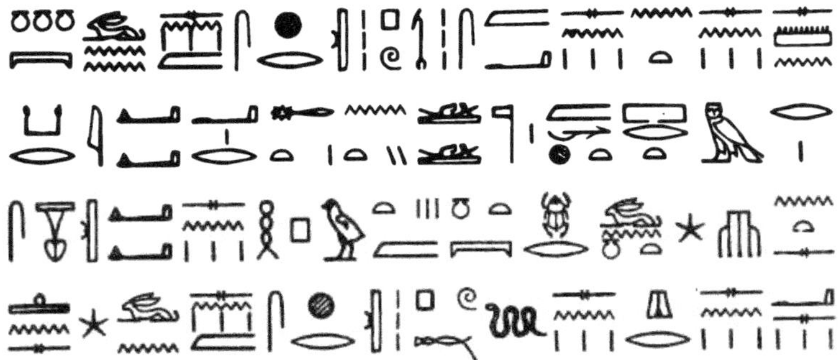

The gods who bring Disks and Stars for Rā.

Of the four gods bearing disks it is said:—

"Those who are in this picture carry the disk of Rā, "and it is they who make a way through the Ṭuat and "the height of heaven by means of this image which is "in their hands. They utter words to the Pylon of "Åkert so that Rā may set himself in the body of Nut "(i.e., the sky)."

Of the four gods bearing stars it is said:—

The gods who prepare the Offerings and Shrine of Rā.

"Those who are in this picture carry stars, and "when the two arms of Nu embrace Rā they and their "stars shout hymns of praise, and they journey on "with him to the height of heaven, and they take up "their places in the body of Nut."

Of the four gods bearing sceptres it is said:—

"Those who are in this picture [having] their "sceptres in their hands, are they who stablish the "domains of this god in the sky, and they have "their thrones in accordance with the command of "Rā."

Of the four ram-headed gods it is said:—

"Those who are in this picture [having] their "sceptres in their hands, are they who decree [the "making ready] of the offerings of the gods [from] the "bread of heaven, and it is they who make to come "forth celestial water when as yet Rā hath not emerged "in Nu."

Of the four hawk-headed gods it is said:—

"Those who are in this picture [having] their "sceptres in their hands, are they who stablish the "shrine [in the boat of Rā], and they lay their hands "on the body of the double boat of the god after it "hath appeared from out of the gate of Sma, and they "place the paddles [of the boat] in Nut, when the "Hour which presideth over it (i.e., the boat) cometh "into being, and the Hour [which hath guided it] goeth "to rest."

Of the goddesses who are seated on uraei it is said:—

"Those who are in this picture with their serpents "under them, and their hands holding stars, come "forth from the two ÅTERT of this great god, four to "the East and four to the West; it is they who call "the Spirits of the East, and they sing hymns to this "god, and they praise him after his appearance, and "SEṬTI cometh forth in his forms. It is they who "guide and transport those who are in the boat of this "great god."

There is no description of the crocodile-headed god Sebek-Rā in the text.

In the lower register are :—

1. Four gods, each wearing the Crown of the South; these are the "Kings of the South in chief,"

The goddesses of the Återti.

2. Four bearded gods, "the WEEPERS,"

3. Four gods, each wearing a Crown of the North; these are the KHNEMIU,

4. Four bearded gods, the RENENIU, , i.e., "those who give names."

5. Four females, each wearing the Crown of the South; these are the "Queens of the South,"

6. Four females, each wearing the Crown of the North; these are, presumably, the "Queens of the North;" these are the KHNEMUT, [hieroglyphs].

7. Four females, without crowns.

8. Four bearded gods, with their backs slightly bowed; these are the gods who praise Rā.

9. A cat-headed god called MÅTI, [hieroglyphs].

The text which refers to these gods reads:—

[1] Var., [hieroglyphs], SAR, Champollion, *Monuments*, tom. ii., p. 539.

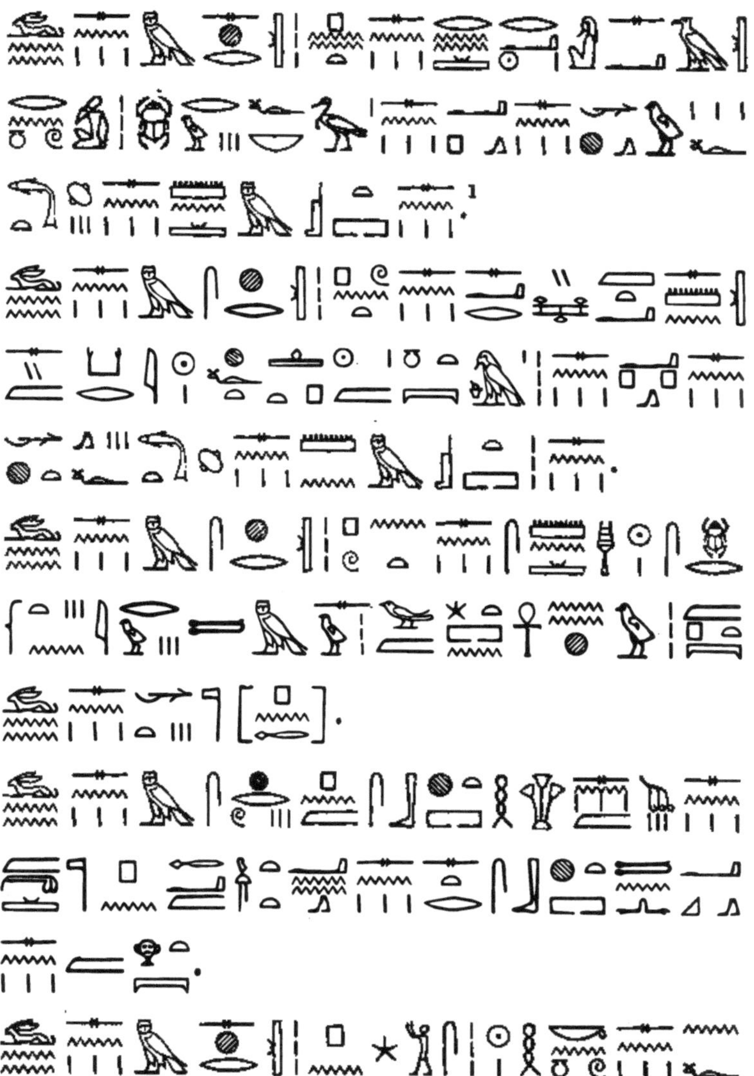

[1] Champollion, *Monuments*, tom. ii., p. 539.

The Stablishers of the White Crown. The Four Weepers.

Of the gods wearing the White Crown it is said:—

"Those who are in this picture are they who stablish "the White Crown on the gods who follow Rā; they "themselves remain in the Ṭuat, but their souls go "forward and stand at [this] gate."

Of the four Weepers it is said:—

"Those who are in this picture in this gate make

"lamentation for Osiris after Rā hath made his appear-
"ance from Ȧment; their souls go forward in his train,
"but they themselves follow after Osiris."

Of the four gods wearing the Red Crown it is said:—

"Those who are in this picture are those who unite "themselves to Rā, and they make his births to come

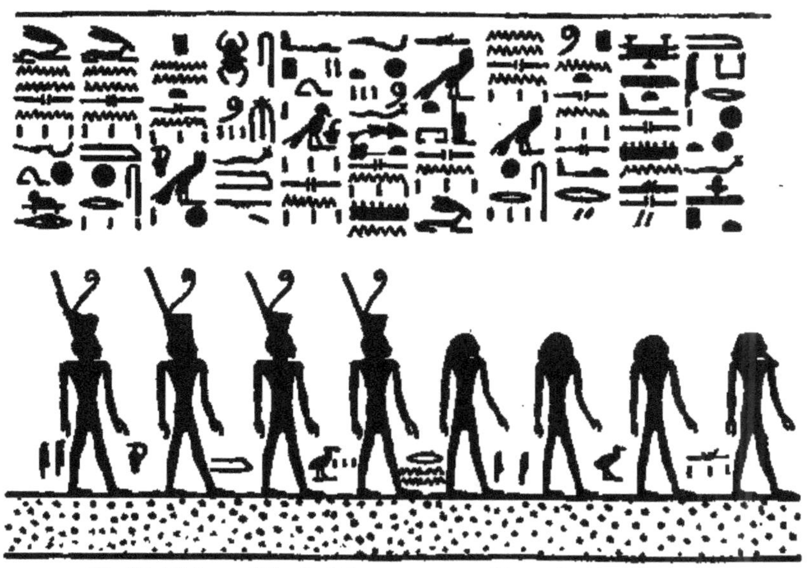

The Stablishers of the Red Crown. The gods who give names.

"to pass in the earth; their souls go forward in his "train, but their bodies remain in their places (or, "seats)."

Of the four RENENIU it is said:—

"[Those who are in this picture are they who give "the name to Rā, and they magnify the names of all "his forms; their souls go forward in his following, "but their bodies remain in their places (or, seats)."][1]

Of the four goddesses wearing the White Crown it is said:—

"Those who are in this picture are they who make

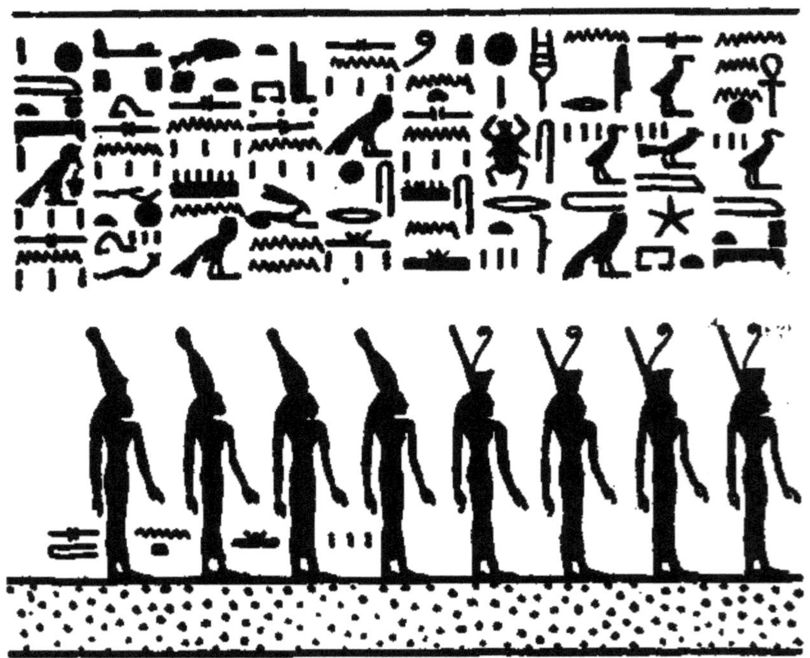

Goddesses who stablish the White and Red Crowns.

"MAĀT to advance, and who make it to be stablished "in the shrine of Rā when Rā taketh up his position "in Nut; their souls pass onwards in his following, "but their bodies remain in their places."

[1] Supplied from the tomb of Rameses VI.

Of the four goddesses wearing the Red Crown it is said:—

"Those who are in this picture are they who stablish "time, and they make to come into being the years for "those who keep ward over the condemned ones in the "Ṭuat and over those who have their life in heaven; "they follow in the train of this great god."

Goddesses who drive away Set. Gods who adore and praise Rā. Māti.

Of the four females who are without crowns it is said:—

"Those who are in this picture in [this] gate make "lamentation and tear their hair in the presence of "this great god in Åmentet; they make SET to with-"draw from this pylon, and they do not enter into the "height of heaven."

Of the four gods with their backs bowed it is said:—

"Those who are in this picture make adoration to "Rā and sing praises unto him, and in their place in "the Ṭuat they hymn those gods who are in the Ṭuat, "and who keep guard over the Hidden Door. [They "remain in their places."][1]

["The warder of the door of this Circle remaineth "in his place."][1]

[1] Supplied from the tomb of Rameses VI.

CHAPTER XIV.

THE GATE OF SEBI AND RERI.

THE TWELFTH DIVISION OF THE ṬUAT.

HAVING passed through the Eleventh Division of the Ṭuat, the boat of the sun arrives at the gateway ṬESERT-BAIU, , which is the last that he will have to pass through before emerging in heaven in the light of a new day. "This great god cometh "forth to this gate, this great god entereth through it, "and the gods who are therein acclaim the great god." The gateway is like that through which the god passed into the previous Division; at the entrance to the gate proper stands a bearded mummied form called PAI, , and at its exit stands a similar form called ȦKHEKHI, . The corridor is swept by flames of fire, which proceed from the mouths of uraei, as before. In the space which is usually guarded by a number of gods stand two staves, each of which is surmounted by a bearded head; on one head is the disk of TEM, , and on the other a beetle, the symbol of Kheperȧ. The text which refers to these reads:

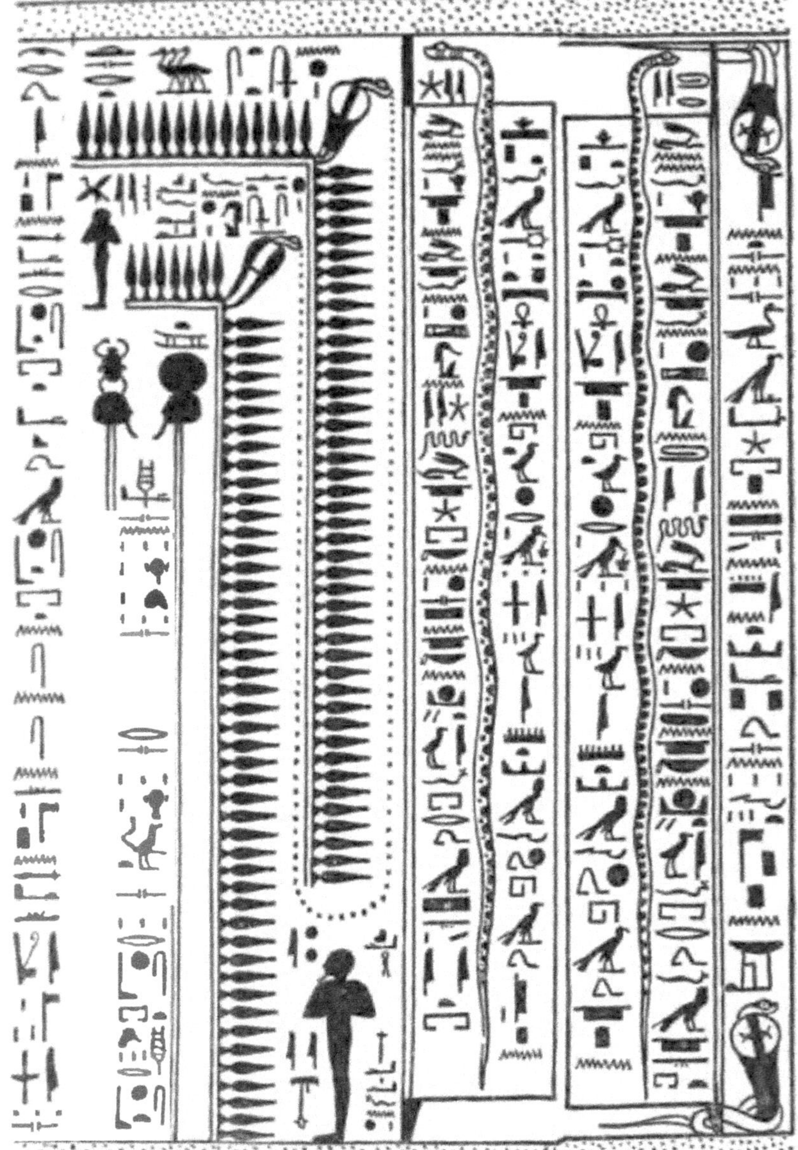

The Gate Ṭesert-Baiu. The doors of Sebi and Reri.

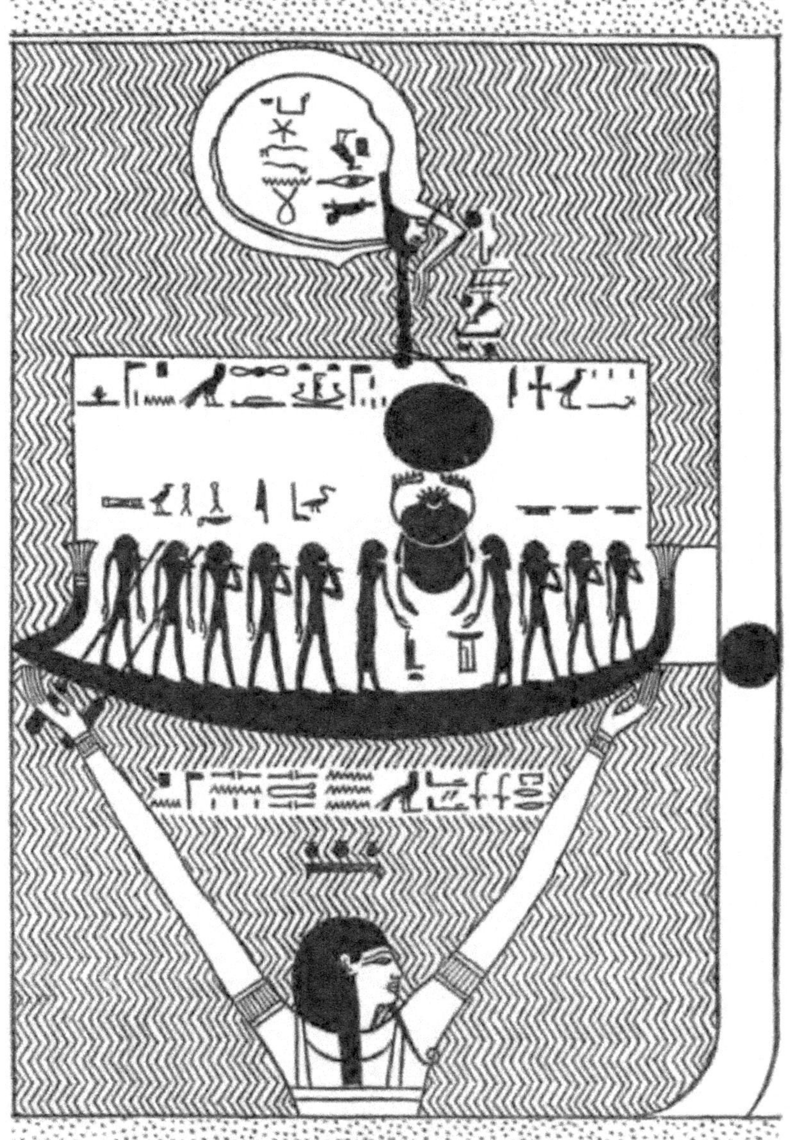

The Sun-god under the form of Kheperà with his Disk, in his Boat, supported by Nu and received by Nut.

, "They stand up on their heads, "and they come into being on their staves by the "gate; the heads stand up by the gate."

The monster serpent which stands on its tail and guards the one door is called SEBI, , and the two lines of text which refer to his admission of Rā read, "He who is over this door openeth to Rā. SA saith "unto Sebi, 'Open thy gate to Rā, unfold thy portal to "Khuti, so that he may come forth from the hidden "place, and may take up his position in the body of "NUT.' Behold, there is wailing among the souls "who dwell in Åment after this door hath closed,"

, &c.

The monster serpent which stands on its tail and guards the other door is called RERI, , and the two lines of text which refer to his admission of Rā read, "He who is over this door openeth to Rā. SA "saith unto RERI, 'Open thy gate to Rā, unfold thy "portal to KHUTI, so that he may come forth from the "hidden place, and may take up his position in the "body of Nut.' Behold, there is wailing among the "souls who dwell in Åment after this door hath closed."

The text, being similar to that which refers to SEBI, is not repeated here.

On each side of the door is a uraeus, the one representing ISIS and the other NEPHTHYS, and of them it is said, "They it is who guard this hidden gate of Ȧment, "and they pass onwards in the following of this god,"

Here we see that the end of the Ṭuat is reached, and the boat of the sun has reached that portion of it through which he is about to emerge in the waters of Nu, and thence in the form of a disk in the sky of this world. Having passed on to the water the boat is supported by the two arms of NU himself, or, as the text says, "These two arms come forth from the "waters, and they bear up this god," . The god appears in the boat in the form of a beetle, which is rolling along a disk; on the left of the beetle is Isis, and on the right Nephthys. The three beings in the front of the boat are probably the personifications of doors, , and the gods to the left are SEB, , SHU, , ḤEK, , ḤU, , and SA, . In the hieroglyphics at the top of the open space above the boat is written, "This god taketh up his place in the MĀṬETET "Boat [with] the gods who are in it," . Away in the waters above, or beyond the boat, is a kind of island, formed by the body of a god, which is bent round in such a way that the tips of his toes touch the back of his head. On his head stands the goddess Nut, with her arms and hands raised and stretched out to receive the disk of the sun, which the Beetle is rolling towards her; the text says, "Nut receiveth Rā," . The island formed by the body of the god is said to be "Osiris, whose circuit is the Ṭuat," .

END OF VOL. II.

www.ingramcontent.com/pod-product-compliance
Lightning Source LLC
Chambersburg PA
CBHW041312240426
43669CB00023B/2966
* 9 7 8 1 6 3 1 8 2 8 2 8 7 *